T0354764

WALKING BOYS

WALKING
BOYS

The Perilous Road to South Sudan Independence

A W A K M A L I T H

WALKING BOYS
THE PERILOUS ROAD TO SOUTH SUDAN INDEPENDENCE

iUniverse books may be ordered through booksellers or by contacting:

iUniverse
1663 Liberty Drive
Bloomington, IN 47403
www.iuniverse.com
1-800-Authors (1-800-288-4677)

ISBN: 978-1-5320-0652-4 (sc)
ISBN: 978-1-5320-0651-7 (e)

Print information available on the last page.

iUniverse rev. date: 08/30/2016

PREFACE

I have been in the United States of America since August 2002. In that time period, many people—friends, colleagues, fellow students, professors, and even relatives—urged me to write a book about all the experiences of the civil war and refugee odyssey I went through in my past in South Sudan, Ethiopia and Kenya. I had shared these stories with them verbally on many occasions, and delivered stories to audiences through public speaking, and even on TV and for newspapers. Some well-wishers begged me to narrate the story into tapes and then have it transcribed and published. However, I didn't take these proddings seriously enough at the time. I resisted. I always thought that I would do it someday, but it was postponed, maybe because I was busy with school and everything else. Yet, I always believed that I would tell these stories to a larger audience in a format such as a book. I just didn't know when.

Endeavoring to write a book was daunting at first. I was a good writer in school in Kenya, and some of my teachers and fellow schoolmates took notice, but I never pursued literature beyond two years at college. Moreover, I knew there were quite a few people, including a professor, who would have gladly assisted in writing this story. However, I did not act on these possibilities. The reason is now clear to me: The story was still incomplete. The Republic of South Sudan was still a region in the Sudan. It was still called Southern Sudan and there was still a country called the Sudan, which was still at war with itself. Part of me knew it was incomplete. Though the story of the Sudan, South Sudan, my story, has been happening for well over 50 years, it still had not reached its completeness.

Then, on January 9th, 2011, Southern Sudanese worldwide voted in a referendum to decide their own fate. I participated in the vote in the United States with some of my South Sudanese friends. It was a joyous and a momentous day. The day we had been waiting for had finally arrived. At this time, I finally decided to put it all down on paper because the Southern Sudanese were beginning a new chapter, a chapter in which their own destiny was now in their own hands. Never again would we put blame on anyone else for our own problems.

I began to write in the summer of 2012 and by the fall 2015, I was done writing it. I have endeavored to remember it all as it happened, from a very young age, and to write it all down as accurately as I can muster. Where possible and for privacy reasons, I have used pseudonyms. However, the narrative is factual and accurate. I hope the work you are about to read has lessons about life that I could share with you, and I hope I have done justice to those who lost their lives in the cause of the Sudan's tragic civil wars. This is as much their story as it is mine.

Juba, South Sudan, 2015 A. K.

GLOSSARY

Anya-Nya —The southern Sudanese rebel army of the first civil war, 1955-72.

Anya-Nya II—Rebel south Sudanese forces who, together with former members of the Sudanese army, formed the SPLA in 1983; also, some of those forces that defected from the SPLA later in 1983 and became a militia force of Nuer in Upper Nile province supported by the Sudanese government; several Anya-Nya II groups over the years were wooed back to the SPLA.

ICRC—International Committee of the Red Cross.

Murahilin—Baggara Arab tribal militias from north Sudan.

NGO—Nongovernmental Organization.

NIF—National Islamic Front, the militant Islamic political party which came to power in 1989 after a military coup that overthrew the elected government

Nuba—The African people living in south Kordofan's Nuba Mountains; some are Muslims, some Christians, and some practice traditional African religions.

OLS—Operation Lifeline Sudan, a joint United Nations/NGO relief operation for internally displaced and famine and served war victims in Sudan. It began operations in 1989. It served territory controlled by the government and by the SPLA. Much of its work in southern Sudan was through cross-border operations conducted by its Southern sector, OLS's Southern Sector, based in Nairobi.

Red Army—SPLA name of fondness offered the minors.

SPLA—The Sudan People's Liberation Army—the Sudanese rebel army formed in 1983 and headed by Commander-in-Chief John Garang.

SPLM—The Sudan People's Liberation Movement, the political organization of the Sudanese rebels formed in 1983, of which John Garang was chairman.

SRRA—The Sudan Relief and Rehabilitation Association, relief wing of the SPLA.

Popular Defense Force—The Sudan Islamist Government-sponsored militia, which included the *Murahilin*.

SPLA-Nasir—The faction of the SPLA that broke away from John Garang's leadership in August 1991, led by Riek Machar and based in Nasir, Upper Nile.

SPLA/United—The rebel movement led by Riek Machar after March 27, 1993, also the name that the other SPLA dissidents adopted after they united on March 27, 1993.

SPLA-Mainstream—The faction of SPLA that, after the August 1991 Riek rebellion, remained under the leadership of John Garang, based in Torit, Eastern Equatoria province, until that town fell to the government in July 1992.

UN—The United Nations.

Sayyid Abdel Rahman al-Mahdi—The father to aSadiq al-Mahdi and former head of the Ansar sect.

Ansar Sect—One of the two main Islamic sects in the Sudan.

Sayyid al-Mirghani—The former head of the Khatmiya Sect, one of the Islamic sects in the Sudan.

Khatmiya Sect—One of the Islamic sects in the Sudan.

Closed District Ordinance—Called the 'Southern Policy', the Condominium Colonial policy of keeping the Nuba Mountains, Blue Nile and Southern Sudan away from Northern influence in view of integration into the East Africa region.

Passports and Permits Ordinance—Law that controlled travel between North and South.

Permits to Trade Order—Limit Arab trading in the South.

Juba Conference—The **1947** conference in Juba, organized by the colonial government—Southern chiefs agreed with northern nationalists to pursue a united Sudan. A crash programme of integration followed, as Southern Policy is abandoned.

Mohamed Ahmed "al-Mahdi"—Grandfather of aSadiq al-Mahdi.

Khalifa Abdullahi—Successor to Mohamed Ahmed 'al-Mahdi'.

Ismail al-Azhari—The first Sudanese prime minister and head of state in 1956. General Abboud overthrew him two years later in 1958.

Sudanization—Policy of giving civil service jobs to the Sudanese by the colonial government in preparation for independence.

Torit mutiny—The rebellion of the Southern Equatoria Corps at Torit in 1955, before the Sudan independence in 1956, refusing rotation to north Sudan. Their action precipitated the first civil war beginning then and intensifying in 1963.

Missionaries Act—The government of Sudan law expelling all the Christian Missionaries from Southern Sudan in 1962.

SANU—Sudan African National Union- the William Deng Nhial political party that first suggested federalism as a form of governing the Sudan, its vast territory and its many ethnic communities. The SPLA/M benefitted from this party's ideology.

Sadiq al-Mahdi—Grandson of the al-Mahdi and the architect of the Murahilin enterprise.

Kerubino Kuanyin Bol—The former SPLA/M 2nd in Command and the man whose forces started the 2nd Sudanese civil war at Bor on 16th May, 1983. Kerubino is among the big five founders of the SPLA/M which include Dr. Garang, Salva Kiir, William Nyuon and Arok Thon Arok.

Salva Kiir Mayardit—The former SPLA/M number four who rose among the ranks to become the 2nd in Command and now the President of the independent South Sudan, Commander-in-Chief of the SPLA forces and the Chairman of the SPLM party.

William Nyuon Bany—The former SPLA/M 3rd in Command and the man whose forces from Ayod joined the rest of the rebels marching to Ethiopia to form the first nucleus of the SPLA. Nyuon rose through the ranks to become the 2nd in Command.

Dr. John Garang de Mabior—The first among the founders of the SPLA/M and the first in the line-up. Garang proved to be an able strategist and a leader whose ideas and organization brought about the independence of South Sudan.

Deng Ajuong—The Commander of the Nile Battalion of the Mormor Division. Deng Ajuong was in our area with his forces to fight the Murahilin.

Tong Akok (Tong Arabia)—The Commander of the Nile Battalion taskforce that fought the Murahilin at the village of Wunlit. He died fighting the Murahilin and his forces were massacred. He is buried there.

Dr. Riek Machar—The perennially rebellious South Sudanese ex-SPLA/M alternate commander.

Dr. Lam Akol—The former SPLA/M alternate commander who helped precipitate, and who became a major participant of, the 1991 coup against Garang.

Paride Taban—Former Bishop of the Catholic Diocese of Torit, one of the bishops who worked tirelessly to help the people of South Sudan.

Caesar Mazzolari—Former Catholic Bishop of Rumbek who did a lot to help South Sudanese.

Vincent Donati – The Don Bosco priest at Kakuma.

Armin Pressman—The German Don Bosco Technical School Director.

Don Bosco—Italian Catholic order active in youth rehabilitation ministry.

Chol Ayuak—Former Commander of the Bee Battalion of the Mormor Division that fought the Murahilin in Twic County.

Macham Atem—The former Commander of the Eagle Battalion of the Mormor Division that fought the Murahilin in Twic County.

Mengistu Haile Mariam—Former Ethiopian Strongman who became pivotal in supporting the SPLA/M.

Yusuf Kuwa—The first SPLA Nuba commander of the SPLA Mountain Division. He was a well-respected SPLA leader who officiated at the 1994 SPLM/A Convention at Chukudum.

Manut Bol—The former NBA legend, Manut became pivotal in supporting the SPLA/M.

TIMELINE

- ❖ **1821**: Turco-Egyptian conquest of Sudan "unified" small independent Sudanese states.
- ❖ **1885**: Mahdist forces captured Khartoum after a long siege; British General C.G Gordon is killed. Al-Mahdi died; the Khalifa Abdullahi took over.
- ❖ **1898**: Anglo-Egyptian forces led by General Kitchener overthrow the Mahdist state in the battle of Omdurman. The two countries begin to establish condominium rule.
- ❖ **1920s**: Sayyid Abdel Rahman al-Mahdi (Father of Al-Sadiq), head of Ansar sect and Sayyid Ali al-Mirghani, head of Khatmiyya sect, are encouraged by the British to reconstitute their movements into political organizations along quasi-secular lines.
- ❖ **1922**: Passports and Permits Ordinance controlled travel between North and South.
- ❖ **1925**: Permits to Trade Order limit Arab trading in the South.
- ❖ **1947**: Juba Conference organized by colonial government—Southern chiefs agreed with northern nationalists to pursue a united Sudan.
- ❖ **1953**: The 800 administrative posts vacated by the British are "Sudanized" as "self-rule" is introduced, with a Westminster-style parliament.
- ❖ **1955**: The Torit mutiny of southern soldiers refusing transfer to the north marks the beginning of the first civil war, lasting 17 years. Killing of northern administrators, teachers and traders in the south follow "Sudanization".

- ❖ **1956**: Independence on 1 January follows growing political pressure and British exhaustion. Ismail al-Azhari becomes Prime Minister of the first national government, formed by the conservative Unionist and Umma parties.
- ❖ **1958**: Economic crisis and growing parliamentary division precipitate military takeover headed by General Abboud. Abboud dissolves the political parties and institutes a state of emergency.
- ❖ **1962**: Missionaries Act expelled Christian missions from the South.
- ❖ **1963**: The Anya-Nya movement for southern secession is formed.
- ❖ **1964**: The Abboud regime steps up military action in the south. A general strike and popular uprising brings down the military regime. Transitional government headed by Sir al-Katim khalifa.
- ❖ **1965**: March—most parties from north and south attend Round Table Conference on the "Southern Problem" organized by Professor Mohamed Omar Bashir.
- ❖ **1965**: Parliamentary elections are held; government formed under Mohamed Ahmed Mahjoub, an independent turned Umma Prime Minister. Authors father sustained three bullet wounds as he escapes the Wau Massacre.
- ❖ **1966-67**: Aged 30, Sadiq al-Mahdi is elected as MP, becomes Prime Minister.
- ❖ **1967**: Sudan sided with the Arab world and declared war on Israel.
- ❖ **1967-present**: Period of consistently lower rainfall than previous long-term average.
- ❖ **1968**: William Deng Nhial, leader of SANU is assassinated.
- ❖ **1969**: May—A group of officers led by Colonel Jaafar Mohamed Nimeiri takes power in a military coup with leftist and Communist support.
- ❖ **1970**: Joseph Lagu becomes sole leader of the Anya-Nya.
- ❖ **1972**: Addis Ababa Agreement ends 17 years of civil war. Signed by Nimeiri and Joseph Lagu following talks between Khartoum and the South Sudan Liberation Movement, it is based on regional autonomy.
- ❖ **1974**: Riots in Juba follow rumors that Egyptian farmers will be settled in the area drained by the prospective Jonglei canal.

- **1978**: A joint Sudanese-Egyptian project is launched to construct a canal through the Sudd marshes of the South. Oil is discovered in Southern Sudan.
- **1978**: The author is born at Chong, Twic County, Warrap State— Particular day is unknown.
- **1980**: Jonglei Canal construction begins.
- **1980**: The author is in Wau with family.
- **1983**: September—Nimeiri introduces "Sharia" or "September" laws.
- **1983**: South is "redivided" into three regions, and the single regional government is abolished. Civil war resumes when on May 16th, Major Kerubino Kuanyin Bol 105th troops at Bor, southern Sudan, rebelled thereby starting the SPLA.
- **1984**: Jonglei canal work is halted by SPLA activity. First appearance of Murahilin occurred in north of Twic County.
- **1985**: The author traveled to Wau with military escort. The author is at Heilat Denka with family. The author started school at Catholic Church school at Heilat Jadit in Wau. The SPLA started Rumbek Campaign.
- **1985**: April 16th—Nimeiri is overthrown, after a popular uprising, headed by the "National Alliance for National Salvation" led to a military coup by defense minister, General Abd al-Rahman Swar al-Dahab.
- **1986**: March—Koka Dam Agreement in Ethiopia, between SPLA/ SPLM, represented by Kerubino Kuanyin and northern National Alliance.
- **1986**: The SPLA TuekTuek (Woodpecker) battalion captured Rumbek. Wunlit village is burned to ashes. Murahilin massacres the SPLA Nile Battalion soldiers at Wunlit village. The same Murahilin group at Wunlit wounds the author's Grandfather. The author escaped from Wau and traveled back to Twic County. Wunrok is burned to ashes by Murahilin-shops had all their goods destroyed by fire. The erstwhile Wunlit villagers who became SPLA Eagle Battalion soldiers arrived at back at the village- received with a joyous welcome. The author's father, coming from Wau, reunited with family at the village.

- ❖ **1986**: April—Elections—Sadiq al-Mahdi becomes Prime Minister of a coalition Umma/DUP government.
- ❖ **1987**: Sadiq al-Mahdi abandons Koka Dam Agreement on receiving arms from Libya and Iraq, declares a state of emergency and begins a policy of arming militias of Baggara as parallel force.
- ❖ **1987**: January—The author's grandfather died at Wunlit around January of his wounds.
- ❖ **1987**: February—Murahilin at Paliet, south of Wunrok, fought with the SPLA, take children—two boys, brothers, who were sick.
- ❖ **1987**: March—A report details the kidnapping and enslavement of Dinka women and children as part of the militia raiding pattern in northern Bahr al-Ghazal.
- ❖ **1987**: September—The author began the trek to Ethiopia.
- ❖ **1987**: December 26th—The author arrived at Panyido Refugee Camp.
- ❖ **1987**: Mengistu Haile Mariam imprisons Kerubino Kuanyin Bol, the SPLA/M 2ND in Command.
- ❖ **1988**: Famine in Southern Sudan, growing since 1986, becomes intense: Deliberate "scorched earth" and relief denial policies of government, militias and SPLA are the primary cause of food shortage, compounded by drought, floods and pest infestations. The author started attending school at Panyido.
- ❖ **1989**: The author attended military training for disciplinary purposes
- ❖ **1989**: February—Army issues ultimatum to Sadiq demanding progress towards peace and disbandment of militias.
- ❖ **1989**: April—Sharia laws are frozen; a date is set for a constitutional conference on 18 September 1989.
- ❖ **1989**: June—A military coup on 30 June thwarts the peace process.
- ❖ **1989**: December—War escalates in the South; large shipments of arms from China, ordered by Sadiq, are paid for by Iran.
- ❖ **1991**: May—After the fall of the Mengistu regime in Addis Ababa, some 300,000 Southern Sudanese are forced to return to Sudan from border areas in Ethiopia, and are bombed by the Sudanese air force. The author fled Ethiopia for Southern Sudan-arrived to Pochalla.

- **1991**: August—SPLA Commanders Riek Machar and Lam Akol lead a "creeping coup" attempt against Colonel Garang. They say Garang is too authoritarian and lacks political direction. The coup is unsuccessful but leads to the formation of a breakaway "Nasir" faction.
- **1992**: February—The author fled Pochalla. The Toposa militia at Magos attacked the author and group.
- **1992**: March—Khartoum launches its largest-yet offensive against the SPLA. One aim is to cut off sources of relief to civilians in SPLA-held areas. 100,000 people are displaced.
- **1992**: Nearly half a million displaced people and squatters are forcibly expelled from their homes in the Khartoum area to desert camps with inadequate water, food and shelter.
- **1992**: May—After the government captured the SPLA-held town of Kapoeta, some 22,000 Sudanese seek asylum across the Kenyan border, including 12,500 unaccompanied minors. The author fled Narus for Lokichoggio, Kenya.
- **1992**: June—SPLA infiltrates Juba city and briefly captures the military headquarters on 7 June.
- **1992**: August—The author and group arrived to Kakuma Refugee Camp. The author started schooling at under-the-trees schools at Kakuma.
- **1992**: September—Catholic bishops from SPLA-controlled Southern Sudan accuse government troops of genocide, and call on Catholic bishops throughout East Africa to press for international consideration for Sudan.
- **1993**: January—An estimated 60,000 people are said to have died from kala-azar (leishmaniasis) in Panriang, bordering Upper Nile and Bahr al-Ghazal.
- **1993**: February—Pope John Paul II stops over in Khartoum.
- **1993**: March—SPLA-Mainstream attacks anti-Garang (SPLA-United) leadership meeting in Kongor. Veteran politician Joseph Oduho is killed.
- **1993**: April—The Opposition National Democratic Alliance meets for five days in Nairobi and announces a "historic" agreement on religion and the state.

- **1993**: August 18th—US State Department adds Sudan to its list of states sponsoring terrorism.
- **1993**: September—The heads of state of Ethiopia, Eritrea, Uganda and Kenya establish a committee to resolve the civil war in Sudan, in their capacity as members of the Inter Governmental Authority on Drought and Development. Bashir accepts the initiative but warns against foreign intervention.
- **1993**: November—Hassan al-Turabi flies to Afghanistan, ostensibly to mediate between warring Islamic factions.
- **1993**: December—The Opposition National Democratic Alliance fails to agree on a common response to the question of self-determination for Southern Sudan. Thousands of militia fighters died in Southern Sudan and the Nuba Mountains.
- **1994**: January—Archbishop of Canterbury flies to Southern Sudan for three days. A diplomatic row over his cancellation of a visit to northern Sudan leads to the mutual expulsion of ambassadors from Britain and Sudan.
- **1994**: July—SPLA-United commanders Faustino and Kerubino advance into Wunrok, northern Bahr al-Ghazal. Battles with SPLA-Mainstream lead to 1,000 mostly civilian deaths; both factions loot possessions from local people.
- **1994**: The wanted Venezuelan terrorist known as Carlos the Jackal is captured in Khartoum and taken away by French forces. It emerges that in addition to assisting Khartoum obtain right of passage for its armed forces through Central Africa, Paris has made available satellite photographs identifying the positions of the SPLA in Southern Sudan.
- **1994**: September—Bashir claims some of the IGADD states convening peace talks in the Horn of Africa are "not neutral": there is deadlock over the issues of self-determination and the separation of state and religion. Garang endorses the IGADD declaration of principles.
- **1994**: October—Over a hundred civilians are killed in an attack on Akot by Riek Machar's "Southern Sudan Independence Movement" forces.

- **1994**: December—Chukudum Agreement—Umma Party and SPLA Mainstream concur on "self-determination" for South using existing boundaries.
- **1995**: September—The author is persuaded by fellow Sudanese refugees to travel to Dadaab Refugee Camp in North-Eastern Kenya to seek resettlement abroad.
- **1996**: January—As the move was unsuccessful, the author moved back to Kakuma.
- **1996**: November—The author sat for Kenya Certificate of Primary Education, KCPE at Kakuma.
- **1997**: March—The author started high school education at Bakhita Center
- **1998**: USA launches a missile attack on a chemical plant in Khartoum assumed to develop chemical weapons possibly in coorporation with the Al-Qaida terror network.
- **1999**: Sudan start an export of oil assisted by China, Canada, Sweden and other countries. Gadet assassinated Kerubino Kuanyin Bol in the Unity State area.
- **2000**: November—The author sat for Kenya Certificate of Secondary Education, KCSE.
- **2001**: February—The author moved back to Kakuma, and got accepted to go to U.S.
- **2001**: September—The UN lifts sanctions against Sudan to support ongoing peace negotiations.
- **2001**: October—Following the New York terror attacks, USA puts new sanctions on Sudan due to accusations of Sudan's involvement with international terrorism.
- **2001**: More than 14,550 slaves are freed after pressure from human rights groups.
- **2002**: July 20th—The government and SPLA signs a protocol to end the civil war.
- **2002**: July 27th—President al-Bashir meets for the first time with SPLA leader John Garang. Ugandan president Yoweri Museveni has arranged the meeting.
- **2002**: July 31st—Government attacks SPLA again.

- **2002**: August—The author arrived at the U.S. city of Rochester, N.Y.
- **2003**: January—The author started university education at SUNY (State University of New York) at Monroe Community College.
- **2004**: September—The author continued university education at the University of Rochester, a private school.
- **2005**: January 9th—Comprehensive Peace Agreement (CPA) signed between Khartoum Government and Southern rebels.
- **2005**: March 15th—United Nations Security Council agrees to send 10,000 peacekeeping soldiers to Southern Sudan.
- **2005**: July—Garang sworn in as first Vice President: constitution gives South a degree of autonomy is signed.
- **2005**: August—Garang killed in plane crash after visiting Ugandan ally Museveni. Salva Kiir succeeds Garang as First Vice President of Sudan and President of Southern Sudan. Widespread clashes between northern Arabs and southern Sudanese.
- **2005**: September—Power-sharing government formed in Khartoum.
- **2005**: October—Autonomous government formed in the South in accordance with January 2005 peace deal.
- **2006**: September—The author graduated with Bachelors degree from the University of Rochester, New York.
- **2007**: October—SPLM accused Khartoum of failing to honor the 2005 peace deal and temporarily suspends participation in Government of National Unity.
- **2007**: December—SPLM resumes participation in Government of National Unity.
- **2008**: June—Arbitration over Abyei: al-Bashir and Salva Kiir agree to international arbitration to resolve dispute over Abyei.
- **2008**: September—Census Results to be announced; Southerners reserve the right not to be bound by the results.
- **2009**: July—North and South Sudan say they accept ruling by arbitration court in The Hague shrinking disputed Abyei region and placing the major Heglig (Panthou) oil field in the north.
- **2009**: December—Deal reached between leaders of North and South, on the terms of a referendum on independence due in south by 201.

- **2010**: January—Al-Bashir says he will accept referendum result, even if South opts for independence.
- **2010**: March—The author traveled back to Southern Sudan to meet family.
- **2010**: April—Sudan's first multiparty nationwide election held in 24 years, since 1986. Al-Bashir gains new term as president of Sudan; re-instates Salva Kiir as First Vice President of Sudan and President of Southern Sudan.
- **2010**: September—The author attends business school. UN Security Council calls on all sides to ensure that the 2011 referendum is peaceful.
- **2010**: November 15th—The author participated in registration for referendum voters.
- **2011**: January—The people of South Sudan voted in favor of full independence from Sudan, the author participated in the referendum vote.
- **2011**: February—Fighting broke out near Abyei.
- **2011**: March—Government of Southern Sudan said it is suspending talks with the north, accusing it of plotting a coup.
- **2011**: May—The author graduated from the University of Rochester's Simon Graduate School, and traveled back to Southern Sudan.
- **2011**: June—Governments of north and Southern Sudan signed accord to demilitarize the disputed Abyei region and let in an Ethiopian peacekeeping force.
- **2011**: July 9th—Independence Day.
- **2011**: September—South Sudan's cabinet voted to designate Ramciel—a planned city in Lakes State—as the future capital.
- **2012**: April—After weeks of border fighting, South Sudan troops temporarily occupied the oil field and border town of Heglig (Panthou) before being forced to relinquish the town by the International Community. Sudanese warplanes raid the Bentiu area in South Sudan.
- **2012**: May—The author began writing memoir. Sudan pledged to pull its troops out of the border region of Abyei, which is also claimed by South Sudan, as bilateral peace talks resumed.

- ❖ **2012**: July—Country marked first anniversary amid worsening economic crisis and no let-up in tension with Sudan.
- ❖ **2012**: September—The presidents of Sudan and South Sudan agreed trade, oil and security deals after days of talks in Ethiopia. They planned to set up a demilitarized buffer zone and lay the grounds for oil sales to resume. They failed however to resolve border issues including the disputed Abyei territory.
- ❖ **2013**: March—Sudan and South Sudan agreed to resume pumping oil after a bitter dispute over fees that saw production shut down more than a year earlier. They also agreed to withdraw troops from their border area to create a demilitarized zone.
- ❖ **2013**: June—President Kiir dismissed Finance Minister Kosti Manibe and Cabinet Affairs Minister Deng Alor over a multi-million-dollar financial scandal, and lifted their immunity from prosecution.
- ❖ **2013**: July—President Kiir dismissed entire cabinet and Vice-President Riek Machar in a power struggle within the governing Sudan People's Liberation Movement. Civil war erupted as ex-vice-president, Riek Machar, plotted a failed coup d'état.
- ❖ **2014**: August—Peace talks began in Ethiopian capital Addis Ababa and dragged on for months as fighting continued.
- ❖ **2015**: February—General elections due in June are called off because of the ongoing conflict.

CONTENTS

ACKNOWLEDGEMENT

I would like to express my gratitude to the many people who provided me support while working on this book. Thank you to all those who assisted in the editing, proofreading and design, specifically Prof. Laura Nyantung of the University of Michigan, Katie White Lesczinski, her brother Tim White, and mother (Mom) Kitty White, Mike Latona of the Catholic Courier, Dominic Dut Mathiang and many others who read the manuscript at various stages. All the errors are mine.

I would like to thank my wife, Christine, and the rest of my family, who supported and encouraged me.

This book is dedicated to all the South Sudanese people, the people of the Sudan and all the rest of the people everywhere who in one way or another have a part in the stories told in this book, including: Awak Ring Mathok, Akol Lual Lual, Lual Baguoot, Majok Baguoot, Santino Mabek Dau, Madut Majok Ngor, Emannuel Athiei Ayual, Bol Agau, Abraham Chol Majok, Agook Mayik Riak, Machok Mou, Machar Buol, Peter Bior Kuch, Achak Deng, Bol Deng, Deng Deng Amer, Lat Mathou, Angelo Ugwak, Victor Deng Ngor, Tong Akol, Dominic Dut Mathiang, Ayuel Deng, Ring Madit, Awach Anei, Isaac Bith Madut, Adhar Lok Aguek, Yom Madut Malith, Garang Malith Mel, Ajak Kuol, Matiop Bior Kok, Acho Acho, Diangbar, Aher, Malak, Dhor Aher, Rung Madit, Deng Akec, Deng Dut Ring, Nyuol Mangok Ayuel, Nhial Makerdit, Deng Mtoto.

This book is also dedicated to the late Tong Akok of the Nile Battalion, of the Mormor Division of the SPLA, who led his soldiers into Wunlit as the first to arrive at our village to face the Murahilin, and who died in the process, along with group of his soldiers. You are among the very first heroes to me. I always wanted to be like you.

This book is also dedicated to Kiir Mayardit, Kerubino Kuanyin, Dr. John Garang, William Nyuon, Deng Ajuong, and Manyiel Ayuel.

I also dedicate this book to Ann Marie and Jerry DeLuccio. Thank you for your kind and generous support throughout my studies at the University of Rochester. This book is also dedicated to Dayle Bird and Susana Remito. You were the first to welcome me to Rochester, NY. Thank you for teaching me how to drive. It was all worth it.

Last but not least: I beg forgiveness of all those who were with me over the course of the years as we walked and suffered in the Sudan, Ethiopia and Kenya, and whose names I have failed to mention.

MAPS
SUDAN AND SOUTH SUDAN

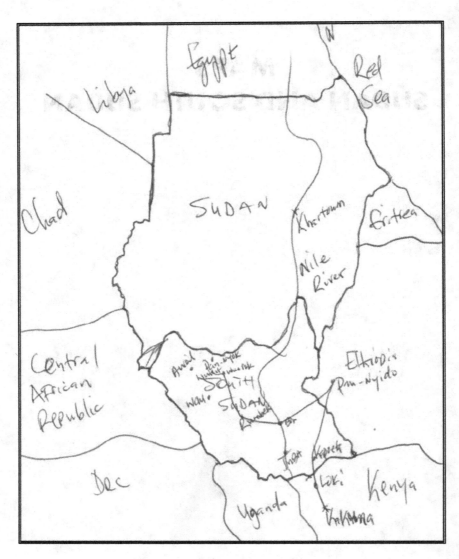

Gogrial to Pan-Nyok

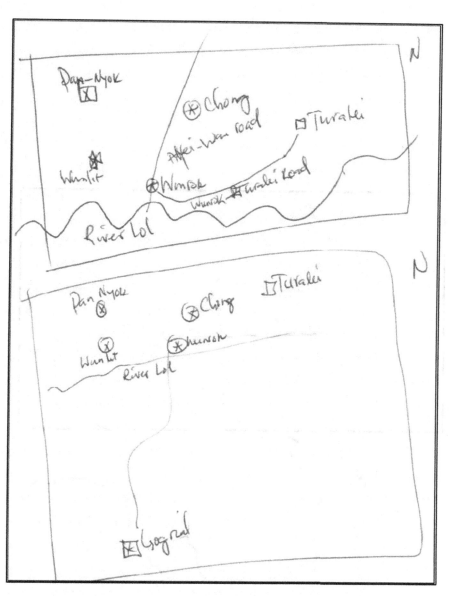

Wau, Gogrial, Wunrok, Wunlit, Pan-Nyok

xxix

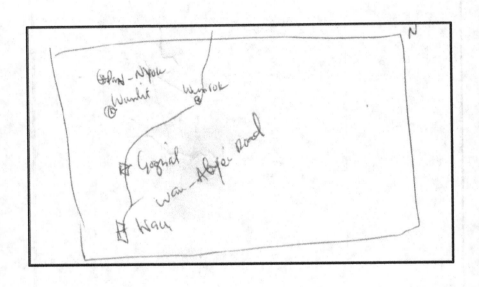

INTRODUCTION

The world is vast. Conventionally, it is composed of seven continents: Africa, Antarctica, Asia, Australia, Europe, North America, and South America. Africa, the second largest continent, has 54 sovereign countries. The Republic of South Sudan became one of these in July 2011. This book reveals, in a first-hand account, the horrors that preceded the establishment of South Sudan.

Here you will find personal reflections on the tragic war between two conflicting societies, Arab and Islamic on the one hand, Christian and African on the other, though the dichotomy was not so clean-cut. You will also discover more about the differences and similarities among these people.

Many of my friends, colleagues and relatives urged me to write such a book. It took me all of 12 years to finally put it down in written form. This is my story of coming face-to-face with these horrors of war, which erupted in 1983 and lasted until 2005. The story spans a period of 18 years beginning at age 5 at our home province of Bhar el Gazel, Southern Sudan region of the former Sudan.

The narration of the story begins with an attack at night against a group of 'Lost Boys'—children, mostly boys, displaced by war and traveling back from Ethiopia into the Sudan and onward towards the Kenyan border. After escaping the war from their home villages and towns throughout Southern Sudan and parts of Northern Sudan in the later 1980s, they travelled to Ethiopia, separately or in small groups, to form a larger group of boys and women and children. They found a restive peace under the communist regime of the Ethiopian dictator,

Mengistu Haile Mariam, only to be displaced once more after the overthrow of the regime by the Ethiopian rebels in 1991.

The refugees were pursued back into the Sudan by Ethiopian rebels, combined with elements of the Sudanese Army and allied militia. The refugees spent the rainy season,[1] from May to December 1991, at Pochalla with the SPLA repulsing waves upon waves of these attackers to secure Pochalla. However, in January 1991, Pochalla could not hold any longer—the refugees would have to leave as the dry season approached, to seek shelter elsewhere in Southern Sudan, disperse back to their homes in Southern Sudan or seek refuge in another country, possibly Kenya and Uganda. After escaping an attack that led to the capture of Pochalla,[2] just a month earlier in January 1992, by the Sudanese Army,[3] the boys had reached Magos.

The night attack happened at the small village of Magos, close to the Kenyan border. The attackers were members of a local ethnic group, the Toposa, who inhabit the area, and were trained and armed by the Sudanese Army in the nearby town of Juba, the largest town in Southern Sudan and the autonomous regional capital. The Islamic government of Sudan decided that arming local ethnic communities and urging them to fight each other, and to specifically attack the Dinka, the largest ethnic community in Southern Sudan and the backbone of the SPLM/SPLA, was a good counterinsurgency strategy. It worked well, but it was mostly civilians, the displaced refugees, children and women who bore the brunt of this policy.

I was among that group of boys sleeping in the open. Though the attack was horrific, leaving 9 boys and a sentry as causalities, it was not the first time. The attacks had become routine for us. They were expected. The question in my mind was always 'When will it end?'

This book narrates my turbulent journey, from northern Bhar el Gazel, in Southern Sudan, across the Nile River to Ethiopia, from Ethiopia back to Southern Sudan, from Southern Sudan to Kenya

---

[1] The typical rainy season is from April to September
[2] The Ethiopian-Sudanese border town
[3] Combined with allied Ethiopian rebels and Anywak Militia

and then finally to the United States. I have endeavored to recount the significant events that I faced, and the lessons learned. My hope is that you, the reader, will not only find the tragic side of humanity in these pages, but also the redemptive. Amidst the strife, evidence of the goodness of humanity is laid bare in these tragedies. This is a story of war and peace, of tragedy and hope.

CHAPTER 1

BANDITS

The phone rang one frigid afternoon in October 2010. I was sitting in a chair in the apartment I shared with a friend, Isaac, in Rochester, New York. I decided to pick up the phone.

"Hello!"

"Who is this?" I inquired.

The voice sounded familiar. The caller was Deng, a longtime friend from my walking days in the bushes and plains of Eastern Africa. I was grateful to answer the phone. "How are you, my friend?" I said in greeting.

"I am great, man. How are you doin'?" Deng replied. We laughed and joked for a few moments before the conversation turned more serious. "It would be nice if you could gather a group of five Sudanese from Rochester to join with us here in Syracuse; we will rent a van and another car…"

"Why?" I cut him off, intrigued.

Breathless, Deng almost shouted on the other end, "Don't you know we have to vote? We have to fire the final bullet!" Deng went on, "We want to travel in a convoy to get to Boston, Massachusetts in a week's time to register to vote in the January 9th, 2011 Southern Sudan Referendum. There you have it."

I quickly agreed to gather those friends. Just like the Biblical tale of the Roman Emperor Tiberius Augustus ordering all the Jews to go back to their towns of origin to be counted, likewise, all the people of

Southern Sudan and of their descent—abroad or inside their native country—would gather at designated points inside Southern Sudan, Northern Sudan, and other population collection points abroad. Massachusetts happened to be one such chosen location.

Southern Sudanese in the Northeast US had the option to go to Washington DC., Boston, or to cross the border to Toronto, Canada to be eligible to vote in the self-determination referendum that would decide the fate of the region and its people once and for all. Regardless of the venue, the crux of the matter was the decision we were about to make. As mundane as it may seem, the task of voting was rather momentous. Yet I was treating the forthcoming vote too lightly—and I was not the only one.

On the face of it, arriving at this point took nearly 50 years of warfare between the Southern Sudan region and the Sudan Central Government, and cost an estimated 2.5 million lives, 4 million more scattered abroad, and untold destruction to everything that was ever put together inside Southern Sudan. The toll of arriving at this day of self-determination was immense, and memories of years of suffering were still vivid in my mind. Two days after surges of bone-tired travelers arrived on foot and by lorries from Pochalla to Magos in February 1991, the swelling numbers of refugees in this little Sudanese town, coupled with the local Toposa community, overcrowded the place. Movement was everywhere. Around the camp, people exchanged meat products for jerry cans[4] (plastic cans entirely emptied of oil contents), soap, salt, grain and so forth. It was a fair and friendly trade conducted between the Toposa—mostly women—and the refugees, a majority of whom were lost boys.[5]

The Toposa were peddling their wares, specifically goat meat, beef, mutton, and bush meat[6] to the travel-weary boys in exchange for blankets, cooking oil, corn, beans, spare clothing, and jerry cans.

---

[4] Plastic cans entirely emptied of oil contents
[5] A band of 12 to 16 year-old boys; I was 14
[6] Also, probably donkey or zebra's meat as we later discovered that the Toposa and the Turkana probably ate zebra and most likely the donkey meat

Nothing was amiss. We were amazed at how friendly the Toposa were, given all the tales of their animosity we were told. A burly Toposa, known to be associated with the Sudan People's Liberation Movement,[7] wore sandals and bed sheet typical of the Toposa and like those worn by the Maasai of Kenya. We were told he had the ear of the Big Man himself, Dr. John Garang. The burly man appeared quite jovial and I was curious to find out what he thought about the legendary Toposa animosity; but I would never have been allowed to approach him. The young soldiers around him, protective yet sociable, must have been his minders. We felt safe. As the sun set on the achab,[8] the final Toposa had left for their manyattas[9] dwellings outside the little post. We prepared for the night. No word can describe the weariness after our long journey: on foot from Pochalla at the Ethiopian border in the Northeast all the way to the middle of the Tikling Desert and then by Kenyan trucks to the Southeast village of Magos, closer to the Kenyan border. Except for the hum of nearly 16,000 boys, the place was finally peaceful. Our groups dispersed to sleep in the open, closer to the bushes just outside the little station.

Magos was not really a town by any meaning of the word. Rather, it was a soldiers' encampment, used by both the Sudan Army and the SPLA alternately. There was a guard stationed a few paces closer to the shrubs at the outer perimeter of our sleep clearing.[10] It never occurred to me that there would be any trouble that night.

As the boys' commotion faded to slumber, the land was eerily quiet except for the unceasing twittering of crickets. I was simply grateful for sleep, which was no option on our trek from Pochalla. We needed to evade pursuit of the combined Sudanese Army and allied militia, which included the Anywak and what was said to be elements of the new Ethiopian Army. The Army was seeking to capture our group and turn innocent boys into Muslim fundamentalists. My thoughts, as the

---

[7] The SPLM-Sudan People's Liberation Movement
[8] An impenetrable thicket
[9] Kraal-like huts
[10] I came to learn of this arrangement later on

3

sleep took over, raced back to my times in Wau and at our village; I feared that our trajectory was moving us away from the path leading to Bhar el Gazel, our home province inside the then Southern Sudan. Our destination was a mystery. Months earlier, upon leaving Ethiopia, I was elated at the prospect of returning home after five years in the Ethiopian camp of Panyido. Though it soon became clear that we'd never see home again.

Being in the Toposa country, without conflict, we had begun to hope that the group had been sufficiently won over by the international community—the Churches and the SPLM—never to harm us. Before we got to the area, we knew what kind of activities the Toposa militia[11] were capable of. Yet we hoped never to experience these firsthand.

These swirling thoughts calmed, and finally I slept.

Hours later, in the darkest part of the night—around midnight—there was intense commotion. Everyone awoke and ran toward the center of the encampment. It was surreal. I somehow found myself sprinting along with the crowd, unaware of what had catalyzed the stampede. Only the swift footsteps of the group compelled me.

In a danger zone, like this civil war, we instinctively found protective cover before investigating what caused the disturbance to the peace. In nature, upon hearing the slightest snapping of a twig, an antelope rears its ears to ascertain where the possible danger is coming from, before warning others in the herd. Then, the herd bolts to safety. Our case was a reverse of the situation: we ran before investigating. Never to be outdone, I ran along with the crowd. However, my bed cover became tangled in a thorn shrub a few paces away, an encumbrance that gave me a moment to pause and fully awaken. I decided to stop and return to where I had been sleeping—trying to figure out what had happened. I lay down on my mat spread to slow my breathing, racing heart, and thoughts. Nothing made sense.

---

[11] See also Human Rights Watch, "CIVILIAN DEVASTATION: Abuses by All Parties in the War in Southern Sudan, (New York: Human Rights Watch, June 1994), p.279 for a story about this Toposa militia attack at Magos

A group of boys passed by me, carrying another boy on a mat, spread like a gurney. The victim was groaning in pain. One of the boys carrying the mat said, "He was shot in the stomach and the intestines are out." We were shot at.[12] As I laid down on my mat, amongst the chaos of more stricken and fatally wounded boys being carted by, my mind somehow wandered: my family; the danger I had endured; where we would go next. Sleep was over. We were headed into the unknown. I had escaped death that night as I had numerous times before. Did God have a hand in this? Did he want me to survive for a reason? I was yet to find out.

As I sat in the apartment, conversing with my friend Deng, I knew what needed to be done.

---

[12] After scouting the camp during the day, measuring the strength of the SPLA troops, the Toposa bandits, who numbered less than three gunmen, came back in the middle of the night. The first bullet went through the head of the sentry-they knew were the sentry was-then a barrage went through the sleeping boys, killing and wounding the few that rose first and who were close to the edge of the clearing. The SPLA response was swift, so the bandits melted into the thicket before any more damage was done. By the time I awoke, the attackers were gone, even the guns had gone silent.

CHAPTER 2

WHAT GIVES

"The day to have a free Southern Sudan is finally close, my friend. We need to speak with one voice and loudly enough that the whole world hears," Deng emphasized.

We were well aware of the immense sacrifices endured so that Southern Sudan could achieve self-determination. My friends and I needed to perform this crucial deed for Southern Sudan, and also, for ourselves: participation in the vote would decide whether Southern Sudan should become a free, independent nation, or remain under the Old Sudan, with terms set out in the CPA.[13] To my comrades, preserving a united Sudan completely nullified our journey. Southern Sudan could not concede. Our road had been too long, our sacrifices too immense.

The year was 1987, September, when it became clear that we could no longer cling to life as we knew it in my village of Wunlit and surrounding lands. Nomadic Arab raiders, known as the Murahilin, continued to pillage the countryside. Our cattle were seized. Our children and women were taken into captivity to be used as unpaid domestic servants[14] under squalid conditions in Northern Sudan. Men, elderly and infirmed, were murdered. Everything else was burned. For

---

[13] CPA, called the Comprehensive Peace Agreement, is the negotiated Peace Agreement that brought the Second Sudanese Civil War to an end in 2005

[14] Some said slaves

over three years, beginning in the dry season of 1984, Northern Sudan's Baggara Arab tribe had conducted punitive raids in the rural Southern Sudan region of Northern Bhar el Gazel.

Those devastating raids were supported by the Sudan Islamist government based in Khartoum. The Fundamentalist Islamic government had found that the raiders were a potent force in its counterinsurgency effort against the Sudan People's Liberation Army[15]——SPLA, a Southern Sudan based insurgency outfit whose stated aim was to rid the Sudan of the Islamist regime and to install in its place a new democratic and secular government for the multi-ethnic and multi-religious country, the Sudan.

With few Southern Sudanese insurgent contingents of the SPLA, the area was mostly defended by sparsely armed local ethnic militia, generally acting as reconnaissance scouts. They were no match against the superior Murahilin raiders, whether in training or weaponry, even though the ragtag defenders were determined to keep the raiders from taking their land.

But before those ferocious raiders arrived, a momentous event had been initiated for the people of Southern Sudan and the rest of the marginalized communities of the Sudan. On May 16th, 1983, a battalion of the Sudanese Army, formed of mostly Southern Sudanese absorbed members of the Anya Nya I,[16] had rebelled.[17] The Battalion 105 forces, on May 16th 1983, under Major Kerubino Kuanyin Bol, stationed in the town of Bor on the Eastern bank of the Nile River, led the fight that day against the rest of the Sudan Army in the vicinity of Bor and from nearby Juba. The rebel troops had then gone to nearby Ethiopia to begin a war of liberation for the people of the Sudan, in

---

[15] SPLA–The Sudan People's Liberation Army

[16] Joseph Lagu was the head of the Anya Nya I forces. The *Anya Nya I* rebellion granted Southern Sudan an autonomous government and earned the region a restive peace lasting until 1983.

[17] *Anya Nya I* was the rebel force that had started the civil war against the British-Egyptian Colonial Administration jointly ruling the Sudan till 1956, a rebellion that had lasted from 1955 to 1972, culminating in the Addis Abba Peace Agreement

general, but mostly for the oppressed peoples of Southern Sudan and the rest of the marginalized ethnic populations in its peripheries.

Unbeknownst to most people in our village, a civil war had begun and its consequences would so alter the landscape that twenty years later, nothing would be the same. The new war was a continuation of the old war that was fought between the two foes. History was repeating itself.

The immediate dangers now confronting the villagers were the ferocious raids spearheaded by men on horseback from Northern Sudan who gave no explanation for their brutality. We, the civilian inhabitants of the area, had fallen in the middle of a war fought between two very powerful armies and their equally powerful militias.

Our village and its surrounding areas had become rife with danger— and staying there meant a life of constantly trying to evade the raiders. We could not live that way. We needed to go somewhere else. Yet nearby Southern Sudanese towns like Wau no longer offered safety nor amenities. The towns in our region were under blockade by the SPLA army. Nothing went in. Nothing came out.

The Khartoum-controlled Sudan Armed ForcesSAF, the armed opponent of the SPLA, also enforced the blockades. However, the SAF would encourage civilians to come to the towns to be persecuted. The situation was so acute that basic necessities like foodstuffs, salt, soap, razor blades, and clothing were impossible to find. I realized this quickly, as I needed to give up having my head shaved, and eventually went without any descent clothes.

The market for the Dinka cattle had also dried up, depleting our cash, so that we couldn't purchase the necessary goods. The dire situation kept the adults up at night. And there was no rest during the day when we were on guard or on the run.

The decision to abandon the village was never taken lightly. The year before, in 1986, some members of the village, who had already been displaced from Wau decided to relocate to Ethiopia, after some of them were captured, snared in the Murahilin raiders' dragnet in the countryside. Others remained, though, deciding to take their time to see if they could suffer the wrongs, while evading the raiders within the surroundings of their villages, as had been done by their ancestors since the advent of the Islamic conquest of the Sudan.

Soon though, the risks of staying in the village began to outweigh the risks of leaving. Families began marching to Ethiopia in record numbers to swell the ranks of the SPLA; but most never made it back to their villages because the SPLA had other plans in mind for them, which didn't involve sending them back to their villages loaded with guns and ammunition. It was rumored that some soldiers, former villagers who had gone to Ethiopia to acquire guns for fighting the Murahilin invaders, would try to go AWOL to return to defend their villages. The SPLA did not support such actions, and deserters were often executed. Desperate, families and individuals continued to go to Ethiopia for survival, and men joined the SPLA to somehow return armed to fight the insecurity that had invaded their lives.

The economic blockade was a way to arbitrarily create famine, and force the country people, the backbone of the SPLA, to leave the countryside and join the government-run towns inside Southern Sudan, or to go to Northern Sudan where the displaced would be kept in squatter camps and generally mistreated or neglected. It was a scorched-earth policy aimed at wiping out a community. The main architect of that policy was the then Prime Minister ASadiq AL Mahdi. He had vowed that he would teach the Dinka, the most populous ethnic community in Southern Sudan and the main community from which the SPLA drew most of it's members, a lesson for their rebellious ways. But the Dinka kept resisting and kept joining the SPLA in masses. In 1989, ASadiq was forced out of power as his plan failed.[18] His plan not only had the opposite effect, but his government was also weakened by the emboldened SPLA/SPLM, militarily and politically.

For the local population of the region, keeping one step ahead of the raiders was the way to stay alive. Every year as the dry season

---

[18] His scorch-earth policy, of genocide and of forcing the country people to abandon the country-side and to relocate to the government-run towns, had failed because the country people swelled the ranks of the SPLA and the refugees in Ethiopia instead

approached in December and January, families prepared for their dry season escape routes, hiding places, evasion techniques, and information networks. Cattle, their main resource, were swiftly herded southward the moment the rains stopped, the harvest was taken in, and the land soon dried from floods. The grain would be put into underground granaries that were sealed off and discreetly marked so that they could be accessed after the danger had passed; or, grain was, hidden on tree canopies in the forest.

Life had become a matter of survival for the communities of Southern Sudan starting in 1983. By 1987, refuge was being sought, either by escaping to Ethiopia, or by joining the SPLA. This was our time to depart. Whatever the cost, fleeing to Ethiopia was better than waiting to be captured or killed. Escaping was our only chance for survival.

CHAPTER 3

THE LOL

"I am inviting you to journey with us to register and to vote together. Our country needs to be free from the Khartoum oppression," Deng added. I thought of our escape 23 years prior: At that time, I had no say in who was to travel with me, no understanding of what exactly my journey would accomplish on a larger scale, or where I would end up. "We are the ones to finally do it, brother," Deng urged. Our community had been suppressed by grave danger for too long. It was time to be free.

On the day of our escape, in September 1987, our relatives, neighbors, and members of the larger community were gathering for the long and feared journey to Ethiopia. I had steeled myself for the journey. I had witnessed the raiders' carnage and had run for my life with my family. I had also seen the few SPLA soldiers, who had been allowed by their commanders to return to our area, combat the raiders. They conducted their operations with competence and courage. I wanted to become a soldier. But how?

The people in our traveling party were to converge on the village of Wuntit, about a three-hour walk from our home village of Wunlit. Wuntit is right over the banks of Lol River, the region's main waterway. Travelers from surrounding villages swarmed Wuntit. We would spend the night in a relative's house and depart the next morning.

Our group consisted of nearly 50 people—men, women, and children—all related in some manner. Our group was abuzz with rumors, counter-rumors, and bits and pieces of truth about the journey. We shared a palpable fear, but also a keen enthusiasm and hope. Our overarching goal was to reach Ethiopia alive, and the risks of the trek were never lost on us.

At that time of year, the Lol River was still full of water from the rainy season as well as backflow from the Nile River. The Lol, emanating from the Mountains of Central African Republic— specifically, from the Nyamlell River in Aweil West, South Sudan— empties its water into the Nile River at Lake No until the Nile overflows around September and October. The backflow then pushes the extra water from the Lol into the countryside, flooding the low-lying areas and watering the pastures for the Dinka cattle the year round. Flood waters can sometimes reach the neck of a six-foot tall adult. The abundant waterway also provides much needed fish to the inhabitants of the Lol River Valley.

The river, which loses most of its flood and rainy season water to evaporation during the high heat of the dry season, is used to water the cattle, the mainstay of the Dinka. It is one of the major tributaries of the Nile River and it runs from west to east towards Lake No, the confluence point with the Nile. For the Dinka in Wunlit village and in the rest of Twic County, the Lol River is a major artery of the Nile that regulates most of the life throughout the year and it is, therefore, a vital water system for the area.

The Lol River is a critical resource for the region. When there is little rain in the Central African Republic's Mountains and low water levels in the Nile, limited floods destroy the pastures. Cattle die, leading to famine in the countryside. Though this was not a particularly flood-stricken year, the river was bursting with water to its banks, full of aquatic riverine life like crocodiles, hippopotamuses, and fish. Acacia, chum, tamarind trees, ferns, and other native trees populated our side of the banks. The people of Wuntit, as most Dinka in the area, were subsistence farmers, pastoralists, fishermen, hunters, and small-scale traders.

On the other side of the riverbank, across from the elevated village of Wuntit, was the low lying valley. The valley was full of water and awar grass[19] that nourished the cattle. Several trees were scattered beyond the valley.

It was in this village that we spent our evening preparing to depart early the following day, heavy with worry, and torn with grief over separating from the family members we were leaving behind.

---

[19] *Vetiveria Negritana*

CHAPTER 4

THE LION

"This is the final journey, as you know," Deng continued, "for us, the martyrs, and the wounded, and for southern Sudan." I knew that it would be less harrowing than that first journey.

"It is like that last straw that broke the camel's back, but only this time, it will right what is wrong with the Sudan," he added. Indeed, I would be forgiven had I refused to make the first journey in 1987, but never would I be forgiven if I refused the final call. It was simply my sacred duty to fulfill. I would make calls and persuade those who needed convincing. I was going to get that group of five.

Yet, when we embarked on that initial journey in 1987, we were keenly aware of the dangers that laid ahead. For once, the Nile River and its swamps[20] were a formidable barrier to ford across. It was rumored that it would take seven full days in the boat to cross the swamps, and the Nile River itself. Imagine being jammed in a canoe or a dugout for seven full days, with crocodiles and snakes hitching rides on the passing water hyacinth, circling the boats, or swimming below the water's surface looking for prey; the great hippopotamus prowling in the dark waters. The Nile is deep and there would be no rescue if a boat were to capsize.

Then came the desert. It was rumored, perhaps by those who never really wanted to be a part of the journey, that the desert was so vast that it would take more than eight days to cross over on foot; and not

---

[20] Collectively, the *Sudds*

a single drop of water was to be found in such terrain. Your own urine was the sole liquid available to quench your thirst.

Predatory land animals posed another threat—especially, the feared lion. Without a spear, club, or gun amongst the group, we would stand little chance against such a powerful beast.

Then there were the ever-present threats faced from the hostile ethnic communities along the way. The most fearsome was the Murle, a nomadic group in Jonglei. Without hesitation, or apparent motivation, they would massacre unarmed civilians, especially members of the Dinka. They would slaughter everybody except little children, who would be adopted into the tribe to increase their numbers.

Our group also risked encountering garrison towns along the way. The government-controlled towns like Rumbek, Tony, Bor and Pibor were of particular concern because they were on the exact route we were to follow. Being untrained civilians traveling on unfamiliar routes, we would need better guides, perhaps SPLA military personnel, to navigate us away from those towns and the minefields surrounding them. We could easily lose our bearings and wander into those areas, occupied by the feared Sudan Armed forces.

Another concern was the sheer distance from Bar el Gazel, closer to the border with Chad, all the way across the vast country of the Sudan into Ethiopia. This distance was especially daunting for women and children. How could one walk every day, nonstop, for three months without rest? Exhaustion would be inevitable, survival uncertain. This distance might only seem surmountable to an experienced SPLA soldier, or the bravest civilians.

Our final concern was the hunger we would face along the way. We carried no money and had no other way to secure goods, or replenish resources. We had no pack animals to carry our food rations, and no cattle to sacrifice, to provide us with a feast. SPLA soldiers were welcome to impose taxes on the communities they were traveling through. Such a tax would be in the form of foodstuffs like dairy products or livestock. We could never attempt such a move.

These impending dangers, coupled with the pain of separating from our families, led to a heavy evening of unspoken worries. My friend,

Ayuel, started narrating a powerful story. Dinka children always tell stories for each other before bedtime, just as many children are read books at night. These stories are usually about animal characters and in this case, it was a lion. Looking back, this story seems unsettlingly relevant to our existence then.

"A man traveled the forest looking for the lion that had killed his bull, Maker[21]. The lion was feared by all the cattle keepers in the area. It had killed cows before and no one had been able to kill it. The lion made his abode in the very deep forest. Any attempts to hunt and kill him ended with the hunters getting lost in the deep jungle, only to fall prey to the ultimate hunter, the killer lion.

The man sang as he walked the forest searching for the lion, '*Kuany roric ku ror aken kan yok eben*, (I have traveled through forests but never through such a strange forest).'

'*Na yin ya yin aken Kan yok Na yuom e ran bi ya kuin keda*, (You too are a stranger; I would love to chew on the bone of a human') the lion replied."

Ayuel narrated, "The man met the lion in a fight. Then, the man came out of the forest after the fight with the bones of his cow to show the cattle keepers. '*Wun wun tiengke chon Makerdie yo*, (People at the cattle camp, come to see the leg of my Maker)' the man sang.

'*Makerdu yen ci ngo nok*, (What happened to your Maker?)' the cattle keepers sang back.

'*Makerdie yen aci Nyituil[22] chuet gua nok eh*, (My Maker was killed by the lion Nyituil and so I killed him!)' replied the man."

Though we were terrorized by the situation ahead of us, that night I was simply entertained by the story. Lion stories are ubiquitous among the Dinka and are used to instruct little children of a moral: stay close to your mothers, and do not wander into the lairs of wild animals. Dangerous lions and other wild animals were a reality to us. Still, our party was resigned to the journey, whatever it would bring. We were leaving no matter the odds.

---

[21] Black and white bull

[22] The lion's name is Nyituil-meaning hungering after or in want of meat

CHAPTER 5

WUNLIT

"Do you think they can bar any of us from registering?" Deng questioned. "It is said that we must show proof we are Southern Sudanese. I don't need to prove to anyone that I am a southerner."

The Southern Sudan Referendum Commission, SSRC, stipulated that to be qualified to register, one must have been "Born to parents, both or one of them belonging to one of the indigenous communities that settled in Southern Sudan on or before the 1st of January 1956, or whose ancestry is traceable to one of the ethnic communities in Southern Sudan.[23]" Meeting such a requirement was never going to be any harder.

Born in 1978 at the village of Chong—present day Wunrok Payam, Twic County, Warrap State of South Sudan—my youthful innocence kept me from fully understanding the situation around me for some time. As is the practice among the Dinka, the first two children of a newly married woman can be delivered at their maternal grandmother's house instead of at their father's house. The educated members of the community often preferred to deliver in a safer environment, however, and because of this practice, my elder sister was born at the hospital in Wau. That was never going to be the situation for me.

I was born at my mother's home village of Chong—the second among what would be six children, three boys and three girls. I later

---

[23] Southern Sudan Referendum Act 2009, Chapter 4, Part 2, sec. 25, #1-5, p.14

learned that my father had desperately wanted a son first and was disappointed when my sister arrived. So disappointed, in fact, that he did not want his second child to be born at the hospital in the provincial town of Wau where he worked—in case it was another girl. That concern turned to joy when he learned that his son had been safely delivered at home in the village. It was then that I earned my status: the first-born son, though second to a girl.

The Dinka honor a first-born son, who might become heir to the father's name and family fortune. Girls, meanwhile, are to be married off to establish new families, caring for home and children. They still remain part of their father's lineage, though, and retain the family name. The Dinka view those with no family as being outcasts, or worse still, being dead.

My maternal grandfather, Mayen Deng Cyer, was the Chief of the nearby Adiang Mayom community, a section of the Twic Dinka who inhabit the present day Twic County. Chief Mayen Deng Cyer was a much-respected leader to his people; a righteous and a just man, in character, leadership, and faith.

By the standards of the time, my mother's family was wealthy with a lot of cattle. I still remember, in the foggy eyes of a young boy, seeing calves playing about in the field in the soggy grounds and witnessing herds of cattle at dusk at Chong before being tethered to their wooden pegs. Milk was abundant and life was good for a child growing up.

Chong is a strip of raised ground, running east-west, about an hour's walk north of the town of Wunrok. This land is slightly higher than the surrounding area, which floods during the rainy season and during the annual floods prevalent in the Nile River valley. It is also bordered by seasonal swamps and a meandering stream. Initially just a clearing, it is also surrounded by trees and was frequented by elephants, giraffes, buffalo, and other game. The animals would stay mostly overnight to dry themselves off after bathing in the nearby swamps. This activity led the strip to become a beaten-down patch of land before my grandfather took it over to make his second home. He named it Chong, which means 'to be trampled underfoot'. The large herds had shaped, and helped name, the land.

My true home, however, is Wunlit village. My paternal grandparents lived in Wunlit, and because the Dinka are counted paternally, I considered it my home too. The best way to describe Wunlit's location, perhaps, is by its proximity to the well-known little town of Wunrok, which is to the east—about two-hour walk. A 20-minute walk south of Wunlit brings you to the Lol River.

Wunlit, as with most other settlements in South Sudan, was chosen as the village center and place for dwellings because its raised ground protected houses from the inevitable rains and annual floods. Although the frequency and temerity of the floods has reduced over time, the place was once swamp-like. By my own reckoning, I assess the village was founded about 200 years ago. In jurisdiction, Wunlit village falls under the present day Pan-nyok Payam, of Twic County of Warrap State. Pan-nyok, the town and the Pan-nyok Payam center, is about an hour's walk northwest of Wunlit.

The history of the village, a mixture of legend and fact, traces its founder as being Awak Rum. This man is the clear ancestor of my community, the Panawak, and an eighth generation ancestor to me. It is stated that his father Rum or Rumdit[24] emigrated from areas east of Twic County and that his forebears emigrated from further afield in South Sudan in the present-day greater Tonj District, in the same Warrap State. Perhaps as evidence of this emigration, in the Tonj District, most of the ancestors of Awak Rum still call the place home and there is even a village named Wunlit there. That village became quite famous for the 1999 Wunlit People-to-People Peace agreement between the warring Nilotic[25] communities of Dinka and Nuer; their ancient conflicts were increasingly militarized by the SPLM/SPLA politicians. The Wunlit village in Tonj was the venue for that breakthrough peace agreement, which was the precursor to the Sudanese Comprehensive Peace Agreement, the CPA, leading to the end of the Second Sudanese

---

[24] Rum the Elder

[25] The Nilotes are the Nile valley area people, with similar characteristic bodily features, cultures broadly similar and languages that carry similar meanings. The Nilotes inhabit swathe of territory along the Nile from Sudan, South Sudan and all the way into Uganda, Kenya and Tanzania

Civil War in 2005. Awak Rum must have striven to name his new home after his ancestral village in Tonj. But, the similarities end there.

It is amongst the community of the newer Wunlit village, in Twic County, that I grew up as a boy. My family and I spent time in the neighboring villages of Chong and Wau—places that I still hold dear—but my birthplace and true home is Wunlit.

A typical Dinka boy in the village in the 1980s would have very few articles of clothing yet an assortment of tools depending on his age and his level of involvement with cattle-keeping chores. Spears, clubs, and sticks were used to lead cattle, and fight off attackers and wild animals like hyenas. Young boys were known to fight each other with clubs and sticks, though they were also expected to work hard and contribute to the family.

Chores required of a Dinka boy varied depending on his age and family wealth. They involved looking after the cattle, calves, goats, and sheep, farming, housing construction, running errands and looking after children, especially younger siblings. I was never spared any chores. I started out with farming. My job was to act as a watchman for our little farm during the planting season. When the crops planted had germinated, I would sit under our thau (Heglig-Balanites Aegyptiaca) tree to keep watch over the farm, with sorghum seedlings knee-high. I was especially watchful for goats and cattle. I would keep one eye guarding the farm, while the other eye was on the games then at play.

Boyhood was never dull, and there were always chances to play. Games involved fighting other boys, wrestling, fishing, fruit picking, hunting,[26] got,[27] and going to dances. When not working, Dinka boys were always playing or inventing new games.

Neighboring cousins would often play the game of cattle keeping with me. This involved using the empty shells of snails as cows. In their various shapes and coloring, a collection of them would act as the cattle capital of a very rich owner who would then proceed to arrange them

---

[26] Especially for small wildlife
[27] A hockey-type game played on hard ground with sticks

in a gol.[28] You would succeed by remembering the particular coloring, which you would use as the name of that particular kind of cow to prevent your friends from stealing it. Such games were elaborate and we would be engrossed in them until sunset. I remember being proud of my effort to guard our garden, despite the games, knowing full well that my family, especially my mother and elder sister, worked tirelessly to till the whole farm.

Our games often resulted in mishaps or injuries that sometimes caused rifts in our little group. As a young boy, I was sometimes called on as a peacemaker because I had a capacity to be impartial and fair. I recall one time, though, while playing under the famous Rual (*Kigelia Africana*) tree in Wunlit, where I accidentally caused an injury to my best friend and cousin, Chol, and this led to acrimony within my family.

The *Rual* tree, *Rual Makam*, is a large tree with broad leaves and dark red flowers that produce oblong inedible fruits. The tree existed when the village was founded around it, and has long been used to shade the village elders when socializing and while settling village disputes. The Rual tree is sacred to our local Dinka, the Parum community, and we are forbidden to cut any part of the tree, which explains its longevity.

Since the village's founding, the tree has witnessed countless episodes of children fighting and playing. During one particular day during my boyhood, my friends and I were engaged in a game that included running through the branches—which was quite precarious for younger climbers. Occasionally, someone would be bitten by a wasp hidden among the leaves, or worse yet, fall and sustain minor injuries. The Rual tree branches are exceptionally light and would break easily with the slightest of weight, just like the branches of the Mango tree; and that was why the climbing of the Rual tree was left to the daring and the truly mischievous boys.

It was during this game that I wanted to practice spearing at the Rual fruits with my fishing spear even though it would be frowned upon by an adult nearby. I prepared to spear at least one of several fruits

---

[28] A particular way of arranging cows, tied to wooden pegs stuck to the ground, according to size, gender etc.

hanging like stalagmites from the ceiling of a cave. I threw my spear and missed the fruits. When it came down, the unserrated spear lodged in my cousin's foot, just between the bones of the upper ankle. Although it avoided damaging the bones, the spear wound was deep.

After removing the spear, which was confiscated by the judges of the moment, I prepared to defend myself. The news had already traveled home and I received word that my Mom and uncles were going to issue punishment. What better way to avoid punishment than by simply staying away from home? I believed that my absence would concern my family, since there were many dangers—namely wild animals—for a child alone in the wilderness. My hope, therefore, was that they would value me more, and sympathize more, if I failed to reappear at home.

When I made the threat, which was quickly relayed to my adoring mother, I was welcomed back at the house that evening without incident. The victim, my friend and cousin, had confirmed that it was purely an accident. That, coupled with my threats to spend the night in the nearby forests, saved me from severe punishment. My punishment came from within: the guilt of my carelessness and how it could have caused greater injury to my dear cousin. And the people at home and around the village never hesitated to point out such a mistake. Most important, I did continue a friendship with my cousin. Sometime later, while fishing, he speared one of my fingers. Though it was less severe of an injury, we considered it a draw.

CHAPTER 6

FAMILY ROLES

"Almost every family in South Sudan has lost a family member in the long war, some never even know how their relatives lost their lives, either in active combat in the SPLA trenches or due to the spinoffs of the war. How can we bring closure to these families? How can we collect all the scattered bones in order to memorialize them?" Deng lamented.

As my Father was an accountant, my Mother was a farmer. During Wunlit's farming season, my Mother and Sister, the main farmers, would start tilling the land, with me tagging along. After my initial job of guarding the seedlings, I would guard our families' goats and sheep. By the standards of the village, our livestock and farm provided for a relatively wealthy household; and this was in addition to my father's town profession. Taking care of the goats came easily to me because once I had the goats under trees, they would graze while I played games. A simple shout could keep them in one general area. Tending goats and sheep together proved more difficult. While I was herding goats one day, I was faced with an unexpected dilemma for which I was entirely unprepared: our goat was about to deliver. I instinctively pulled the baby's feet as they appeared, and a few minutes later the cream-colored goat was born. I came home with the little kid proudly upon my shoulders and the doting mother goat behind me; upon narrating the ordeal, everyone was happy with how I had handled the situation except for one caveat: Did I make it breathe by blowing air into its nostrils? I had failed to follow that precaution, but the kid was thriving nonetheless. I had succeeded in being a goat-keeper.

I later started looking after calves, the tougher of the two, because one must never allow calves to meet their mothers and suckle before milking in the evening. If the keeper failed in this regard, he might get shut out of the house or sleep on an empty stomach if the milk was needed for a demanding toddler. I can boast that only once did a calf ever suckle from his mother under my watch.

Cattle keeping among the Dinka is as old as the Dinka themselves. Perhaps the first thing God gave to the Dinka after creating them was the rope to tie down a cow and to tether it to a peg. This form of livelihood is what the Dinka learn from the beginning and continue doing until they drop dead. The moment a boy was weaned away from his Mother, he would be forced to look after calves and goats, learn how to milk cows, fetch the delicate grasses for the very young calves, and pick up cow dung to spread in the sunlight to dry. The dried dung would be burned in the evening, to keep away the insects. He was expected to look after domestic livestock, even defending them from wild animals. The girls would be taught how to milk cows and complete other chores around the house.

A Dinka man (or boy) is most comfortable when he is standing with one of his legs perched on the other in a particular way, while his cattle graze contentedly nearby. With his height, he can see far afield— looking out for danger while making sure the cattle get the best pastures. He will never rest or seek comfort unless his cows are tethered and watched over. The cattle economy is so vital that it is a status symbol among the Dinka.

Growing up, Chong and Wunlit were not my only homes, just as farming and keeping livestock were not my only chores. My family also maintained a home in the town of Wau. We would travel between the village and town every season—farming in Wunlit and then attending school in Wau.

Traveling between our home village of Wunlit and Wau was treacherous. We would follow the route from our village on foot to Wunrok, where there would generally be a truck traveling to Gogrial and then on to Wau. The journey would start very early in the morning and last until late afternoon. The shoddy roads were handmade by conscripted public laborers appointed by local chiefs. Maintenance occurred only when the roads were eroding, and never on a regular basis. As the central government rarely assessed or repaired the roads, their condition depended on the mindfulness of a chief who may ask his subjects to contribute manpower. And as such, the road was usually damaged and awfully bumpy. Motion sickness was not uncommon. There would be occasional rest stops at the villages along the road where vendors sold foodstuffs like boiled eggs, fruits, and milk; and where there were water wells where the travelers could drink to quench thirst.

My first recollection of Wau was our home in the Number Three section of the city—a housing complex for government employees. The huge compound, made of red ironstone bricks, contained several houses arranged in a row with common areas. Families would increase their dwellings by building thatched roof huts or tukuls or rukuba. As government housing tended to be congested, some well-to-do families would have better housing in the sections just outside town. One of my aunts—whose fearsome dog I remember vividly—owned such a dwelling and we would travel to her house often.

In 2010, upon returning to Wau for the first time in 24 years, I could neither find our former house nor make out the landmarks. And though atop the nearby hill now sits the new Kenya Commercial Bank, I can still look out and remember scenes from our childhood there in the 1980's. I still remember my elder sister going to school next to Medan Isaac, or the Isaac Stadium—even though I could no longer find the school or the stadium. I vividly recall being left at home while my sister went to school, as I was too young for school at the time.

One day, I got so bored that I decided to go call on my sister to come home. I went and stood outside the classroom of her girls' school and shouted for her to come out. The noise got the attention of the teacher and the other girls. The girls started insulting me in Arabic, insults which I don't quite remember now. Feeling indignant, I picked up a stone and hurled it through the open window into the classroom. I don't know if anyone was injured but my sister shouted that I should run. I didn't. Instead, the teacher got a hold of me and started beating me. Running would have shown that I was in the wrong so I stayed and was punished for my unruly behavior.

On a number of occasions, I went to church with my sister. The Catholic Church cathedral in Wau is a huge structure compared to the other buildings. My sister, in effect, became my first evangelizer. She told me the story of Jesus: "Jesus' mother, Mary, was expectant of Jesus in heaven but she decided when the baby was due, to come to earth for Jesus to be born. So, when she was ready, all the outcasts of the society, the lepers, the sick, the handicapped and so forth, came to witness the delivery of the baby. When the child was born, all those who had gathered were miraculously healed of their ailments.

Then, Maria was urged to return the baby to heaven, but she refused and remained on earth till Jesus became an adult. Then, the bad people colluded and killed Jesus by nailing him to the cross. Then, God raised him up to heaven, along with Mary", she narrated. And in my child's mind, I thought he was cut into pieces through the joints, without breaking his bones and then the bones nailed to the ground.

I likely had this thought because of the Dinka Altar.[29] The Dinka build a shrine made of strong pieces of timber arranged in a circle. Even though there was always a crucifix in the church, it never occurred to me that that was how Jesus actually died. Hung too high for a young boy like me, I merely thought it an insignificant statue. I didn't truly understand how Jesus died, and I wonder if my sister truly did either.

At the Wau Catholic Church, an incident occurred that left the entire town abuzz. My sister and I had gone to church one very early Sunday morning. It was Palm Sunday, I believe, because the whole congregation had marched into the woods to collect palm fronds. While the church was in prayer, an attendant went upstairs to operate the electricity. Somehow, there was a short circuit and someone was electrocuted. In the midst of a solemn song, and heavy incense smoke, sharp noises emanating from upstairs alarmed the churchgoers, who

---

[29] See also Godfrey Lienhardt, 'DIVINITY AND EXPERIENCE, The Religion of the Dinka', 1961, part 2, p.259

stampeded out of the building. Amazingly, I only sustained injuries to the knees and hand during the ordeal. Up to now, I am not sure if the electrocuted attendant died or survived.

Every year, during the dry season[30] and rainy season,[31] our family would travel between our rural Wunlit home and our urban Wau home, a movement which gave me an exciting and challenging contrast of locales. In Wau, there would be many chances to play and fight with other boys, in quite different ways than in the country. I could find myself playing soccer or making car toys in the town, among other forms of entertainment. There was a chance to go to school too. But, in the country, you could go fishing, hunt small animals, look after cattle, calves, and goats and then fight with other boys or play games like got.

My best friend in Wau was Maluk. He was a little older than me and was more familiar with the ways of Wau than I was, given my nomadic lifestyle. On occasion, he would take advantage of my naiveté and penchant for fairness.

One day Maluk and I were sent to the market together to buy bread and other essentials for our families. It was the first time for me to be sent on such an errand and I relied on Maluk to make sure I bought the right items at a fair price. However, I ended up spending all the money I had because after having bought what I was sent for, Maluk told me that the goods he was bringing his family were smaller than mine and I thought that would be unfair. So I gave him part of our family's money to equalize the groceries and my mother was none too pleased. I would later learn the true meaning of fairness.

At around this time the Sudan Armed Forces trainees were running around Wau, training in shorts and white shirts with heads shaved. Sometimes they would climb on the electricity poles and sing songs

---

[30] Involving seasonal changes from September–to–October–to–November—the Autumn season, then December–to–January–to–February—the cold-dry winter season, then March–to–April—the hot-dry winter season—collectively the dry season

[31] Starting from May–to–June—the Spring season, and then July–to–August–to–September—the Summer season—collectively the rainy season

which were quite unintelligible. It was Nimeiri's time.[32] Nimeiri ruled the Sudan till 1985 when he was overthrown in a popular uprising in the streets of Khartoum. He was the President of the Sudan in 1983 when the SPLA rebelled. The rebellion was directly attributed to him. He had violated the key principles of the Addis Ababa Agreement that brought to an end the first Sudanese Civil War in 1972. He violated, in particular, the principle of Southern Autonomy in 1983, famously quipping of the Addis Ababa Agreement: *'La Koran, La Injil'*—It is neither the Koran nor the Bible! When An-Nimeiri discovered that Southern military officers leading battalions of the Sudanese army formed from former Anya Nya forces and stationed in Southern towns, were planning a rebellion that would lead to the break-away of Southern Sudan—a direct result of his usurpations—he decided to have those officers along with their battalions relocated to Northern Sudan. This plan quickly unraveled the Southern Planned rebellion. After most of the rest of the battalions in Southern towns acquiesced and were successfully relocated to Northern Sudan, Major Kerubino Kuanyin stationed at Bor with Battalion 105 acted quickly on May 16th 1983 to stave off the move. He ushered in the SPLA.

Wau was becoming a melting pot of Sudanese multiculturalism. The major Islamic culture was becoming apparent in towns; I recall the first time witnessing public mourning and burial of a murder victim (likely killed by some authority). The body of the deceased was put on a bed, covered with white cotton clothing, and then carried in a procession toward the burial grounds with ululating. I wondered then why such a scene was unfolding, and I wonder now if it still occurs given that the Islamic influence is now largely gone.

Staying at our uncle's house across the road from the UN compound, before we moved to our own house, my cousins and I would stand by the roadside every day to bid "Kawaja Morning" to the white woman passerby on a motorcycle. My cousin Maluk had told me that it was a fun form of greeting. We would stand waiting solemnly for the rider,

---

[32] Field Marshal Mohamed an-Nimeiri was the Sudanese dictator that took power in a military coup in 1969

counting every minute to ensure that she would never go a day without us bidding our 'morning' greeting. The graceful rider would reply back "Morning!" with a wide smile but never stopping. What went on in her mind?

She probably thought of us as innocent boys, who had nothing better to do except stand by the roadside to bid her good morning. She surely must have felt sorry for us for never being in school. Indeed, I do believe my cousin Maluk should have been at school then though I was not yet enrolled. This was going to change in a short time. But, curiously, it never occurred to me to marvel at a white person and see her as somebody different. She was a charming curiosity to us, just as we were likely a charming curiosity to her. She must have been working for UNICEF. In 2010, I was walking on the road in Wau when I saw another white woman in shorts and sandals. I was bemused because that reminded me of my time with my cousin Maluk. How much has changed? I now speak better English!

During that time in Wau, my family decided to move to another part of the town—Heilat Dinka (Dinka Borough), because my father got another job with the UNICEF agency. Then, it was decided to enroll me at the new Catholic school being built in the nearby Heilat Jadit (New Borough). I was accepted for afternoon and Saturday sessions. Most other pupils were already knowledgeable in the English alphabet, Arabic, and Dinka. Even though I was behind the other students in this regard, I befriended one boy. When I explained to him that I did not understand most of what was being written on the board, he offered to take my exam for me. I quickly accepted his offer, thrilled that I could continue to focus on playing, not learning.

One day, as I was approaching the school well to get a drink, one of the boys made sure that I didn't get anything from a girl who was there holding the water jug. He challenged me, instead, to a fight on the nearby hill. *"Kede namshi inaak fil jam el jebel ashan ti shuf!"* I accepted the challenge and we moved to the hill, with the girl and several more spectators in tow. When we reached the hill, the girl scooped two generous handfuls of earth, one in her right palm and the other in her left palm, saying those were our *madida* (or porridge). The symbolism was that if we were ready for a fight, then each of us would slap the porridge off of her hands—signaling that we did not want *madida* and were ready to fight. Slapping off the madida meant someone was not sickly and in need of the nourishments; instead, he was healthy and able to fight.

I slapped mine off and my adversary followed suit. It must have been amusing for our girl but then the school bell sounded and as we had been warned, if one was late, you would go through a beating even worse than the one you might get from a hillside opponent. We both ran back to the school and so ended our intended fight. From that day, I was free to drink from the fountain without any problem and I played, prayed, and attended classes with everyone else.

But when the exams came, my friend was true to his word. He did both our work and the following day our papers were back—mine with a nice drawing of the head of a cat in red ink at the top of the page where the teacher's mark should have been. My friend had filled the paper with some writing in blue but it apparently was all wrong—I didn't know. I thought it was all perfect. I ran all the way home to show my father how well I was doing at school. But upon seeing my paper, I got a spanking. It was the first time my father had spanked me and I was simply puzzled. At the time, my father only showed me that my name was spelled wrong. About three years later I finally learned what the head of a cat on a term paper meant: a zero.

Our house in Wau was located just next to the UN compound, which included the UNICEF office. At those times, UNICEF was engaged in providing clean water to the town's population by placing water-pumps in strategic population centers around Wau. One of these water-pumps was next to our new house when we moved in. The large UN compound running the entire length of our block was fenced in with meshed wire and we could see the German made Mercedes trucks full of tubing and metal encasing for the wells. There were also drums of fuel for the trucks. Nearly every day, the compound was busy with workmen either loading or unloading the various spare parts for the water-pumps using cranes and so forth. We marveled at it. The same tubes, now rusted and neglected, were still there in 2010, 24 years later,

CHAPTER 7

FISHING AND SINGING

"All that happened during our struggle must be written down for the world to know. No one knows for sure the tragedies we have faced. They say that there was genocide in Rwanda and Darfur but they never talk of Southern Sudan. How many bones have you seen?" Deng lamented.

The Southern Sudan Referendum Commission, SSRC, was charged with the task to end an historical problem. The question was: Was the Sudan going to remain united under the terms of the CPA or would the people of Southern Sudan choose to secede to create their new country? In the minds of Southern Sudanese, the right choice was obvious; but the area had so many internal problems that some Southern Sudanese thought it might be better to maintain the Sudan as a united country. Ethnic tensions always remained under the surface and a large concern. However, Northern Sudanese had shown the people of Southern Sudan time and again that they never wanted them as equals in the affairs of the Sudan.

A liberated Southern Sudan would be free to rewrite its history and to celebrate its many cultures whereas a Southern Sudan within a united Sudan would lose its identity to the dominant Islamic Arab history and culture. The choice was ours to finally show in a ballot box no matter the consequences.

As we made seasonal trips between the town and the village, I became acquainted with relatives and friends of our family. While in Wau, I was asked to accompany my grandfather to the home of my uncle in Heilat Jadit, which was close to the Grinti military barracks. On this particular trip, we could see the Sudan Army at parade. The home we visited was perched upon a higher ground overlooking, to the right, a small valley of the River Jur running North of Wau. The tall grasses of this valley reminded me of our home village of Wunlit.

My grandfather's travels depended on me and I never disappointed him or my family. I must have realized he was a very important person and I learned a lot from him concerning the situation at the village and our community in general. I also got to tell him the rubbish young boys narrate about places like Wau. And when he was attacked and fatally wounded by the Murahilin about a year later—after they found his briefcase which contained a military uniform from his time in the British-instituted Southern Sudan guard force-the Home Guard—I sought to honor him by participating during the funeral, though as a young boy, I didn't realize that he was gone for good. Even two years later, I participated in efforts to maintain his shrine. I know my father respected him, and would have braved a storm to be with his father.

Upon returning from Wau to the village, for the rainy, farming season, I was able to learn firsthand how fishing is done by the Dinka. One year, an uncle decided to fish at our family's fishing ground, which had been handed down from generation to generation. The grounds had been left dormant for several years, with nobody volunteering to perform this traditional, important activity. And since I was ever inquisitive, I was going to be with my Uncle at every turn of the way.

Going through the preparations for the fishing season, the rieth grass was fetched and the first kind of net for the very small fish was made. This particular net, called akolkou, was like a placeholder until the fish riding the flood had time to grow to larger sizes for the real fishing to begin. The fishing grounds in the toc, or swamp, were prepared by heaping the mud onto the ridges that were built and maintained every year there was a flood and fishing was done. This process required the exhausting work of digging the mud and heaping it onto the ridges to leave only the channels opening to the deeper parts of the toc, where the fish would be flowing into the nets. When the fish were plentiful enough in the grasses of the flooded toc, the fishing season began. At night, the able-bodied fishermen would be at the mat, the fishing ridges, and our particular family mat was situated at Aweet, a seasonally flooded swampland.

At night, schools of fish would quietly follow the channel into the fishing net and, would eat the leaves of the bitter *adhoth* tree, placed there to trap them. The fishermen would wake up in intervals and go slowly through the water without causing any waves in the water system, something which could warn the school to rush off the way they had come leaving an empty net. The fisherman would approach the *rok*, fishing net slowly and deliberately and then with a quick movement, raise the *rok* high from the water. He would empty the fish into a basket placed on stilts and then replace the *rok*, making sure that there was no opening to the other side of the ridge. The fisherman would go back to the mat abode, which invariably was a mound under a tree farther away from the mouth of the mat.

The process would be repeated throughout the night, trapping and catching more fish. The darker the night, the better the catch; and so during the day and during periods of the full moon, the catch would decrease. When it was light enough, a dark form approaching, albeit silently and without a stir, could be seen, or sensed, by the fish, who would dart away. So we focused on trapping the fish during dark, moonless nights.

The men and boys at the fishing camp would pass time by singing songs circulating in the dance spots throughout the region, and telling each other stories passed down from generation to generation. The songs' lyrics captured life, its ugliness and its blessings, as well as tales of the community's history. Some of the songs I happened to hear where about the *Murahilin* raiders plying the countryside in the dry season and the carnage they left behind. The songs were also about those Dinka who gave them guidance to areas only the Dinka would know were filled with cattle. Those traitors were particularly loathed and considered the lowest members of the group—so low that attacking them was a contemptible action for they weren't even worthy of punishment.

The songs also talked about the heroism of the young men who fought the *Murahilin* raiders. Lyrics conveyed the atrocities committed by the few SPLA contingents who were already present and actively fighting the *Murahilin*, but who were also looting wantonly in the countryside for goats, sheep, cows and other goods.

> '1. *Koc wan ci dong aci lok a banybai acin ke luel, cuet*
> *e thok yen aluel, kek e naak e monydit tau bai na pen*
> *wengde* (Those who remained behind have become
> leaders, looters of goats and beaters of old men for
> refusal to part with cows).
> Ref: *Ka ye riak, yen akuath areth, aye riak yen a nak e*
> *wet ken rot det* (The old men get arrested and beaten for
> refusal to part with their cows or goats).
> 2. *Garang Mabior* (To you Dr. John Garang Mabior).
> 3. *Kuanyin wen e Bol* (To you Kerubino Kuanyin Bol).'

The song was a complaint to Dr. Garang and Kerubino Kuanyin, the SPLA leaders, about what their army was doing in the countryside—stealing property and beating men upon refusal.

For the Dinka, songs are primary ways to convey experiences and tell stories. Songs are passed down like valuable books. To know about what happened at a particular time, you only have to listen to Dinka songs, along with a bit of helpful commentary by a Dinka village elder. Though some of the stories were fictional, they were used to impart knowledge about human behavior and convey how to act morally.

One ubiquitous Dinka story is that of Chol Mong. The basic story is commonly agreed upon, but individual narrators tend to embellish it, depending on the moment and the audience. All agree that Chol Mong was a huge man who ate a lot. He is depicted refusing to defend his family's cattle because his wife had failed to give him enough milk, as she kept the milk in a big gourd to use for the extraction of the important cream. Instead of asking his wife to provide him more milk, he kept quiet and then decided to look for a way to make his wife provide more milk.

As narrated, "Chol Mong colluded with a group of men from the neighborhood to arrive at his house with shields and spears at the ready one evening at the time when the cattle were tethered to their pegs and the evening embers aflame, as if to raid the cows. Chol Mong wanted them to drive the cows away with him following later to return them. He convinced his friends that there was a very important matter he wanted to have solved between him and his wife and that such a participation by his friends was what was needed, no more, no less.

The men obliged and waited for him to return to his house. At the right time, they appeared brandishing clubs, and holding spears and shields, proceeding to untether all the cows and to make off with them. Upon seeing the unfolding scene, Chol Mong's wife came in rushing to warn him to follow the cows knowing full well that the husband was quite capable of doing the deed. But, he simply told his wife, 'Ask your gourd to go bring them back.'

This puzzled the wife. How could a gourd follow the cows to bring them back? But she quickly realized that what her husband meant was that he was upset with the way she was handling milk. So, she promised to give him more milk than she put in the gourd. This pleased Chol Mong so much that he promised right away to bring back the cows, which he did."

Such stories were shared to pass time and for entertainment. I believe Chol Mong is a much maligned legend, if he ever lived,[33] for he is made to bear the exigencies the Dinka would find extreme in their own behavior. Any human behavior the Dinka think is extreme or funny; one will find Chol Mong to have attempted it in one of the narrated stories. For instance, while the Dinka think gluttony is bad behavior, they make Chol Mong the master of gluttony. The same way, he is made to be the most clueless person you could ever find.

---

[33] Chol Mong, the legend, actually lived

CHAPTER 8

EMBLEMS

"I don't think the Arabs will allow Southern Sudan to go peacefully. And to think of it, I also believe the international community is not in a position to support us should it come to war" Deng claimed. In September 2010, the then President of the autonomous government of Southern Sudan, Salva Kiir Mayardit, had asked the world community, at the UN General Assembly in New York, to prepare for a new country in the Sudan. The choice for Southern Sudanese, in the upcoming referendum was a foregone conclusion. But, there were still barriers on the way to gain such an outcome. Indeed, while Southern Sudanese prepared for nationhood, they were also preparing for war, just in case it came to that.

Spending time with the elders of the village was something encouraged because by being close to them, we learned the stories and the history of the Dinka. Being inherent priests, the Dinka elders' blessing was always sought after. One of the village elders who I came to revere was Mordit. He was a relative of my grandfather and a venerable authority when it came to saying prayers and blessing the people. I knew him well, and when we were brought to him for blessing, I would notice what he was doing and wonder what it meant. Back at the Wunlit village one evening, after the sun had set and the cattle of the whole village were gathered in one place just next to our house, the old man came to pass his blessings on the cattle before they were driven to another rainy season cattle camp, a higher ground and a place far from the village farms. At such a time, everyone was told to get out of the cattle camp for the spiritual elder to call upon God and the ancestors to bless the cattle, but by me being a tiny fellow, I could slip back to observe what was going on. Not that I might never have been seen, but if I was spotted, the response would probably just be "Let him learn!"

A flaming torch and a bunch of spears were in each hand. He also had a bowl of water and green twigs from the tamarind tree,[34] all for the blessings. He walked around the tethered cattle slowly and deliberately, uttering words of prayer and singing and chanting songs of blessings, asking God for the health and good fortune of the cattle and their owners. When he was done, he put out the fire, threw away the water and then he was gone.

Growing up at the village, the elders, friends and relatives of my grandfather, were very nice to me and would often bestow blessings on me. The elders of the Dinka communities are seen to possess the powers of priests in which each man has the power to pass on God's blessings for health, long life, good fortune and general wellbeing. I was probably one of the most blessed in the entire village because almost all the notables in our community had put a hand on my shoulder, or put their spears on either of my shoulders, and uttered words of blessings and prayer. I attribute my escaping through a lot of trouble later on, to those blessings. Many times I've told myself it could have been me, but then it was not. There was one elder, though, who was at loggerheads with my grandfather. I should have expected this man to utter curses upon me, but instead, memorably, he blessed me.

There I was, chasing after our calf that had run away, refusing to be driven back to our home. I ran after it through the grass, across the dry streambed and off to the old man's house, right through the compound where I got into an altercation with the housedog. The dog barked so loudly that it got everyone's attention and had to be held back so that it didn't bite me. "Who is that?" the old man inquired. He was told that the dog was barking at the grandson of his contemporary. Gingerly and

---

[34] *Tamarindus indicus*

eagerly, he commanded, "Come here, my son!" I was brought to him to receive blessings for he was ailing, and losing his eyesight. He laid his hands upon me and asked God to protect my feet wherever I went and to increase my blessings beyond measure, in health and life. Then, I was off after the calf, making sure that we made it home.

Another traditional aspect of life within my community was the funeral ritual of the elders, mostly men. Men in that community, when gone, are buried in very elaborate process and through a traditional funeral ceremony full of prayers and customs. When I was quite young and not very sure of what I was seeing, the father of our current chief got sick and died. That night, the drums kept on beating in a particular way to signify that he was still hanging onto life. In the early morning, he died, and the drums started beating in a different tenor and different beat.

At ten in the morning, the village was full of warriors carrying shields, spears and clubs and doing the war dance. They were displaying how they fight, singing the traditional community war songs, and chanting the blessings and prayers. That is as much as I could witness, for I was not allowed close to the household of the deceased because I was too young. However, when my Grandfather died from wounds sustained from a Murahilin attack, I was older and was brought to witness the ceremony. A bull was to be slaughtered, and since my Father was absent, I acted in his stead. I was made to symbolically take the long spear and then, being helped by an adult guiding my hand, to cut the throat. At first, I had my heart in my mouth and must have completely held my breath, but after the symbolic gesture, an adult took over to finish the action and the process went on, whereupon the women fetched me to keep me away from the actual burial.

In conducting the funeral, the sacred wood of the akoc tree was used to build a sturdy bed inside the grave, and then the skin of the bull was used to build a platform and the body laid in it, sewn up and lowered down. Finally, a ram was placed in the grave, buried alive, for the afterlife. The grave was then filled up while the singing of the traditional funerary songs went on, ending in a crescendo as the ground was covered up. It was done by the able-bodied, particularly the young men who had recently become adults by having markings on their foreheads. The process would be both solemn and joyous for the Dinka celebrate a life well lived in courage. Dhor, or solemn funeral, was a right earned by certain old men, but it wasn't an occasion for wailing. It was a celebration.

In the Dinka countryside roam many large animals, including the elephant, the buffalo and the rhinoceros. There are such potentially lethal threats as lions and leopards, crocodiles and venomous snakes. And there are insect pests like mosquitoes and tsetse flies. The Dinka have evolved in this environment, and learned to coexist with these creatures. The various animals that seem dangerous never really touch the people who share the surrounding environment with them. For example, you might find that among some sections of the Dinka, the lion is a friendly animal, which has been emblemized and respected. The lion is venerated. It is not uncommon for an animal, or even a community of animals, to befriend the Dinka, and to even recognize who are the actual members and who are non-residents of the area. The people in such areas refuse to kill their emblems and would go on to respect them and treat them like members of the family. The animals also learn to return the favor.

This balance exists because the communities have lived side by side, maintaining a friendly regard, for generations. The animals learn to respect this balance, in the way that a pet respects the family that it becomes a part of. And the Dinka respect the balance so that if a member of the community kills an emblematic animal, intentionally or mistakenly, this person would then respectfully offer some sacrificial animal like a goat or a cow, in return, to the animals.

This practice is so good for conservation that it carries over to how the entire environment is treated. For instance, the rivers, lakes and streams contain aquatic life including the fish that are very important in the diet of the people, and the water, which is good for the grasses and the cattle. Responsible use of this water is very important. The sources of water are conserved, and fishing in them is usually regulated, with the chief of the community deciding when to permit fishing to go forward in a way that allows the fish to grow back for the next fishing season.

The same goes for grasses. A particular area should never have too many cattle grazing and destroying the roots of grasses for the next season.

As a little boy, I was able to talk an uncle into acquiring a spear for me, made specifically for my hand, light enough in wood and metal so that I could carry and spear fish with it. On one fishing outing at a 'marsh at the edge of small lake, I encountered a strange force of nature with my spear. I jabbed the spear through the reeds in the lake and struck something which quickly caused my right hand to become paralyzed. Despite stiffening fingers, I was able to pull out the spear, and found two fish, pierced through and connected by the weapon. "*Der!*" the electric fish, a knowledgeable friend shouted. I ended up releasing the fish because I was still stunned by the electrocution but I had learned something about the wonders of nature. That was my first education in electricity.

While the Der fish gave me a scare, I once innocently almost provoked a much direr reaction, from a lolling snake. I was playing under the huge tamarind tree at my maternal grandmother's place in Chong. It was the rainy season and the grasses that germinate early on were spreading into every crevice, hosting, and hiding, many creatures. Under the tamarind tree, there was this patch of green grass that was still close to the ground but had spread over a relatively large area. I decided to jump around that patch of grass, jumping from one end to the other. In the background, I could hear a slight hiss but paid no particular attention to it, since I couldn't see the source, and was unaware of what could be making a hiss. While I went on jumping back and forth, the hisses increased in intensity, growing louder each time I jumped over the grass patch. Suddenly, my Grandmother called, "Come here!", simply because it was time for some rest. She hadn't seen the snake, but I did glimpse it, before running off. I almost froze when I saw the snake's head above it's coiled body, with a very big puffed udder, poised to strike a victim. I am grateful that my Grandmother called me inside.

Another almost disastrous situation was when I was out at the nearby forest looking after goats and happened to be traveling on a footpath, looking to my right. Momentarily, I saw something that looked like an old dead cow's horn among the grasses that had grown all round it on the side of the road. I thought of stopping to pick up the horn as something to play with. Without hesitating, I bent to gather it with my right hand. Suddenly the horn slithered away! I was struck by surprise. The snake simply disappeared into the tall grass and I was left without any remorse for not acquiring a horn to play with, for it could've been my death. I recall this incident any time that I come in contact with a snake.

Another natural phenomenon that left a strong impression is lightning. Because South Sudan lies on mostly flat, grassy savannah, the plateau is susceptible to lightning strikes, which occur often and can be quite severe. The Dinka believe that the lightning strike is actually an act of God, an instance where the Almighty has decided to wreak destruction. This is seen as a way to show His power to remind the folks in case they have forgotten who He is and to also take back anybody He wishes to take back. The Dinka would never try to do anything to stop lightning as a destructive force. In fact, the Dinka would first go look for a ram to throw into the burning property as an offering before attempting rescue. Moreover, unless the victim miraculously walks out from the burning house, invariably a cattle byre, dazed (lightning strikes happen mostly for comparatively large buildings), none goes in to remove anyone. God pushes out any one He wishes to save from a lightning struck property. A ram is what one should look for.

It is interesting to see the contrast at Wau, where the Catholic Cathedral has the important copper wires to conduct lightning strike charges without causing damage to the precious church. A proposal like that to the Dinka would be laughed down. A friend I met recently told me how his father almost lost his life by being struck by lightning inside a cattle byre and that the mother, instead of allowing the children to go rescue the father, was crying, "*Tethiei, tethiei, aci Wa loi!*" (Blessing, blessing-my Father (God) has done right!). The suggestion was that God decides, and people must rejoice in his actions whether those actions are destructive or constructive.

Living the year round inside South Sudan, as I did from May 2011 to March of 2012, gave me a sense of the seasons and how the people in the region live within such an environment in time. Before I left the village in 1987, my ability to understand the seasons was inadequate. So my recent stay there was an opportunity to make sense of what it must have been like when I was growing up there in South Sudan.

In South Sudan, the floods begin in October and last through late December. As the New Year begins, the moisture dries up slowly, and the grasses gradually die. Into early January, it turns very cold at night, a chill that goes to the bone. It becomes cold and dry, and this is quite oppressive because a person loses body heat and body moisture, unlike in the winter cold of the western hemisphere, where the air remains moist and doesn't carry the risk of dehydration. South Sudan in January becomes almost a cold, desert environment. This is the cold part of our winter. The hotter and drier part starts in February and lasts to early April.

By February, the land has lost all moisture, and the dry season sets in. The grasses turn yellow and the sunlight grows intense, as the air quickly becomes warmer. A traveler would require immense amounts of water intake to remain hydrated during this time.

By March, the cold and dry winter has completely ended and it is full-blown dry season (the hot and dry winter), with everything being beaten on by the heat of the intense sunlight and by the vigorous winds, changing directions almost every hour. This lasts from the beginning of March to the end of April; which is the hotter and drier part of winter. At this time, every rodent, snail, snake and even the lungfish is hibernating in underground burrows, in dry riverbeds and river valleys and, waiting for Spring and the rainy season in April. At this time, the grasses are dry and can catch fire quite easily. They are often intentionally set alight to make way for new growth for the animals. The trees would have lost their leaves in late February, then regenerated new leaves by April, at first drops of rain, turning everywhere bright green. The trees also start to grow flowers. This happens in April, and foretells the beginning of the long rainy season, or Spring and summer. Sometimes, the winds might bring the smell of rainwater. It is said that the cows smell the coming of the rain in the air and seem to move with some energy as if expecting a better breath of air and life which was about to materialize.

Indeed, by late April the rains become heavier, and by June the rainy season has commenced in earnest. This season, which lasts through the end of June, is also our Spring. The rain sometimes falls continuously for days, though there are periodic dry spells. This is the farming season and the time when there is abundant milk from the cows. The rain begins falling more intermittently while the crops grow and the farming season progresses. The greenest part of the year is from late June to July, August and September, and it is the Summer Season. By September, the crops, especially the dura (sorghum), are ready to harvest. During this time, the rivers have already breached their banks, sending their excess water into the countryside as floods watering every grass, shrub and tree and sending out schools upon schools of fish for the birds and the humans.

Early in September, the annual floods begin to increase after the rainwater had already soaked the countryside and the rivers started overflowing their banks. Pretty quickly, water from the rivers flood the grasslands giving water to their roots. After September, fishing camps begin to haul in their biggest catch as the fishes try to follow the water levels.

By October, the floods are at their highest, and the crops have been harvested to avoid flood disaster. September to October are the months of the Autumn Season. This is the harvest time, with the trees teeming with fruits.

In summary, the seasons are: *Rut*—Cold and dry winter,[35] *Mai*—Hot and dry winter,[36] *Ker*—Spring,[37] *Ruel*—Summer[38] and *Anyoc*—Autumn and fall,[39] in that order.

* * *

---

[35] *Cold* and *dry* Winter–November, December and January
[36] *Hot* and *dry* Winter–February, March and April
[37] Spring–April, May and June
[38] Summer–June, July, and August
[39] Autumn and Fall–September to October

While growing up in the 1980's, our family would leave after the harvest season, returning to Wau so that my siblings and I could resume school. We stayed in Wau from September until early May, then returned to Wunlit again for the farming season. In traveling to Wau, the ferry at Wunrok was a very important Lol River crossing vehicle. Sometimes, we would use the canoes plying the river, but the ferry was where the vehicles crossed. The ferry was vital for all of us, and served us well, until 2006, when a bridge was erected to span the river.

The Lol ferry, as I remember it, was a huge steel platform crossing the wide river. It was used to ferry cars, livestock, and all people who preferred not to have to boat, or swim, across. The ferry had a chain affixed to it and tied to two metallic beams on both banks of the river. Powerful men would then pull on the rope, while in the ferry, to move the huge metallic slab from one side of the river to the other. These days, the rusting steel is left on one side of the Lol banks, while people happily cross the Lol over the new bridge built after the Sudan peace agreement that brought to an end the war. When I saw the important landmark recently, it looked so small and insignificant. I must have grown too big. However, I think it should be housed in a museum rather than be left to rot beside the river.

In South Sudan, the Savannah grasslands cover large expanses as far as the eye can see. Indeed, the grasslands are so vast in certain areas that you see only this rolling terrain, and the sky above, for miles around. These grasslands are very important to the local economy because they provide pasture to the herbivores, including the livestock which are so valuable to the people. And the grasslands provide grazing grounds for numerous wildlife, including tens of thousands of antelopes and gazelles.

The grasslands also provide grasses for the roofs of the huts, or 'tukuls', the dwellings of the population. These days in places like Wunrok, during the dry season, one can see women carrying bundles of grass for thatching the roofs of houses. Grass is a freely available roofing material utilized by the population. The grasses cover the land, preventing the soil from being washed or blown away, and leaving bare, unfertile grounds. The grasslands seem endless, though there are eventually virgin rain forests increasing southwards. The rain forests provide wood for cooking and for building. The rainforests are also places that bring in rain and cover the soil to prevent soil erosion and desertification.

* * *

Just before leaving for Ethiopia, in 1987, the weather changed in a way that foretold trouble that year. In the mornings, visibility would be so low that the trees nearby couldn't be seen. The fog would persist almost the whole day, along with lower temperatures, which made the air damp and cold. This was quite unusual in the sense that, though fog was common that time of year, it was usually mild and would last only a few days. However, the coming of the Murahilin raids seemed to have brought on a change to everything, even the weather. But, when the fog and the cold were gone, just before Spring, there appeared another new phenomenon: swarms upon swarms of the bird known as amour.

Those birds were virtually unknown to us previously, yet they began having a resurgence all over eastern Africa in 1987. That year, we saw them throughout our journey, until arriving in Ethiopia that December. The birds would move in swarms, with deepening little twittering sounds. Masses of thousands upon thousands would fill the sky, blackening it as they passed overhead. Swarms would colonize the tree canopies until whole branches fell off from the weight! And to make matters worse, the ground was littered with the droppings of what seemed like a million birds. The droppings piled up under, and on the surface of, the trees, coating everything black and white. Then, suddenly, many birds just fell to the ground and died. Where they came from, and what they were eating, was a mystery to us. Their presence was a wonder for the villagers. The following year, although we continued to see the birds, they were never so numerous again.

CHAPTER 9

BECOMING A MAN

"I have heard that Khartoum is preparing to confuse the registration process. In Khartoum, they have prepared non-Southerners to register as Southerners, and then asked them to remain home during the voting day. They intend to ruin the process so that we won't reach the 60% turnout of registered voters needed for the vote to be considered legitimate. They are also planning to bar Southerners in North Sudan from registering. They might try to do the same here," Deng said. It was bad news.

The SPLM party had issued a cautionary warning to those abroad to not register because the SPLM couldn't guarantee fair play. But the host countries prevailed: The process was going to be free, fair and credible no matter where the voting took place. During the process, there would be independent international observers, like from the Carter Center that would monitor the registration and the voting throughout the voting venues, including in host countries. The host countries would also guarantee security. The international press would also be on hand. These were the guarantees promised by friendly host governments like the U.S. It was good news.

The young men of the village were ready for the generational rite of passage: scarification. Markings are incised into the forehead to show that one has ascended from childhood and young adulthood, to adulthood. For the young men, it was time for real manhood, where the fear of pain, and indeed any fear or weakness, was left behind. A select few young women also received markings as their rite into adulthood and womanhood. For each, the process was a test that one had to pass unflinchingly without bowing to pain.

Of course the candidates would experience pain, but it was essential that they could endure this pain without flinching. This was the mark of having passed from childhood to adulthood, for the life of the Dinka was often pain and toil, and if someone was weak enough to bend to the pain of life, then such a person was simply not an adult. Therefore, one absolutely must not flinch at pain during this rite. It was considered a generational shame to oneself and one's family to show pain, in any way, whether by shedding tears, jerking one's head or attempting to flee or hide. Such an attempt was cause for disownment by the family, and by the whole community, who cared about that person. The person would be expelled from the community. Sometimes, the family might swallow the shame, then pack up with their own and go join another far-away community altogether. The Dinka country is littered with such stories.

Yet, if you were to endure the pain unflinchingly, the family and the community would rejoice in your victory over pain. One became an adult who could be relied upon to defend life., Still, as narrated to me recently by a friend; "Just because one surpassed the pain during that time, it isn't an indication that the person would never fear pain again. It was a manifestation and a demonstration that pain could be endured. To tell you the truth, I could not accept to go through it again".

The process is a mark of passage and I think it is a process one conquers when one is prepared for it. So, whoever shows signs of pain has not been properly prepared. Other Nilotic communities, specifically the Nuer and some Dinka, do markings on the face very early on, just at the time when boys reach puberty. I think this is to compensate for their lack of steps of initiation, equally pain intensive, as a first traditional step that are done very early, a process which culminates in the markings on the forehead. The North-Western and Western Dinka, as well as the Jur-Chol, situated in the states of Warrap, Northern Bhar el Gazel, and Western Bhar el Gazel of South Sudan, begin with circumcision for the boys at about age 5–10, then followed by the removal of the lower front six teeth for both boys and girls around ages 8–12. Finally, scarification follows at puberty. Except for circumcision for boys, the removal of the lower front six teeth and the scarification are common for all the Nilotic communities of the Dinka, Nuer, and Jur-Chol (The Luo).

The young men returned from the far away village to the sound of a bugle booming, with their heads shaved and foreheads covered with the green leaves of the pumpkin. The smell of blood was quite distinctive and the men were quite proud. Older boys who were eligible for the rite of passage but had somehow failed to head the call- and therefore considered cowards but not yet outcasts until they have completely refused the rite, in which case they are expelled from the community- would try their best never to get any closer to the group that had just undergone scarification to avoid being beaten terribly with the clubs.[40] A strike to the head would leave the victim with head problems for the rest of life. The clubbing skill was a skill practiced like practicing sword fighting techniques; the very best became as famous as swordsmen would be known. Scarification, as a rite of passage, is still practiced as I write. Not only is it a way to put tattoos of decoration on the forehead, but it is also a way to bring the initiate face-to-face with the pains rampant in life, making them adults as it were.

Once the young men have been marked, they are initiated into adulthood and ready to be married. But before marriage, they first gather all of the cows that they are planning to send to their in-laws, and milk them. For months, the young man does little besides enjoy this fresh milk; the fresher the better, and in very large quantities. The aim is to gain enough fat to beat all others in a competition called toc. And when the time comes to showcase the toc candidates, the whole community comes out to look at the competitors and to pick out the winner, who remains a legend among the community. Sometimes, though, a candidate becomes so fat that he dies once he resumes moving. When this happens, people don't mourn him, not even

---

[40] The initiates would carry clubs and with practiced skills, fight as a group. The victims were invariably those of their age-mates that have somehow avoided the painful rite of passage

the parents, but rather bury him in a cow dung mound, without the mourning ceremony, but rather in a joyous one, while the cattle camp moves on to new camp and grassing ground.

At around this time, the young men also begin to find partners. The young men are allowed to court as many young women as possible; the young women are allowed the same as well, with the process culminating in the young man picking the bride among the various girlfriends. The families would then concur or demur. Since the choice of the families is paramount, it behooves the young suitors to suit widely and carefully. Sometimes, this process would go on for years for some. It is a mutual process.

As the women in the village transition to adulthood and marriage, many compose songs about their new communities and families. The songs are generally full of praise and thanks for all the good things happening in their lives. However, there would be an outside professional composer who the women would tell their particular stories to. They would share the feelings that they wanted to express in the songs, whether of joy or of sadness, and he would create the song for them. The composer would then have to be paid, and the person who usually would foot the bill would be a kind friend of the song owner. The resulting songs were typically sweet, with verses pleasant enough to charm a serpent. For me, it was simply interesting to know where all of the beautiful, wonderful songs came from. So, when the composer arrived at the village, I was one of those who followed him around to see how he brought forth songs.

At the meeting where the women shared their stories with the composer, I never caught what the women were saying, but I was there and absorbing the situation in general. The composer went out for a while, then came back and began teaching to the gathered the verses of a song he had just created. The women immediately joined in and began ululating, expressing their happiness and approval. I wanted to see how this man created songs.

When the composer went outside for yet another round, I was secretly behind him, keeping a small distance from him as he stood under a tree silently. He was composing with grunting beats "genggeng…", trying out the beats, I now realize. He took notice of me and, perhaps fearing the theft of his art, ordered me to leave him. I believed that I had seen how he did it and so I left and went back to the byre where the women were staying. I made sure that I was one of those who got the songs right fast enough to help them sing the songs afterwards.

Unbeknownst to me, my effort had earned me the right to be praised in song alongside the rienythi, the young men of the community who had undergone scarification and graduated into adulthood. Perhaps the rienythii who took time to notice the praises, and their names, in the song, might have just pushed aside the inclusion of this child's name. But, there my name was, in the lyrics. Apparently, I took it to heart, because I still remember the song. I even reminded the now older women of the village about the song in which I featured prominently, on my recent trip to South Sudan.

* * *

Around 1986, when it was thought I was ready to look after cattle, I was given the responsibility. Yet since I liked to play, like all boys do, I attended a dance one evening in a village next to ours, during the time when the harvest was almost over, and people attended dances at night. The dance went on the whole night, until sunrise. I stayed so that I could boast that I had spent the whole night at the dance, without pulling a wink. I only went home when our village party went home. And just about as soon as I returned, it was my time to take the cows out for grazing, and to herd them, making sure that they never strayed into anybody's farm.

Unfortunately, and before I knew it, I was seated under a tree watching the cows grazing peacefully, so peacefully that I dozed off. When I came to, my father was standing right over me, shouting "Get up!" It was 5pm, and the sun was almost down! How did that happen? I had been asleep since around noon, while our cows had traveled to some farm eating ripened grain. The owner had recognized the cows, and drove them to the chief's court, where my dad was at council to lodge a complaint. My father only got the cows back after a lengthy talk. Only the intervention of the chief, who helped calculate how much damage was done, saved our cows. He made my father promise to repay the owner with the same amount of grain destroyed at the farm, from our own produce once the harvest was over. It took only five hours of sleep, from the time I dozed off in a slumber, to the cows slipping off to the distant farm, to the time the farmer driving them to the court, until my dad was demanding that I wake up. Knowing that I had made a terrible mistake which I had never committed before, I stood right in front of him, contrite, listening to what he had to say.

My friends, who were as shocked as I was, urged me, by use of hand gestures, to run off, because they knew very well that the punishment was lashing. My dad was of course grabbing the lash, so, taking a cue, I was off in a sprint! That evening, I came back, stepping as if every step would broadcast my presence, but I found that my family was not interested in punishing me. They knew that I was not ready for the cows yet, but a lesson was learned.

CHAPTER 10

THE THREE ARMIES

"Do you remember that song about the three armies? It went, *'Tek nhom e diak, bi dek jesh e Muraahilin, ku dek jesh e junub, ku dek jesh Arab Malual e Monyjangda, kidit aci ok ja yok* (It is divided into three: Murahilin bandits, SPLA army and the Sudanese Army, oh, Dinka, we are now in trouble). I don't believe the world knows that the Janjaweed in Darfur are actually those Murahilin. After all that Murahilin destruction, do you think we can ever share the same country with the Arabs?" Deng asked. Southern Sudanese, and other marginalized Sudanese, had seen enough since the Sudan's independence from Great Britain in 1956 to have pessimism about the prospects of a united Sudan. Although ideally the Sudan could be unified, in reality the Sudan was becoming increasingly factious, with unity seeming more unpalatable and unworkable. Separation was the better option for peace. The Sudanese arrangement was "too deformed to be reformed," as declared by Dr. John Garang.[41] For 22 years, the Sudan, and especially the Southern region, burned. Armies were too numerous to count. It took six years of the CPA for the SPLM and its leadership to whittle down the armies to two. Yet, the experience was never forgotten.

The so-called Murahilin, Arabic for nomads, were a militia outfit, devised, trained, armed and told to conduct raids inside Southern

---

[41] These definitive Garang declarations were delivered mostly in speeches and popularized by the members of the SPLM/A and the rest of the Sudanese public

Sudan by none other than Sadiq al-Mahdi, the great-grandson of Sayyid al-Mahdi,[42] who picked up the Murahilin enterprise from Suwar al-Daab and Jaafar Nimeiri. Sadiq was prime minister of the Sudan during the late 1980s, after the overthrow of the military dictatorship of Jaafar Nimeiri. Sadiq al-Mahdi also ruled the country once before in 1960s.

During the period of slave trading in the 18th and 19th centuries, the Baggara Arabs, cattle-keeping tribes from Southern Khordufan, would raid southern Sudan. At this time, before guns had reached the region, long spears were the primitive assulting weapons. The Baggara remained a loose-knit band until Sadiq al-Mahdi opted to train them—the Murahilin[43] became sophisticated beginning in 1984 onwards-as part of the Popular Defense Forces,[44] alongside the regular army, and then sent them southward. This was part of al-Mahdi's program to prosecute the war against the SPLA, and to deny it a base, as it were. The Baggara were thus transformed into the Murahilin.[45] Their pay was the loot in human beings, and the cattle they would take, from Southern Sudan.

The raiding was so well organized that during the dry season in Southern Sudan, typically beginning in December or January, the Murahilin raiders would ply the routes between Southern Khordufan and Northern Bhar el Gazel and into Upper Nile, with raiding parties passing each other on the way. Those raids would go on until the first drops of rain appeared in April or May.

From 1984 onwards, the annual appearances of the raiders would begin at the northernmost tip of the then Gogrial District of Bhar

---

[42] Al-Mahdi, the great-grandfather of ASadiq, was the Sudanese Arab nationalist who fought and briefly took over and ruled the Sudan in the 19th century. Sayyid al-Mahdi died before the Anglo-Egyptian alliance retook the country.

[43] The Baggara were a political base for aSadiq

[44] See also Human Rights Watch, "CIVILIAN DEVASTATION: Abuses by All Parties in the War in Southern Sudan," (New York: Human Rights Watch, June 1994), p.34 for a slightly different view about the Murahilin

[45] The *Murahilin* were motivated by the immense loot in human beings, cattle and the chance to fight the infidels. For us, the *Murahilin* were simply our mortal enemies hell-bent on robbing, killing, and enslaving us and also invading our country. They were our ancient and very well known enemies.

el Gazel and then spread out to the town of Wunrok. The first causalities were in a place called Aruet Malual Chan, part of present day Twic County. Those victims thought that they could face the new menace with spears and shields, as they were used to from olden days, only to discover that the brave local traditional militia could not contain the threat. Men were mowed down by the dozens, with some captured. Some survivors started composing songs about certain militiamen who had run away from the fight, saying that such an act was cowardly! "*Tong wa Moy wan nek Maral Kondokdit yen ket ariocku le rip, arioc ca ben kat ca ok nyang piny* (We remember the fight of last dry season in which the Murahilin killed the Spiritual Leader, Kondokdit; when the fire burned and the cowards ran away leaving us behind)."

The song disapproved of these militia members who withdrew during the fight against the Murahilin. Yet the Murahilin, on horseback and camels, and using deadly modern rifles against the spears and shields of the local foot militia, was not a fair match. A very important leader was killed and many young men were also killed or captured during this battle, but the song still admonished those who ran away, whether as a matter of tactic or otherwise. How could someone, however brave, with a bundle of spears and a shield, fight someone on a horseback, fitted with a modern automatic rifle? It was simply suicidal to continue confronting the raiders. But confront them the young militiamen did, and they paid the price, even if those who somehow survived the ordeal thought that those who saw futility in holding on and withdrew were cowards! Maybe they were, but there is a reason to believe that they must have been smarter.

Stationed at Wunrok, however, was a local police force, comprised of southern Sudanese, mostly former Anya Nya I members. This force responded to the Murahilin raid and, were it not for them, many more civilians would have been massacred. The battle between the Wunrok Police force and the first batch of victorious raiders took place at Pan Abiy, home of the SPLA's Kerubino Kuanyin Bol, who was at that time number two in the SPLA hierarchy, and also the home of the respected Fr. Dominic Matong Majok.

During their campaign, the raiders decided to relax at Pan Abiy, slaughtering goats and having a feast, while their pack animals, the horses and camels, munched on grain. Unbeknownst to the happy raiders, the Wunrok Police, with their few personnel carriers and machine guns, were approaching. By the afternoon, the Murahiliin were running for their lives back to northern Sudan, with several causalities on their side. Victory was claimed by the Wunrok Police, whose bravery was romanticized in local dance songs and folklore like this one: "… *Tong Pan Abiy ngot kec we mor nhiim Maral, Jur Maral* (Murahilin, have you now forgotten the fight at Pan Abiy)?" The victory came at a price.

Casualties among the Wunrok outfit included their leader, Bol Mayol, and two of his comrades. These fallen officers were buried at Wunrok, seemingly forgotten, but their heroism protected the northern Gogrial District before the SPLA stepped in to deal with the raids. The locals who were watching the fight at a safe distance later got to demonstrate how the battle went on. They were impressed by the police from Wunrok, though the police were generally not liked. This was part of the reason why the locals sought guns to fight the Murahilin raiders. Yet when the SPLA finally reached the area, and a call went out for all the local militiamen, which meant every young man of fighting age, almost everyone left to go to Ethiopia!

It is not clear to me what the raiders had been doing after the chase by the Police, but the Wunrok Police post was later closed down! The raiders never made another show of force at the local scene, because my only way of knowing their raids, at least before the war had intensified and I had grown older, was through the talk of the chatty villagers. During the dry season, when the Murahilin raiders might have made a show, my family would be in the town of Wau, only to return in the rainy season when it would be treacherous for the raiders to venture southward into the insect-infested and waterlogged Southern Sudan. Not only would their pack animals never make it because of the insects, to which the local animals had developed immunity, but the raiders themselves would never attempt to make it because of the rain and mosquitoes, not to mention the threat of the local militiamen who would then have concealment in the lush greenery of the trees and grass, and the benefit of the large water covering the country. Indeed, it is because of these that the Arab Islamic Conquerors have never been able to succeed in conquering Southern Sudan.

The threat of the Murahilin remained close to the people of Twic County. The presence of the raiders was felt in Abyei, the nearest Dinka land in North Sudan.[46] For some people in North Gogrial, it seemed that the Ngok Dinka were actually in league with the Murahilin, and there was truth to that. During the famine of 1986–87, women and young men entering Abyei from southern Sudan to buy goods, including grain, clothing, and salt, would have those same goods robbed on the way back by members of the Murahilin, in league with some Dinka speakers, who were made up of Ngok Dinka, and even with some members of the Dinka within the Gogrial community.

The travelers to Abyei would take with them cattle to be sold at the market there. Abyei, after the blockade of Southern Sudan by both the SPLA and the government, was the only town accessible from southern Sudan, where goods could be found to avoid the famine and starvation raging on. The terrible famine was exacerbated by the SPLA looting of the countryside and of any strategic stored grains. While the local population was starving, most armed SPLA soldiers plundered whatever goods they desired. There were some heroic Dinka men among the SPLA, though, who still maintained the decency and uprightness to refrain from looting. Those Dinka endured hardships similar to the villagers.

Not only was it just strategic grain reserves, the SPLA had also depleted the countryside of goats, the animal of choice for meat for the local people for the month of July, the time when starvation would set in, affecting those who failed to prepare for it every year, as I was told by a local recently. Not only that, but the SPLA would also strive to confiscate some of the cows being driven to Abyei to be sold there. The SPLA would confiscate some of the items brought back by the travelers as well. If anything, what the SPLA was doing was uncontrolled taxation of the hapless starving population, which was really worse than what

---

[46] Abyei is approximately 100 miles north of Wunlit

was being done by a government tax collector. SPLA soldiers, in groups or individually, had the power of the gun in a civil war whose rules were said to have vanished: "*Long aci loc dhoth!*" ("The law has unhinged the peg like that cow which is no longer tethered to a peg"; a quite an understandable metaphor.). But, the SPLA were fighting a tough war, it has to be said.

And not to be outdone, the Murahilin with their supporters and guides, mostly some dishonorable Dinka, would also loot, assault women, and kill villagers. Only stealthy escape from the town of Abyei, invariably arranged through shrewd locals would carry villagers to safety. And even then, the Murahilin, supported by the SAF in Abyei, would still lay ambushes among the trees outside town to trap the escapees, killing many men and women, the same way they did it in Wau. The civil population was caught in between, and this happened so many times that it ceased to be a surprise. Another popular song[47] regarding the Murahilin mistreatment of the Dinka at Abyei was "…*Adiang Mayen Deng. Jat kith a ku jat lou a nyamor you, Akuei wen e Deng, riny Adiang aci yup e lou, Adiang Mayen Deng, e oh, lou, lou, lou aca Adiang cuop akot cot…*" (…Adiang Community, of Chief Mayen Deng. I have carried a sack of goods and the beating with a bamboo stick near River Nyamor. Akuei, son of Deng, men of Adiang Community have been beaten with bamboo sticks; e oh, bamboo stick, bamboo stick has forced Adiang Community to sit under palm trees).

My next encounter with the Murahilin raiders happened around 1986 or 1987, at about the time when we finally began our journey to Ethiopia. At the end of 1985, just after the harvest, my family and I went to Wau. We stopped at Wunrok where we awaited a truck going to Wau, but none arrived. We had to walk on foot all the way to Gogrial. I don't know how long it took, but it seems it was a little more than 24 hours.

In Gogrial, I was surprised to find that there was absolutely no power, unlike in Wau. People would use lamps to light their way at night. The SPLA was tightening its noose around the area pretty fast.

---

[47] These songs were very popular as dance songs

Several SPLA Battalions were in the area, unbeknown to me. Going from Gogrial to Wau was now untenable because the SPLA was between Wau and Gogrial and the whole town of Wau was encircled and under siege. Anybody who was thinking of traveling between these towns would better travel in a convoy of vehicles with military escorts.

Luckily for us, the commissioner of the Gogrial District, who happened to be from Twic area and was a military man not yet in the ranks of the SPLA, was going to lead a convoy of civilian trucks and military personnel to Wau. This was going to be our way to Wau. The SPLA was still just a rebel outfit, not unlike the famous Anya Any I who had disappointed the southerners. No one, besides vulnerable civilians at the mercy of the Murahilin, was in a hurry to join their ranks. Certainly not an established military officer or a civilian in the backcountry, like in Southern Gogrial District.

Our convoy headed south to Wau, with military personnel embedded on the civilian trucks, on their own trucks, and on military vehicles. While en route, the villagers who knew the commissioner well and respected his leadership, came out in numbers. Some came bearing many cattle to give as gifts to the commissioner. Some cows were slaughtered right there for the commissioner to step on, and the meat loaded onto the vehicles to be consumed in Wau. There must not have been an SPLA in those parts. So, apart from an SPLA assault on the way, and the fear of mines, we sailed into Wau that afternoon. The military wanted to make sure that we were debriefed first before being allowed into the civilian quarters, because they were so worried about defection. After being frisked, asked a few questions, mainly who we were, where our homes were, and whether we were ever in the military, we were allowed to disperse.

It so happens that if you were to stand at Grinti, the military barracks in Wau, and then look south towards, and beyond, the rest of the town of Wau, the view is exotic. Wau is full of hills and valleys, and Grinti is on one of the highest hilltops overlooking the area. The view stretches out to valleys and raised hills, a series of undulating troughs and peaks alternating as far as the eye can see. I saw the same view in the Ethiopian Refugee camp of Panyido.

While in Panyido, Ethiopia, standing at the south end of our original Group II dwellings, and looking south towards the river, the same view as that in Wau can be witnessed. I looked for this same view in Nairobi, and in Rochester, New York. If you are in Mendon, New York, on a higher hill, looking north, or if you are in Rochester on higher ground, looking south, you see the same view: a series of cascading hills and valleys. Certainly if you are near the East View Mall in Fairport, New York, and you look towards Mendon,[48] you witness the same view![49] Why is it important?

In 2010, though I was not allowed to stop at *Grinti,* we passed alongside this rolling terrain on our way to Wau, and the view was as magnificent as I remembered. 24 years had elapsed since I last visited the area, and the town had seen many changes, yet the terrain was still as splendid. Back in 1986, looking out at this landscape, I didn't realize that the events of the coming year would forever alter life for me and all other South Sudanese.

A few months later, the SPLA Battalion called TuekTuek, the Woodpecker Battalion, captured the strategic town of Rumbek. Suddenly, it looked like Wau was going to be overrun by the SPLA. Certainly the Radio SPLA in Addis Abba made sure that there was enough information on the waves to let Southern Sudanese, and the rest of patriotic Sudanese, know that a new political wind of change was blowing and that they better be on board. The military in Wau was on edge. There was a general curfew from dusk to dawn, and if you were found outside at night, you were dead by daybreak. Everything was happening so fast that the town was shaking.

Our house, being on the road that led directly to *Grinti* and just a five minutes' drive from it, was in a vulnerable position. Every night and day, the *Magirus* trucks of the army, with their fearful, whining sound, made rounds about our house. This became especially bad

---

[48] About upstate New York geology- this is considered characteristic glacial topography. The valleys and peaks of the Mendon area are thought to be primarily the result of the retreat of the last ice sheet ~15,000 years ago.

[49] Ice sheets never reached Africa, so the geology around Wau has formed in other ways. It's interesting to note that it appears similar to upstate New York.

when the army's contingent that went to Rumbek to try to recapture it, were repulsed with heavy losses. Every southerner in Wau was in immediate danger. One time, there was a search declared by the military declared for the whole of Wau. Every household in every neighborhood was exhaustively searched, and if someone was found in possession of anything that seemed militaristic, SPLA sympathetic or politically sympathetic to Southern Sudanese causes, such a person was killed. We had soldiers at our house searching everywhere, but they found nothing. Every morning, prominent Southerners would be found dead outside their homes at daybreak, and you were wise to never go to Grinti to inquire about it, even if you were a soldier in the army! It was worse if you were in the police, wildlife or prison forces, because those forces were made up mostly of Southerners and absorbed former Anya Nya I soldiers and therefore, by definition, SPLA sympathizers. They were lucky to still be considered legitimate organized state forces because they were only being tolerated by the main army.

Some days, intrepid SPLA soldiers would carry out a raid in Wau in broad daylight! The forces in Wau would start to shoot everywhere randomly. On days like that, the town's civilian population bore the brunt. It became so bad that nothing would enter Wau, either through the railroad or through the air or by road from the North. Wau was under siege! An airplane that somehow came through, probably from Khartoum, was ready to land at the Wau airstrip and was making a landing pass on the side of Grinti when an SPLA missile missed it by a few inches with a very loud whoosh heard by almost our whole side of town. The airplane quickly managed to make a landing in one piece, but when it was time to leave about an hour later, it did something that those of us watching found very interesting. To avoid being an easy target, the airplane rose slowly over Wau and made concentric circles while gaining height until it was high enough to spring away.

The SPLA now blocked all entrances to Wau. The SPLA also prevented the Sudan Army from getting out of town for campaigns in the rural areas or in the other towns like Rumbek. The consequences for attempting to leave Wau were stark. The Sudan Army further prevented civilians from leaving the town and the SPLA in turn stopped any civilians who might have wanted to come to Wau to buy a few consumer goods and to sell some goods of their own. In Wau, there was now a lockdown, and the perpetual sounds of gunfire, either initiated by the SPLA or Sudan Army. We would hide under our beds, day or night, to stay safe.

My family was fortunate in a way, because our neighbor, a man named Ayok, was a member of the Sudan Army and more often than not, he would guard our house and would inform our family of any searches that were to be carried out on the civilians by the Army. If searches turned up weapons, bullets, or anything that resembled a military device, the owner would immediately be arrested, and surely face a secret extrajudicial execution. Searches and arrests were random and frequent, and almost anything could be used as justification for execution. For anyone arrested merely on suspicion or rumor of possessing weapons, the soldiers would often check the shoulders of these captives to see if there were any marks made by a belt for hanging a gun. We lived in fear.

Worst was when a brother would fight a brother allied on the other side of the war and families were divided among those who joined the SPLA and those who remained at the Government-held towns. This caused a lot of strain in family relationships, some of which still exists today. Two sons of my great uncle were arrayed on both sides this way. The first son was a trained army officer for the Sudan Army and was stationed at Wau's Grinti Barracks, while the other son joined the SPLA and was stationed outside Wau right next to the Grinti Barracks, where the two forces exchanged fire on a daily basis. This did so much to rattle the nerves of our extended family. How could such a thing be and why shouldn't they just join one side, preferably, the SPLA side? But, professionalism and loyalty frowned upon simple family affiliations. And so, the two brothers kept at it, but thankfully both survived. The Sudan Army officer is now retired and living in the countryside, never having joined the SPLA, while his brother is now a member of the disabled SPLA veterans: Two proud patriots.

Everyone realized that it was time to leave Wau, but the military seemed to have calculated that the civilians in Wau must remain, to act as human shields should the SPLA attempt what they had seemed set on: attacking Wau! Our families had to find a safe passage out of Wau. Some relatives decided to relocate to Khartoum. So, searching for a safe corridor out of the country, it was determined that the only possible way was through the aid of the local fisherman, or Awatia, across the adjacent River Jur. One such fisherman was contacted to arrange for a safe passage back to Northern Gogrial District for us.

* * *

Our family, consisting of my Mother, Sister, younger Brother and I joined together with numerous extended family members, and a few others, and prepared to leave Wau together. I later gathered that we numbered about 50 people in all: women, children, and a few men. Our determination was to leave the town of Wau at all costs and to go back to our rural villages situated in the Northern Gogrial District of Bhar el Gazel, the present Twic County of South Sudan, to escape the crisis in Wau.

That afternoon, we went over to the house of a relative where we would be meeting the fisherman to discuss our secret passage out of Wau. Our group congregated until it was late in the afternoon, when the fisherman arrived to be introduced to us and to spell out the terms of agreement, namely a safe passage for us at a fee.

The fisherman was well versed in secret passages out of Wau and would lead escapees out of town at night, from his house just across the river. But there was a catch: our families were not sure if the fisherman was working for the Sudan Army or not. Some fishermen were traitorous, and seeking bounty. We were accepting potential danger. The fisherman could simply lead us to a clearing, after leaving the town, and then call in the Sudan Army security to arrest us. He would then get a huge reward. So, to guard against this, the fisherman was given some reward up front, and told there would be more reward upon leading us to safety. We also felt some assurance about this fisherman, because he was known to our families and trusted by a few. Yet we still knew that we were running a risk.

The fisherman had discovered that at midnight, there was always a change of guard, and that there was a window of opportunity between 12pm and 6am, when the area was free of the Sudan Army guards. The guards returned to the main Wau garrison of Grinti, only to have their replacements arrive six hours later. This knowledge was, no doubt, proprietary, with the fisherman among the few who knew it, apart from the Sudan Army, which is why we were paying.

In the late afternoon, as the sun was setting, casting long shadows, we embarked on our escape, setting off to quickly cross the River Jur. If caught, the fisherman was prepared to give the excuse that we were his family, and were simply returning to our home across the river. After crossing the shallow river, with water low in certain places because it was the dry season, we arrived at the fisherman's residence and stayed at his house until midnight, lounging and generally trying to catch as much sleep as possible without making any sound that could cause the Sudan Army, which had informants everywhere, to be suspicious.

And when we were all woken up and told to prepare for the dash beyond the confines of Wau and beyond the reach of the feared Sudan Army, at just past midnight that night, we did so in quiet. It was whispered to us that at some hour's walk ahead of us, away from the home of the fisherman, was the Sudan Army keeping watch on the road through the teak tree forest. This forest, called *Nyin Chum*, which was near the eastern perimeter of Wau, on the eastern bank of the Jur River, had only a few passages. These passages were well known and, it was feared, well guarded by the Sudan Army.

We moved very fast and very quietly along the path, under a dense canopy of trees, but with no undergrowth, fortunately, moving with the fear that the Sudan Army might still be at their post in the forest. We were so afraid that even children were unusually quiet, something that the older children chuckled about. The fisherman had told us that the journey would only last about an hour until we would be in the clear. Freedom was just a breath away.

Six hours later, we were still searching, with our fisherman guide, for a passage through. We were completely lost in the pitch dark forest. Just then there was a sickening stench, a stench that I had never experienced before. Then we saw it- a large pit, looming in the dark. It was a pit containing the dead bodies of those unfortunate enough to have their fisherman get lost, or to have the Sudan Army suddenly appear before them. Instantly, the need to quickly get away from the area intensified. And to make matters worse, we now began hearing the familiar, feared whining sound of the Sudan Army's Magirus trucks, like the sound made by the mosquito. The deathly sound grew loudly near and clear.

Mercifully, the eastern horizon revealed the glimmer of daybreak. All of a sudden, we knew the passage to freedom. We ran through the forest for our dear lives. A few seconds later, there was shooting into the forest, but we were sheltered in the woods and we would not be stopped, not even by a bullet. To this day, I have no idea where the fisherman went, or whether he received his reward, since I never saw him after that. I would thank him if I saw him today.

We walked through the forest for hours, until late that afternoon, when we came upon a village. We were accepted into the home of a villager, but first we deposited our belongings outside. These belongings included white nylon sacks of wheat flour, rice and sugar. We had no idea of the insecurities awaiting us, outside of the confines of Wau. There was the sound of an airplane circling overhead for a few scary moments. We were becoming familiar with the infamous Sudan Air Force's Antonov bomber. Luckily, the Antonov flew off after the belongings were quickly moved away. Did the Antonov see the sacks? I will never know. We were even told not to look up at the Antonov, because it had the ability to magnify the human eye and could therefore make one the target. Such were some of the myths involved in our induction into the self-reliance of the countryside.

Later that evening, we walked to another village which had a good schoolhouse, where we spent the night. Then at dawn, we moved again. We continued on like this for many days. I was becoming numb and our trudge was growing tiresome.

Then, one day, there appeared a few men carrying guns ahead of our party. Someone came rushing back from far ahead to tell everyone to lay low. For a few fearful minutes, we thought we had run into another Sudan Army ambush. Should we run? But the situation was quickly brought to calm as the men told us not to be afraid. They told us they were SPLA soldiers and then they started asking for medicine from us, invariably penicillin, which we didn't have, or so I think. The men were on a patrol and they told us to veer right because they were on a reconnaissance to the town of Gogrial. We were close to Gogrial! Later, we were ushered in to meet the battalion commander, CDR. Deng Ajuong,[50] who hailed from our home district. The soldiers particularly welcomed the little boys jovially, and made sure that we were the center of attention.

They said we were the future of the country. We had become the Jesh Amar.[51] For a small boy who was trying to get some attention from his family, and trying to solve the problem of being crowded out by a sister and a little brother, it was definitely the recognition sought. The stay in the country was becoming quite promising. There and then, I grew fond of the SPLA soldiers whom we treated as our heroes and heroines and as our big brothers and sisters. I have to say that I have not lost that fondness even though I do believe the present SPLA is not what it used to be. But, I think, in a way, I became inducted into the legion of the SPLA and was happy to enjoy a sense of camaraderie. I became the Jesh el Amar- the continuation of the SPLA. I started dreaming of becoming an SPLA soldier some day when I grew up.

In the days following, we reached Wunrok, where it was made known to us that our home village of Wunlit, to the west, had been destroyed by the Murahilin raiders that dry season while we were in Wau, trying to stay safe from the Sudan Army. Just at about the time when we were escaping from Wau, the second batch of raiders were wrapping up their campaign right at our village among the ruins and the few mud walls still standing! Vast destruction had occurred, including the killing of prominent members of our community, among whom were SPLA's Nile Battalion soldiers, and Taskforce Commander Tong

---

[50] CDR. Deng Ajuong was the overall Commander of the Nile Battalion of the *Mormor* Division

[51] The Red Army was a name of fondness offered the young boys by the SPLA

Arabia. My paternal grandfather[52] was also seriously wounded and left to die by this particular Murahilin cohorts—he died a few months afterwards. The raiding party that had just left could not have done any more damage. After visiting the ruins, my mother informed us that the village was now desolate and songs were already being composed about its destruction. Invariably, the Dinka would compose songs as a way to edge into memory and history significant experiences, rather than write a book; such songs were the way to inscribe history.

One such song stated, *"Tieng tol nhom rup, tony e Goi, ke ci Jur e Maralin yot. Tieng tol nhom rup, tony e Goi, ke ci Jur e Maralin yot. A yok Tong Akok ke ci yic e bai celic, ke ci yic e riang da kou riang dan Wunliet. Ku nek Tong Arabia, ku nek Bany Mabionydit; Wunlit Goi aci cuony; Jur anguek wiir."* (An observer had seen the smoke from the North as the village of Wunlit was burning, burned by the Murahilin; Commander Tong Arabia was dead, and some Murahilin dead were rotting in the water).

Knowing that there was nowhere to stay at our village, our family decided to stay in Wunrok with the rest of my maternal uncles and aunts for a short time, while new dwellings were being prepared. It was expected that another raiding party might be on the way. We were to find out in a few weeks. And sure enough, weeks later, the Murahilin raiders were said to be coming to Wunlit, and nobody knew which way they would go in their march through the Southern Sudan countryside. The soldiers of the Nile Battalion, under Commander Deng Ajuong, who we found deployed around Gogrial, were swiftly sent to stop the raiders. They had reached Thur Adiang, at the other bank of the Lol River, opposite Wunrok, in the evening. The raiders were said to be spending the night at Wunlit. It was also said that the SPLA Battalion

---

[52] The *Murahilin* wounded my paternal grandfather during their first raid at Wunlit in 1986. He died on January the following year. The *Murahilin* had found him still at home and could not run. Upon going through his belongings, they found his old uniforms and insignia from the former *Home Guard* force instituted by the British. My grandfather had served in the World War II at Gambela, Ethiopia. The *Murahilin* thought they had found the father of the SPLA and so fatally struck him on the arm with a poisoned machete, and so delivered a slow, painful death.

commander had sent a taskforce to confront the raiders at the village overnight. Everyone at Wunrok was told to stay put because the raiders could never break through a cordon of an SPLA taskforce to threaten the town! But, our family decided to go spend the night east of Wunrok anyway, just to make sure that we were not the victims of a botched situation.

However, in the morning, everyone was convinced that the commander, Deng Ajuong, must have been right, because as the Sun came up at about 8am, the raiders were nowhere to be seen. Assured, the townspeople started standing down. The notion that the raiders could never break through became credible. My family simply came back to Wunrok that morning. My mother decided to go fetch some water from the Lol River, a five minutes' walk, to make breakfast. She had been gone for a few minutes, and the town seemed to quiet down for a moment, before all hell broke loose!

The sound of a gunshot was heard. At first, there was uncertainty about who had fired it. Was it friendly fire of the Deng Ajuong Nile Battalion, or was it the raiders? It was not long before everyone knew that it was the raiders after all, because the intended target of the gunshots was a villager who had spotted the raiders at the Chief Cyer Ryan tomb, reading the inscriptions. The spotter had started shouting, warning everyone in the town of the Murahiliin presence. The whole town shifted to a crisis mode; everyone was on the run. My mother returned still carrying a jerry can full of water, whereupon my grandmother and aunt shouted for her to empty it out and to join us in running east.

We all ran eastwards, out of the town, with the Murahiliin right behind us, shooting. Being fleet-footed, I was up front, followed by my sister, with my mother and aunt carrying my younger brother, each holding one of his arms, his feet dangling while we ran. Nobody stopped to ask how the raiders broke through the supposed SPLA cordon. It was a race against time. My family wanted me to run to safety. I heard my mother, aunt and grandmother saying "*Kaat!*" (Run for your life!). The raiders were chasing us and shooting in our direction. While I was not truly afraid, due to innocence, the fear displayed by everybody and the shouts from my relatives compelled me to keep running as fast as I could. Still, I barely kept ahead of my family. The raiders were on our heels, and running is all that we could do.

The bullets were flying beside me. I saw dust explosions from shots that struck only the ground, and from missed shots I heard the passing bullets whiz by very close, and whistle at a distance. The grass behind us started to flare up in flames. We were lucky that, somehow, we were never hit. Then, all of a sudden, there was a loud sound, like the shot of an RPG, shot by the remaining SPLA soldiers across the Lol River in Thur Adiang. I later heard the RPG shot was fired into Wunrok. Suddenly, as fast as it had started, the barrage in our direction stopped and shifted southward, towards the river from where the RPG shot emanated. We were in the clear.

We ran as far east of Wunrok, into Amiol[53] as we could, as the raiders pivoted to fight the SPLA across the Lol River. The fight with the SPLA lasted only a few short minutes before the SPLA was dislodged and the raiders were left to ransack, ravage, pillage and burn the town to ashes, including its shops, killing several people. That afternoon, the smoke was adrift in the air over a wide area- Wunrok was burning! It burned through the night and into the early morning.

But at daybreak, the raiders were gone, back to Northern Sudan, by way of our village of Wunlit! Later, when we came back to Wunrok to search through the damage, nothing could be rescued. The shops were reduced to rubble. Even the burned salt, burned in the sacks it was bundled in, was a lumpy white rock, and smelled like burned eggs. How can burned salt smelled like burned egg? Little did I know that salt contains traces of sulfur, the chemical element which was responsible for the burned egg smell. In any case, we weren't going to have any salt, or other new goods, for a while. We would need to make due with what little we had.

We could not make up our minds what the SPLA had become. They were our only protection, and we couldn't understand why they were unable to rout the Murahilin raiders, or at least keep them at bay. Even

---

[53] Amiol is a community in the eastern part of the county, centered around the town of Turalei, the county's capital

the SPLA themselves were beginning to scratch their heads. They were a well-trained force in the mountains of Ethiopia, not lacking in courage. They had been fighting in fields and towns, and had won major battles against the supremely organized army of Jaafar Nimeiri. To be beaten by a band of militia raiders was quite incredible. However, there was an underlying cause.

The training that the SPLA soldiers experienced left them ill suited for combating the Murahilin. Even though the SPLA soldiers were a guerilla force, which was well trained in guerilla tactics, the Murahilin were a rugged group of raiders on horseback that fought with no particular formation, but depended solely on agility and fast mobility. The SPLA, while a guerilla force, were trained mainly to fight a conventional war in fixed positions in foxholes against the conventional Sudan Army. The Murahilin bandits on the other hand were simply mad men who ran around ululating and had a fighting technique that seemed almost chaotic.

It was said that the Murahilin could never fight at night, and that they were incapacitated during rain, because their guns would jam. Yet to combat such a militia, a special force, or a specially trained one, was necessary. Indeed, it wasn't until the SPLA trained such a force that they were capable of overcoming the raiders, finally and thoroughly defeating the Baggara Arab Murahilin menace once and for all! But not before so much damage was done, to towns and to the countryside, with the loss of countless SPLA soldiers and civilians. The SPLA leadership must have been making the necessary preparation for such a force to materialize, because by the time we were on our way to Ethiopia, the SPLA force that we passed on the way, who we expected would meet the same fate as other SPLA units, given their condition, was actually the force that stamped out the Murahilin menace for good.

When our family moved back to the village of Wunlit, we found a village razed to the ground, and the bodies of the SPLA heroes lying now as skeletons in the field. The remains of these tall Dinka men now revealed scarification marks on the foreheads as deep cuts on the skulls. Their lower six teeth were missing, and their long thighbones now appeared extremely long. One wonders about the Dinka pride of never running away from a battle. To run away is thought of as a sign of cowardice, an action that leaves the invader free to plunder and desecrate the land, to violate the living and the dead. Yet to stay and protect the village at all costs had cost so many SPLA soldiers and villagers their lives.

* * *

At around this time, the communities decided that they should form their own irregular militias. It was mandated that the young people begin making uniforms for themselves. Each community would be attired in its own particular colors. All of the young men and women were expected to participate. Uniforms were fashioned, or else bought with goats. Failure to acquire a uniform led to vilification and a fine. It was as if the communities were reorganizing their militia, in their own way. But there was solidarity. It was a very happy grouping and great to see all of the colors of each sub community chosen by the particular group and approved by leaders of the community.

It was a sight to behold, seeing all the young men and women at dances, while also preparing for war and singing about how bad the Dinka then had it: Three armies. The three armies were the SPLA, on our side, the Sudan Armed forces, on the other side, and the ferocious Murahilin raiders, also on the other side and powerful enough not only to cause destruction throughout the countryside but to also defeat the SPLA.

After our final escape from Wau, our village of Wunlit became the center of our life. We lived at the home of an uncle who was lucky enough to have his two huts still standing even though every hut in the whole village was burned to ashes. And even though the Murahilin returned to our district within a month, they didn't come to our village.

It so happened that the raiding group was traveling just west of our village. Perhaps it was assigned a different area of our district. But, nevertheless, a contingent of the SPLA Eagle Battalion, under the command of Macham Atem, was sent to confront them. One very early morning, on the day when the raiders were expected to be west of us, the contingent, in khaki camouflage uniforms, wide brimmed hats and clutching red butted AK47's, came marching in a single file through our village. We prepared to evacuate to go hide in the bushes.

In the afternoon, the battle started. It was over in a short time. The SPLA had won, but suffered some casualties, and many wounded. We came back to our village just before sunset, when another single file of soldiers, the wounded, returned. Some were limping and covered in bandages. They had done a great job, but they were in pain.

At that time two of our neighbors, and their friends, came back from the SPLA training camp at Bilpam in Ethiopia. Before they had left for Bilpam, the two men were mere cattle keepers and simple subsistence farmers, even though they were members of the local traditional militia who would participate in a fight to defend the village and the community at any time. It was probably because of the Murahilin raids that they had decided to seek training and guns from the SPLA in Ethiopia. They were among the first to answer the call of the SPLA for young men to trek to Ethiopia to receive training to defend their communities. There, they became members of the famous SPLA division known as Mormor, one of the largest units in the army.

The two men, along with their three soldier friends, returned to the village with red AK47 assault rifles, as newly minted members of the Eagle Battalion of the Mormor Division. The soldiers returned to find their former homes razed to the ground, and their cattle and other livestock looted by the Murahilin. Yet for the villagers, the sight of these local men returning was energizing. They were proud to see these local folks now ready to defend the land, carrying top-of-the-line rifles and dressed in immaculate khaki uniforms and boots.

The men greeted everyone, but didn't stop there. They decided to go to every home to greet the people at that home by firing shots into the air. Each of the five men visited and made this salute, one at a time. I was among the boys who kept running after them to every home they visited, all the homes where they knew everyone by name and had many shared memories. After a while, the sound of the guns became blended with the friendly chatter of the village. Whereas the gunshots of the Murahilin had brought a sound of death, here the gunshots put us at ease. The gun smoke was quite exotic. We collected the spent bullet casings for toys. The tracer bullet shots, which lit up the night and were seen further and higher into the air, were reserved for special moments. They were fired over the homes of particular important members of the community and over the community shrines. The soldiers visited every household and every shrine to pay their respects by making shots into the air at intervals as each soldier took turns. This process took time, lasting from the very early afternoon into the night. The young crowd running after the soldiers became very tired, but the joy was unmistakable. The village felt that it had its very own true army that had the means to defend the land and the people.

In a short time, the rainy season began.

There was an acute need for the bare, basic necessities like common salt, sugar, soap—virtually everything that was needed for survival—yet Southern Sudan was blockaded. So, it naturally follows that in a short time starvation began to set in, taking a toll on families. The road to Abyei remained littered with the corpses of men and women killed going to or returning with any goods they might have bought. Such tragedies are transformed into songs and folklore, which the Dinka still narrate and sing to this day. The blockade left us famished. Thankfully, though, the harvest was good and we were able to persevere. We would need our strength because the Murahilin raiders were back with a vengeance in the dry season.

This was the time when I really got to know that the raiders were not just something to be avoided but a real destructive force, and that the SPLA soldiers were doing everything they could to destroy or contain the danger. We were in for a rough dry season offensive by the raiders. For the jurisdiction, administration and protection of the whole Bhar El Gazel region, the SPLA had appointed Commander Daniel. Daniel was the former commander of the TuekTuek, the Woodpecker Battalion, of the Mormor Division, which had captured the town of Rumbek and held it for a while in 1986. This had brought the Sudan Army in Wau to its knees (Because every rescue force sent from Wau to Rumbek was destroyed) and led the army to retaliate against the Wau town's inhabitants, which is why we had to escape. Now, Commander Daniel was traveling to Northern Gogrial, not only to meet the communities, but to also investigate the veracity of the danger of the Murahilin raiders. He was not to be disappointed!

In the opening clashes of that season, the raiders fought throughout Northern Gogrial District. In one instance, we left our village while the Murahilin were fighting the SPLA in the nearby village. We went all the way to Paliet Awan, where we stayed for a day or two in hopes that the Murahilin would not reach so far, but they got through. They took the children of a neighbor-the children were sick.[54] We barely escaped capture by running into the nearby woods and escaped by a whisker. During that time, the simple words whispered, "*Maral aci ben*!" (It is the Murahilin) were enough to bring the cooperation of everyone in hiding and evading the raiders.

A story was told to me once, when we were in the safety of the Kakuma Refugee Camp years later. We were thinking about what the Murahilin had done to the people in Northern Bhar el Gazel. A friend of mine narrated the story: "There was once a group of young men who were monitoring the Murahilin raiders' every move, while the rest of the community members sought hiding. The knowledge of the raiders' routes and presence was constantly relayed to the rest of the community members hiding in faraway forests, by fast running couriers. After a long stretch, a group of those couriers were taking a rest under a tree, surrounded by long grasses that concealed them. To give themselves the advantage of height, one member of the group was asked to go to the top of the tree to keep an eye on the raiders, and to inform the group relaxing underneath the tree if he saw the horsemen approaching so that the group may disperse, and to relay the information of the direction and speed that the raiders were headed, so that the hidden crowd may know where to escape to.

This fellow kept a close watch at the top of the tree for some time until he sighted what they all feared—the speeding horseman! He

---

[54] The children, two boys, could not be moved out of their home quickly enough to avoid being captured by the passing *Murahilin*. It was quite unfortunate. The raiders took the children to Northern Sudan.

shouted, 'Maral aci ben!' and instantly his friends took flight. The crowd simply started running for their lives without waiting for the person at the top of the tree to climb down. Seeing that he was being left behind, the thought of running overpowered him, and he ran right off the tree."

He fell down. Needless to say, this was more of a humorous tale than an actual true story, but all of the stories generated by the Murahilin situation remained in our minds, even years later.

CHAPTER 11

A THOUSAND MILES

"In case you are wondering, it is seven hours from Syracuse to Massachusetts. That is why we have to travel right after midnight to be there on Sunday morning, November 15th. So, you should be here in Syracuse at 5pm, and grab a few hours of sleep before we hit the road after midnight," Deng narrated. I was much obliged. We ended our phone conversation. I spent the subsequent week getting everybody together, which was not an easy task. Four of our Southern Sudanese friends were committed to traveling- my roommate Isaac, plus three others who shared an apartment nearby. Yet the trouble was actually getting everyone to travel together, instead of each one planning his or her own journey. The decision for the fate of Southern Sudan was so important that we wanted to be sure that nothing spoiled it. In the end, though, I did get the group together.

When the day arrived for us to start the journey that would take us across the vast country of Southern Sudan and over the Nile into Ethiopia, we carried only a few belongings with us. Our luggage included some clothing, blankets and mosquito nets. We also drove a few heads of cattle for our sustenance along the way, to be supplemented with whatever food we could scrounge. We would acquire supplies with some cash, or through barter in exchange for other goods like watches or pieces of clothing. I don't know the exact number traveling in our party then, but we may have totaled more than 100. Despite the odds, we left with a determination to reach our destination no matter what we faced along the way.

After escaping Wunlit, and walking for a day to Paliet Awan, we had continued on, eventually arriving in Tonj District. A few hours later, we were crossing a swollen river. The water, and currents, seemed overwhelming. A bullet was fired into the water to scare away any crocodiles or other aquatic animals that might try to harm any of us. The river crossing of our whole group took us the entire afternoon, with about five people bunched into a dugout canoe for a single crossing. Our entire group made it across the river just before dusk. After following a path that ran south along the river, our fatigued group stopped to sleep.

The following day we travelled farther south until we came upon an SPLA contingent led by a man named Chol Ayuak, the Commander of the SPLA's Bee Battalion, one of the Mormor battalions, also active in the area. Chol seemed to have been known to some members of our party, and during their conversation, his advice about the routes to travel was taken seriously. We continued on, walking through the afternoon and into that evening, before we slept. We went on like this for another day or two, until we had left the Tonj District altogether and were close to the Rumbek corridor.

The most significant point on the road towards Rumbek is the crossing of the Bhar Gel River. Straddling the river is a sturdy bridge and near the bridge were the wrecked hulks of trucks destroyed by the SPLA. The trucks had been used by the Sudan Army, trying to enter Rumbek from Wau, and were utterly destroyed. They still stood in line, but all bombed out, and the children were prevented from playing in them because they could have been mined.

It took us a few days to skirt by Rumbek. We used a redoubt passing in the forests around Rumbek to avoid the town altogether, making sure that we never got into an ambush laid by the Sudan Army in control of the town. They had finally recaptured Rumbek from the SPLA over the course of 1987, and it was in their hands when we passed by it. Therefore, it was never going to be a port of call for us. In fact, if we ever had gotten lost and stumbled into a reconnaissance mission or cordon of the Sudan Army inside Rumbek, our journey might have ended. We were informed that Commander Bona Bang was in charge of the SPLA around Rumbek, but we never had a chance to meet him. Bang was second in command only to Daniel, the overall SPLA Bhar el Gazel Zonal Commander. For most of us, Daniel was such a big name that we thought we knew him, even though we couldn't identify him had he stood next to any of us.

We came upon the Agar, the Dinka ethnic community that calls Rumbek their home (settled around Rumbek). We found the Agar to be a very amiable community. Our group cherished the little differences discernible in the Dinka language spoken by the Agar versus our group. It was a reunion of sorts. We were members of the same ethnic group, divided geographically, but united in language and everything else. During that time, we saw adolescent boys walking together after having undergone initiation by scarification on the forehead, in the Agar communities we passed through.

CHAPTER 12

NIGHTS ALONG THE NILE

It was Saturday afternoon, and four friends from Rochester and I, were all set to travel the one-and-a-half-hour car ride to Syracuse. We spent the rest of the evening hours before midnight chatting, and catching some sleep. "Did you hear that Ongwec, your friend, has refused to go register? He says that no choice is good choice. He says unity would mean continued Arab and Islamic oppression, while separation, on the other hand, would mean Dinka domination," Deng told me when we met in Syracuse. Ongwec should know better. We no longer refer to his ethnic community by the derogatory term Jurchol, but properly as Luo. He knows we Southerners can work out our problems. We have been trying since before the Sudan independence in 1956. "We are all brothers," Deng added, "and we can't go backwards." At midnight that night, we were on our way to Massachusetts.

On our path to Ethiopia, we encountered many communities. Some resembled ours, such as the other members of the larger Dinka community, while other ethnic communities and cultures differed greatly from ours and spoke different languages. While the journey was necessary in taking us to Ethiopia, to safety, it also became a learning experience for us. Along the way, members of our party encountered people and customs that left us in awe and led us to believe that it was better to have traveled than to have stayed at home. This provided another reason to have made the journey after all. Moreover, it wasn't just the unique people who we met that left an impression on us. The environments were also new, and we saw the impressive southern Sudan wildlife in its variety and quantity, and simply marveled at how rich the land was.

Having left Rumbek and the Agar behind, we proceeded towards Yirol, where we encountered elephants and lions at night. We would walk in a single file whether at night or at day.[55] And while we were traveling in the Atuot and Aliab area one night, close to the little village of Aluakluak, on the road in the pitch dark, we heard elephants close to our path. We saw only darkness, but all of a sudden the silent night was filled with the trumpet sounds of this nearby herd. It was shocking, even dangerous but we avoided them by laying low to allow them to cross and move away before resuming our journey.

On another night, while we were camping in one of the numerous *wuts* (Cattle Camps) of the Aliab, alongside the Nile, we decided to borrow a gun to try to hunt for the hippopotamus along the Nile shore at night, when those creatures were supposed to come out in numbers to graze. But, when our fellow hunters went to the river that night, they found that there was no hippo to be shot. For some reason, the hippo had decided to not come to that spot that night, either because of a change of weather or perhaps for some other reason. Perhaps the folks at that wut passed onto us inaccurate information concerning the timing of the hippopotamus' nightly grazing at the Nile shore.

Our daily journey would usually start at three in the afternoon, and we would walk until midnight, and then sleep. We would pick up the following day at about 6 in the morning. It was simply tedious, and I longed for a time when we would stop or reach our destination. The fun of adventure, kindled by the SPLA, that I felt when we were leaving home, had gone out of it. Resting at one of the villages along

---

[55] The reason for walking single-file while keeping only just a step behind the person in front, a dictum adhered to most strictly at night, was to avoid getting lost and to also get support if attacked by wild animals. In the event there was an attack by wild animals like the lion, or antelopes decided to cross the line, a shout would go out to all to sit down where a person was and to wait until everyone was accounted for before resuming the journey. This happened often, mostly when we traveled at night.

the way, after having slaughtered all of our cattle for beef, and depleted all of our supplies, we were then only surviving on the goodwill of the people we met on the way, and on the good graces of the SPLA bases scattered along our path.

At that point, we encountered many SPLA soldiers coming from the direction in which we were headed. They were coming from Bilpam, the SPLA military training camp in Ethiopia, and going to their deployment points at our home village in Northern Bhar el Gazel. A soldier among them stole a mosquito net belonging to a traveler in our party. Either that or someone else stole the mosquito net, but the SPLA contingent got blamed for it. The mosquito net was a very important article of bedding for any traveler, whether a soldier in uniform or a civilian going to Ethiopia, especially being so near the Nile where mosquitoes were aplenty. It would be a prized possession for anyone, including an SPLA soldier who lacked salary and was surviving on sometimes involuntary contributions from the communities he passed through. Perhaps our fellow traveler shouldn't have left his dear possession on one side of the Lang tree.

But perhaps more noteworthy, along the shores of the Nile, were the series of huge cattle camps that we passed before crossing to the eastern bank of the river. The camps, built around a central area with homely thatch roof dwellings for the cattle keepers, were named after towns in the Sudan, such as Khartoum. Some of the cattle camps were not in use at that time because the season was not appropriate for the cattle to be kept there. It was interesting to travel by night, when the campfires of the next wut would raise a huge haze similar to what one sees when driving towards a large city. It was great to know that we were never really far from our destination, because of the appearance of the light haze showing the location of our next wut, even though the haze could be up to three hours away! It is sort of like seeing a mirage that gives you heart to hasten towards apparent water in the desert, except that the mirage is a mirage, while the haze would be the solid location of an actual wut, with cattle, and men and women.

Soon we entered the swamps, the Sudds, of the Nile. We gathered into dugout canoes made from palm trunks, rowed by the Aliab boys living on the Nile close to Yirol. It took the whole day in the dugouts for all the members of our party to cross the sudds and reach the actual banks of the river itself, and then some more time to cross the Nile proper. The Nile was deeper, and its water currents faster, but it didn't take too long to cross. That evening, we searched and found accommodations at the homes of the dwellers on the Nile River banks. We were fed plenty of corn, mostly dried corn-on-the-cob, for supper. Boiling dried corn-on-the-cob is one of the most unwieldy things to attempt to do. It can't really be done, especially in the absence of firewood. On the Nile, there were no trees for those farmers and fishermen to use for fuel. Building materials must have been hard to come by, even though they still had huts made of grass, wood and mud. They used mainly corn stalks for firewood.

Traveling along the Nile towards Bor, there were several creeks jutting off from the river, with fast currents, but not too deep. The whole trick was making sure that one was never swept away by the rapid current. After we had crossed to the Bor area on the eastern bank of the Nile, we met mostly farmers and fishermen who fished the river, and farmed crops in the lush valleys alongside the Nile. The crops farmed by those folks were mostly corn, cassava leaves and tubers. Upon arriving at the eastern bank, a barter trade commenced between the farmer-fishermen and our group.

Passing through those farming-fishing communities, some members of our group, especially the boys, would steal corn right along the paths through the fields. The paths usually were for the neighbors walking between homes. But for us, it was a chance to harvest a few ripe cobs on the go. The farmers didn't like this one bit, and the village boys who guarded the fields would shout out warnings to their friends further afield at the approach of any long-distance traveling groups. To them we were often simply bar ka dhal, people from Bar el Gazel.

One night we stayed at a home along the Nile, and were joined by a few ladies from neighboring homes, who had gathered to sing and talk about God as taught in their church, in Dinka. Later on, I reflected that the Episcopal Church had done a good job of inculturating the Christian faith, and had taken it to every hut and hamlet in Bor, including the far-flung fishing and farming communities. But that evening I was simply enjoying the singing and chatting about a heaven which was open to all, and a God who loved people. I think women make God seem so personable, nice, and merciful- reassuring for children. Years later, at Panyido, it was no problem for me to attend the Episcopal Church and even to get baptized there, and I believe it was because of the memory of those ladies.

The following day we passed by the town of Mading Bor, cautiously and with great anxiety, because the town was then held by the Sudan Army. By that afternoon, though, we had left the Nile corridor, with the creek at Bor as our last time wading through the water. Approximately 70 miles east from that last creek, the terrain gradually became a little more arid leading into total grassland eastward called the Sahara Ajak Ageer-the Ajak Ageer Desert-with only small scattered shrubs. The water is totally scarce in the dry season with diurnal temperatures reaching 100°Fahrenheit and because of this aridity, people die of thirst when crossing through. It is therefore called a desert though during the rainy season, enough rain would water the grasses and make for a good land for herbivores and the attendant carnivores. We crossed over to the other side, and then immediately veered left, north towards Manydeng, while Bor receded to the south. We traveled towards Manydeng that evening, while being told all about a certain Commander Kuol Manyang Juuk.

Apparently, on that road, no one was afraid of an attack emanating from Bor. It seems that Kuol had subdued the Sudan Army at Bor, so that they never had the nerve to test the SPLA outside of Bor. Indeed, it was at Bor, just about four years earlier, when a son of our home area of Twic County, Kerubino Kuanyin Bol, then a Major leading Battalion 104 of the Sudan Army, initiated the second Sudanese Civil War. This was the reason we were ultimately traveling on that road in that area. So, in a way, we were treading on the grounds where history was made, but for me, and for most other folks, Bor was of no special significance at that point.

We reached the settlement of Manydeng, which was also the base of the SPLA commander, Kuol Manyang Juuk. We spent the day under the trees next to the SPLA Karkon (SPLA Headquarters) which was were the Upper Nile Zonal Command Office of Commander Kuol was located. So, our group must have met Kuol Manyang but I never know this. I didn't know him and there was no formal introduction in which I participated so I probably saw him but never knew. We were welcomed and given some sustenance, and had the chance to witness, for the first time, the SPLA flag and the change of guard in the afternoon at the Karkon. The change of guard was dramatic to me in that those soldiers stood at attention and looked right into the barrels of their AK47 rifles! The bugle sound was also full of foreboding, as if something of great import was happening. Apparently, the SPLA flag had not yet reached back home to Bhar el Gazel, or perhaps I am the one who failed to recognize it. A few nights later, we went over to Ajak Ageer, our staging point to cross the desert to go to Pibor, Pochalla, and then to Ethiopia.

That afternoon at Ajak Ageer, at three o'clock as was usual, the call went out announcing the start of our daily journey. A high-pitched whistle was blown three times, at intervals, with the final third whistle followed by a full throaty call of "*Tarak*!" ("Walk!" or "March!"). This was how the call always went out, and after it was heard, none would stop to wait for stragglers. We walked into the evening, through the night, all the way until morning. That night, I was so sleepy that I was basically sleepwalking. I would be held by the shoulder and shaken to wake up, which kept me pushing on the road. My feet made steps, one-two-three, but my eyes were closed. It was mechanical, and a few times I fell into the ditches made by trucks that had traveled through this desert while it was wet.

The distance through the desert was marked with posts every few miles apart, so the literate among us knew where, and how far, we had traveled before the night set in. But that night while walking, everyone was warned to not lose sight of the person in front. If anyone was to get lost in the desert, they would likely die of thirst the following day, with none to rescue them. Keeping the person in front in your eyesight, never more than a meter ahead of you, was a smart practice. But, suddenly, a lion chasing prey came rushing by and breached our line, briefly creating a gap. The shout went out that everyone must sit down and wait where they were while the leaders went around calming people and eventually trying to reconnect the whole line again, making sure that everyone was accounted for.

Just before the sun rose, we were met by a tractor in the desert. The men in the tractor were friendly and began handing out roasted fish to the children among us. Someone went out of his way to pick out the children and provide something for them. It was a surprise in the desert! And as the sun rose on the eastern horizon, we hastened to the distant spot ahead of us under the few Acacia trees in the barren landscape to look for those barrels of water we were promised the afternoon before upon leaving the Ajak Ageer village,

* * *

Growing up in Southern Sudan, we were all accustomed to walking. The main mode of transportation for the ordinary villager was usually on foot, even for long distances that might take more than a week, or even months, especially in the countryside. And although there were bicycles, motorcycles, pack animals (usually donkeys), and motor vehicles (typically trucks), walking on foot was the most efficient way to travel around, whether in the country or the towns. Walking was never too bad. But long-distance walking, nonstop for three full months, night and day, that was more than taxing! It was simply hellish for the young children.

Yet our endless walk to Ethiopia, and from Ethiopia back to the Sudan and then to Kenya, was always memorable. Later, when I came to the U.S., I told myself that I never wanted to ever walk again, given that I could now afford to hitch a ride in a car. Indeed, walking became so etched in our memories that it shows up in our stories whenever we share such stories with other people, especially Americans. Popular images of us walking in columns upon emaciated columns, conjures the question of how this group of people, including countless children, walked miles upon miles. Indeed, one of our songs was about how we southern Sudanese would walk endlessly day and night. The reason for our determination was that we were no longer willing to remain under the yoke of the Khartoum oppressors.

CHAPTER 13

THE TWO GUNMEN

At daybreak, we crossed the New York-Massachusetts State Line. Deng pointed at a signpost welcoming us to the Massachusetts Turnpike. "Look at that signpost," he said. The picture looked like that of a neighborhood watch. In a short while, we would be close to the registration center.

We walked through a landscape that was barren, save for some shrubs and a few acacia trees, under which we stopped to rest. We had been told at Ajak Ageer that there would be some big barrels that formerly contained oil, but which now would be brimming with water, available for us at the spot. But we had arrived at the spot under the Acacia trees in the Ajak Ageer barren landscape (or the Ajak Ageer Desert) and found that there was none, and there was nobody to elaborate for us as to what had happened. Knowing that unless we trudged on immediately, we would all die of thirst by mid-day, we proceeded at a brisk pace, through the hottest part of the day, with diurnal temperatures hovering around 100° F. We were so thirsty that everyone would branch out if a riverbed was sighted in the distance, to check to see if there was some potable water. But all that we ever found was mud. Every mirage was something to give hope, but it always turned out to be only a mirage. There were some wild animals called ngeer, that resembled goats, running about in herds in the barren landscape, shimmering in the sunlight. On the road, we also found numerous bones of human beings scattered everywhere on the sides of the paths we traveled. If one seeks evidence of genocide in the Sudan, there are enough bones to give testimony, beyond even the stories and memories.

In the evening, just before dark, and after having left the barren landscape of Ajak Ageer behind altogether—we had been walking for what I think was more than 24 hours—we came to another clearing among scattered Acacia trees, where we found a party of two Murle gunmen. One was naked and carried no gun, while the other had a shirt on but nothing else and carried a rifle. Undoubtedly, our group was scared because it was known that a few Murle fighters could decimate a group of people in a short time. In our case, they could probably kill all the adults and take all the children.

We stopped anxiously to see what the gunmen would do. One of them said, "*Kudual areet!*" (This means "greetings to you", in broken Dinka Bor tongue). The unexpected gesture made everyone happy, lifting a whole load of pent up anxiety. We quickly interjected our greetings, quite enthusiastically, in case the gunmen changed their minds and found us unfriendly. More surprisingly, the one who initiated the greeting asked, again in broken Bor tongue, "*La ke e no?*" ("Where are you headed?"). Again, a quick reply was given by the most prominent leader among us, lest we anger the murle. We were simple civilians, fleeing the carnage in the Sudan on the other side of the Nile where the sun sets, and we were headed to safety in Ethiopia. At this, the Murle gunman broadly smiled and said, "*Nhialic athiok areet.*" ("God is near.") He then bade us goodbye. By mentioning God, our fears where assuaged further. We hastened off after the gunmen slipped away. We had encountered wild Murle and survived!

The Murle are a Nilotic community that live within Jonglei state of South Sudan. At that time, the area was under the jurisdiction of the Southern Sudan Upper Nile Province. The Murle are centered around the town of Pibor, yet they roam free in the grasslands, from there to Bor area, Nuer area, Anywak area and all the way to Buma, close to the Kenyan border. The Murle rule South Sudan's expansive plains. Perhaps the most important aspect of the Murle ethnic community is their propensity for raiding their neighbors for cattle and children. Such raids would be so well organized and stealthy that the Murle raiders would be gone before the community they were raiding had enough time to catch wind of what was happening. Some of my colleagues from the Bor Dinka narrated some of the raiding techniques employed against their community by the Murle, and given that I am someone who witnessed raids for cattle and children carried against my community back in Bhar el Gazel, I was a sure sympathizer.

Some of those raiding techniques involved simple adaptation to environmental conditions surrounding the Jonglei grasslands. The Murle would often try to carry raids into Bor communities in the middle of the night, and during the rainy season. The raiding party would travel in a single file, with every person following the leading raider, placing their feet in the footprints of the one in front, so that any person tracking the steps would think that there was a single large man traveling in the area, not a marauding party! And if the raiding party was traveling while it was light out, whether during the day time or under moonlight, the group would tie grass blades around their heads, to look like the horns of antelopes and gazelles, to avoid detection and to fool any witness into thinking that there was a large herd of herbivores traveling the area, a common sight.

And once the Murle had made their raid, the raiding party would employ the tactics of every guerilla outfit making a retreat: The loot, often in cattle or children, would be driven to the rare in the direction from where they came, to be the first to arrive at the central meeting location, while the rest of the raiding party retreated in small groups, protecting each other. Their retreating tactic never involves turning heels and bolting. Rather, they would keep on fighting while retreating in smaller groups. One group will run to the rare in the direction from which they came while the other groups will keep on fighting the rescuers. This will go on until they are all out of range of the rescuers and securely back in their own territory. The raiders will then assemble at the meeting location to share their loot. Those driving the cattle would use whips made of animal skin and smeared with lion fat. The smell would make the cattle go crazy to run towards the direction they were being driven. And should the raiders run out of water, they would simply eat the moist soil found in the drying beds of the few streams, and lowland pools, to escape dehydration. The Murle are so efficient in those techniques that it was narrated that the Anywak, after decades of raids suffered at the hands of the Murle, decided to buy peace by giving all of their cattle to the Murle. To this day, the Anywak cannot be expected to keep any cattle, or so it was said, and yet the Murle have gone ahead attacking the Anywak, anyway, seizing their children whenever they have felt like doing so.

The similarity between the Murle and the Murahilin seemed to coalesce so much so that the SPLM/SPLA refused to consider the Murahilin attacks to be distinct from the Murle attacks. The leadership of the SPLM movement started comparing the two to downplay the lack of response to the Murahilin. This lack of response was not appreciated by most people from Bhar el Gazel and this led to some complaints.

Cattle rustling is rampant and quite ancient among the Nilotic communities of Eastern Africa. Bandits, once armed with arrows, spears, shields and clubs, but now armed with modern light automatic guns, travel from one ethnic community to the next to steal cattle, employing violence wherever necessary. Yet, although the practice is widespread, it is absent among the majority of the Dinka community. The Dinka are the only Nilotic community that rarely engages in cattle stealing or rustling of any kind. It is so rare to take somebody else's cattle that if a cow wanders off and finds itself in somebody else's herd among the Dinka, the owner of the herd protects it and keeps it as his own until the owner finds it. All the progeny of the cow would even be so protected, should the cow spend enough time at the new place to produce calves. Theft of cattle is considered a great crime among the Dinka, not only against the owner, but also against God, and a violation of the unwritten code of conduct among Dinka men who must remain upright at all times. At the present time, cattle rustling is still being practiced by the Nuer, the Murle, and the Toposa, and there is an occasional deadly raid with counter raids by the Dinka to recover the stolen cattle.

When we finally arrived at Pibor, we found that it had been captured from the Sudan Army by the SPLA Zalzal Battalion a month earlier, in November 1987. We arrived into town very early in the morning, and the SPLA guards at the entrance of the town were gracious to allow us in even though we didn't know the military call sign that day. In town, we came upon the Bunia Battalion of the SPLA, a group that was on their way to Bhar el Gazel to face the Murahilin, and it was their condition that made us begin reconsidering where we were going and what we would find there. The evident suffering was so bad that some in our group thought the situation must be worse ahead at our destination in Ethiopia, then back home where we had left.

The Battalion group spent the afternoon in the town. When it was time to leave Pibor to travel towards their target, most soldiers found it difficult to travel. One such soldier was so emaciated and sick that he refused to move. Even upon the urging of his comrades, including a beating by his senior officer, the sick man refused to budge, saying weakly, "I cannot make it." This put his ultimate commander in such a rage that everyone feared the sick soldier would be shot. However, the commander ordered that he be stripped of all his clothing, so his military uniform, which was tied around the waist with a piece of rope because they had no belts, was removed. He was stripped of his rifle as well. The sick man remained utterly abandoned and completely naked. This happened right in front of all of us. The women in our group took pity and one of them took out a woman's underwear to give to him to cover his nakedness. We thought the sick soldier, along with his comrades, was being mistreated by their commander. The commander in question was the same officer that trained them at Dima, Ethiopia. He was a northern Sudanese, captured in war. Later, he did defect to North Sudan.

We traveled overnight, arriving at Pochalla the following morning, Christmas day. We found dancing and celebration all over town. We also found many sick members of the Bunia Battalion, left at Pochalla, everywhere suffering and very emaciated. It was later narrated that they were mistreated very badly during their training in Dima, Ethiopia.

The next day, we walked the whole morning and afternoon. We spent the night somewhere on the River Gilo before entering the Panyido Refugee camp, our final destination, the following morning.

CHAPTER 14

PANYIDO ARRIVAL

"Boston, here we are," Deng shouted as we arrived in Boston at daybreak. I paid no attention because I was driving. I remembered our arrival at Panyido in 1987.

At first, Panyido was mostly just a little rugged camp centered around a small town with very few amenities, and only just one school for the Anywak children, taught in Amharic, the lingua franca of Ethiopia and the language of the Amharic people. There was a shopping center where the main commodity was the local brew, and there were only a few homesteads or farms along the main river at the south side of the village. There were many refugee children, mostly boys, mainly from Jonglei, who had just arrived there. Some more would arrive later from North Sudan, and elsewhere from South Sudan. We also discovered that there were some groups of men who had traveled from the Sudan to Ethiopia to join the SPLA, and they were just on their way to the SPLA camps and training grounds.

Tragically, many of the boys were dying every day and they could not be properly buried. Most of these young boys knew little about death, let alone how to bury the dead, and one could find exhumed bodies lying just beyond the camp, half-eaten by hyenas and lions. The UNHCR arrived and tried very hard to speed up the building of the camp by putting up stores and a camp hospital to treat various sicknesses, including malnutrition and exhaustion from traveling.

Within a few months, the camp was organized into groups with boys placed in several groups of their own, and women and their children grouped alone. The unaccompanied minors' groups served to protect the minors who were placed under the care of several caretaker administrators who also acted as teachers. There was also a substantial local community of Anywak, who are citizens of Ethiopia, even though they are members of the larger Anywak ethnic group, which straddles the Ethiopia-Sudan border. Why the planners of the post-independent Africa thought it would be all right to draw an arbitrary division through these groups, I don't know? International borders largely ignored ethnic boundaries across Africa. Panyido sits on a river which is a continuation of the Gilo River and lies within the Ethiopian Gambella Province.

* * *

At Panyido in 1987, the majority refugee population was made up of unaccompanied minors—mostly boys of below 18 years. They were considered unaccompanied because they were separated from their families and had traveled to Ethiopia leaving their families behind-their families had either remained inside Southern Sudan, had fled to Northern Sudan or had gotten decimated in the carnage.

There were only very few unaccompanied minor girls because in the Dinka culture, there is no such thing as unaccompanied girl. All girls are accompanied and even if they are orphaned, relatives or friends of the family will take care of them as their own. On the other hand, a boy can stay unaccompanied and can even travel alone. A Dinka boy can stay alone in the woods to fight lions. A girl may never sleep outside the house. Therefore, when the war erupted in the Sudan, girls would be bound to families while boys could be found herding cattle far away from home where they could easily get separated from their families. Therefore, there were very few girls in the refugee population as there were fewer families.

Only very few families made it to Ethiopia from Bhar el Gazel in 1987 because of the distance and the dangers. Either the families stayed in the countryside to evade the Murahilin raiders, or they went to the

Southern urban centers like Wau where there was relative safety or went to Northern Sudan, to Khartoum to stay in squatter camps. As a result, there were only very few girls and those girls never feature much in the 'lost boys' narrative because they were mostly accompanied.[56]

There were only very few women with their children among the population. Those children-boys and girls in equal number-were considered the accompanied minors. Of the same age as the unaccompanied minors, they enjoyed the protection of their families,[57] mostly mothers. They were subsequently of less concern to the United Nations, which was the agency taking care of refugees at the Panyido Refugee Camp.

The men were in even fewer numbers. Most of them eventually joined the SPLA training camps at Bilpam and Bongo in the Ethiopian Highlands.

* * *

Of the group that became the first batch of the lost boys, we were the last to arrive at Panyido, just after Christmas day in 1987. Panyido Refugee camp was being established when we arrived there. After a few weeks, it was decided that the whole camp population of unaccompanied minors were to receive blankets. The boys were staying in two large groups based on the major regional divisions back home in Southern Sudan. There was the Jonglei group and the Bhar el Gazel group. The boys numbered about two and half thousands, and the

---

[56] Five years later, at about the time when enough families would have made it to Panyido, because the routes were opening up with the possibility of truck transport as the SPLA won battles, the Panyido Refugee Camp was abandoned and we left to come back to Southern Sudan. Within a year later, we escaped to Kenya. Three years down the road, in 1996, more families arrived to Kenya and then the population of girls increased. However, at that time, the narrative of the 'Lost Boys' was already established. Still, girls were attached to families at the Kakuma Refugee Camp in Kenya and could never be considered unaccompanied even if they were orphans.

[57] My family—Father, Mother, Sister and Siblings and Grandparents all remained in Southern Sudan's Bhar el Gazel Province

camp authorities, headed by Mr. Chan, had procured enough blankets for all of them. The men and the women were not included in the distribution. The camp manager decided that the first group of boys to receive the blankets would be the Jonglei group, who were the larger in number and who mostly never had other articles of clothing, except the few blankets they carried from back home in Bor. The distribution of the blankets to that group took the whole day and was finished towards the evening. The following day, our group, the Bhar el Gazel group, had its chance to get their blankets.

Early that morning, we attended a meeting where the camp manager gave a strong warning to those who might decide to recycle themselves to receive multiple blankets. "If anybody among you has already received a blanket and would now want to receive another, let that person know he will be found out and dealt with very harshly," the camp manager said. We knew he was not bluffing. Most of us decided it was not worth trying, but one person had ignored the warning. We fell out in line and traveled in a single file to where the blankets were going to be handed out. The camp manager was standing on one side and counting everyone passing him. We had to face him as we passed by him jogging. When it came my turn to pass by him, turning my face to look at him so he might identify me, there was right beside him a friend of mine. He could be in trouble.

We arrived at a venue where the camp manager would again be addressing us. We got seated in rows waiting for him to appear. He arrived, along with my friend, who clearly looked to be in trouble. The manager spoke to the crowd of boys assembled. "The person you see here is in trouble. He was issued a blanket yesterday and has come back for another today! This behavior is unacceptable!" he added. We all expected the worst for my friend. He went on, "Cut for me that branch over there," he ordered his bodyguard. We all fearfully looked at the thorny branch. The thought of being caned with a thorny stick was quite unpalatable. Our friend was really in trouble.

By the time it was over, the boy was crying and every one of us had made a decision never to be in a situation like that. We were secretly happy and felt lucky, though, that the thought to violate the camp manager's commands hadn't occurred to any of us. But, we did need more blankets and would do everything to get more, just not that way.

It occurred to me that the boy who received the caning might've appeared conspicuous to the camp manager, and this might explain how he was caught red-handed. This boy was in shorts, in contrast to the other Bor boys who were mostly only covered with blankets. That must have brought him into focus for the camp manager and the manager must have decided that that was a particularly peculiar Bor boy. The image of the boy must have stuck with him, and was reinforced when the boy reappeared. Either that or he must have been in contact with the boy and had known him and his surroundings before the distribution, and upon noticing him during the Jonglei boys distribution, he must have decided to wait to see if he was going to recycle himself. This can explain the strong warning before the day of distribution of the blankets to us. However, I was a happy customer because I did get a very nice double blanket that was a combination of four sheets threaded together and was brand new and good to withstand the cold of the Ethiopian highlands.

CHAPTER 15

SETTLING IN

The registration center was alive with Sudanese exchanging greetings. We joined the lines leading to the registration booths. No one could even ask whether we were Sudanese or not because we looked Sudanese though our papers were strictly checked. Everyone in the room knew what needed to be done and done right. Massachusetts Avenue, on which lie the great Universities of Harvard and MIT, was where our Registration Station was located. Passing on that avenue showed the observer the great dedication to learning by the American people.

Within the group I was first assigned to, Group I, some boys took to fishing with gusto, in the swamps along the river running south of the camp. The river also provided a good place to swim in the afternoon. There would be thousands of boys swimming there at that time of day. The swamps, in the dry season, became our fishing grounds. While I was hunting and fishing, relatively speaking, I could never figure out how to catch fish like the rest of the pros I found myself with in Group I. Indeed, the number one pro was a fellow named Riak who everyone took to calling *Riang Luoth* (Riak of the lungfish), no less.

Riak was this fellow who would quietly disappear for a few hours and then reappear later with a catch of lungfish. How he caught so many was anyone's guess and speculation abounded. He was so good at it that he was never mandated to perform tulba, the baneful manual work that was both a regular work schedule and also could be used as a form of punishment in the camp. He would be given quiet permission to continue his fishing ways any time he so wished, provided the catch was shared between him and our Group lords, the head boys, often older and more literate then the rest, who were put in charge of the boys, to assist the caretakers.

Being boys, misbehavior was pervasive and so were the controls and the punishments, from being caned to being put on a tulba schedule, unlike the regular schedule, as a punishment. But the enterprising fellows like Riak got well out of the way and were rewarded with nothing to worry about except the enjoyable work of fishing for the lungfish, which was eaten with some reluctance, because lungfish is not the tastiest fish. Any fish that doesn't have scales is not a delicacy for the Dinka.

The favorite fishing instrument, the fishing spear, common back home, was made from the metallic pegs of the tents provided by the UN. The procurement of the pegs was a combination of the stealthy unpegging of tents belonging to others, including some camp establishments, and collecting abandoned pegs remaining after tent units were used to make bags by the artisans. The pegs would be melted down by skillful artisans and then beaten into spears, essential instruments for fishing.

The heavy khaki of the tents and the nylons of the sacks in which sugar, grain or any other food items were brought in, would be used to make bags. Those bags were as good as the material they were made from and the skill and artistic level of the manufacturers, artisans with sharp eyes and nimble fingers for good products. The bags would fetch a few Ethiopian Birr notes and so were often unaffordable to the average boy. A boy was lucky if he had in his possession one of those nylon bags which he would use to sew his own bag, often not of the same design or quality of the professional artisans. The artisans were invariably older; typically shoe menders from back home in the Sudan.

The most exciting thing of all at that time, when we were settling down in the camp, was the announcement that Dr. John Garang de Mabior would come by to pay us a visit. The visit was a secret, of course.

We were so happy as we prepared our school grounds to see Dr. Garang, whom we all knew by name only.

To prepare, our class was taught a song by one of our best teachers, Mr. Anyuondit. The song went like this:

> **"Sudan our Country;**
> **Sudan our Country;**
> **Sudan our Country;**
> **Sudan our Country.**
> **We own't, we own't forever."**

Our class was told that we would sing the song during the Garang's visit.

When Garang arrived, he came to our class under the tree in the afternoon. We started singing the song. His entourage, which was made up of two companies of soldiers in two distinct separate uniforms, one company wearing the same bright green uniforms as Dr. Garang and the other company wearing multicolored camouflage uniforms, stood surrounding our seated class. I think Dr. Garang and his crew must have been impressed. We were impressed with the visitors too. Later, we joined the larger group of boys at the school playground where Dr. Garang gave a speech, whose details I couldn't gather. But then he recited the English Alphabet, via a microphone, with us following as he called out the letters "A, B, C…Z". I still think he missed at least one letter but no one else seemed to have noticed. Then he left and we returned to our job of making our shelters and studying the ABCs and Arithmetic.

This was in early 1988. We settled into a life of work, study, play and prayer, of course. We prayed for the Sudan, our families, and ourselves. We hoped that God would bless our country and give us peace and freedom in our own land and that we would one day return to our homeland. We called being in Ethiopia, and anywhere else in the World, being in the bush.

In order to get away from the elements, it was decided to build schools semi-permanently, instead of continuing to study under the trees. The new classrooms got thatched grass roofs and mud walls. The schools were numbered from one through twelve. I was not really that enthusiastic about learning, at least not as enthusiastic as some of my classmates were, but I made it. Sometimes I would be absent or late for class because I went playing or fishing. There were two school sessions, morning and afternoon. I was placed in the afternoon session, which afforded me some time in the morning to go fishing and swimming with my friends before school.

On one of those days, I went fishing with a friend from back home who had a fishing net and knew how to use it. He was a fisherman before and was older and therefore could afford to do what he liked. I came to class a little late that day. I found the teacher writing on the blackboard. The door was always open because the classrooms actually had no doors. So, instead of a knock, one had to clap or clear the throat to announce one's attendance. I clapped to announce my presence. The teacher casually looked at me and asked, "Why are you late today?"

"I went fishing," I replied.

After being drummed into me back home in Southern Sudan, I thought honesty was a good quality to have and I did not fail in trying to tell the truth to my teacher. I didn't expect the teacher to punish me; I was not even thinking of any punishment I would receive. I stood waiting for the teacher because I reckoned that having to wait for the teacher's permission to be allowed to sit down in class was a formality, a show of respect and I did not fail to show him the respect he deserved. I remained standing while he finished writing on the blackboard. However, I was not surprised when he allowed me to attend the class. I expected him never to mind my tardiness.

The following day, I was a little late again, just by about 10 minutes. The Sudanese are not really known for keeping time. When the teacher saw me, he casually looked at me, turned to the class and said, "He probably had gone fishing," and then went on writing on the board. In deference to him and his authority, I had to keep standing, waiting for him to welcome me to sit in class or leave, whichever he wanted. I stood like a tree planted until he was done writing on the blackboard. When he was done, he turned to me and asked, "Why are you late today?"

"I am a little late because I had gone fishing," I replied without so much as a missed breath. This got the teacher angry.

"Open your hands!" He ordered me to present the palms of my hands to deliver the caning punishment: Ten painful lashings of the cane. "Done exactly what I had anticipated!" He kept repeating this phrase until he had delivered the ten lashes. Apparently, he had expected that I should have lied. I don't remember if I was ever late again, but my fellow pupils were snickering and I was left to wonder if I should have lied and said something like "I was sick." Does it pay to lie? This was early in 1988, after arriving in Panyido and I still carried with me the parental admonition never to lie. I should have lied!

At Panyido, the boys, crisscrossing the grass and shrub-covered forests, with thorns and jagged rocks scattered everywhere, and with no bathing soap or better clothing, had numerous infections and wounds, often on the legs, which would threaten to become gangrenous. In fact, some of the wounds were at that level. The UN brought treatment by distributing bathing soaps. The infected ones had to bath often and to have the wounds bandaged. This contributed to healing faster. The Catholic nuns, perhaps following their practice back in India, were quick to take over the treatment of the wounds of the boys at the catholic parish northeast of the camp. Not only would they clean the wounds, but they would also provide meals to the often hungry patients. At that time, none of us could imagine the effort and the love that went into doing something like that, but the sisters were at it as if it was what they were created to do. The sisters, moving about in their saris, and huge rosary beads draped around their waists, were matronly and wonderful to see helping the children. They were steely women of God, no doubt.

Sometime that year, a lion was killed in the camp. The unfortunate lion looked very scrawny and quite emaciated. It must have been sick and therefore unable to secure some prey. Even if the prey had migrated, the lion would never fail to find out where the herbivores had gone to, unless it was unable to hunt. The lion knew where the prey would be and where it would be going at all times. But in this case, the lion was starving, and was easily killed. We came to look at the dead, scrawny, emaciated body at the home of the neighbor where it was killed the night before.

In the wee hours of that night, the unfortunate visitor had made its unwelcome call to the compound. The neighbor was woken up only to spot a lion intruder. He shot it dead. This was deep in the Sudanese refugee housing in what was known as the blocks of Panyido Refugee camp. It was simply amazing that the lion could have passed through, from the outskirts into the very center of town, undetected by anyone. If it had strayed to the unaccompanied minors' group housing, there was no way it would have been dead. In fact, it might have killed one of the boys, unless the security of the camp happened to be patrolling that night around the minors' camp. This was my first encounter with a wild lion. The lion population is ubiquitous in Ethiopia where it feeds on the game there including the amerinya (an antelope).

The regular lion was most common. The lion as a carnivore species was quite common in Southern Sudan until the recent times. Their numbers have dwindled and they are hard to spot these days owing to the civil war and the spread of small arms. However, for the rest of the unaccompanied minors, specifically those from Jonglei, the man-eater, or child eater, Nyanjuan, was a very real phenomenon for them before they left for Ethiopia. There was even a boy in our group who had one of his eyes always covered with an eyepatch because the Nyanjuan bit him in the face and tried to run away with him when he was a little boy. Nyanjuan are short and so they particularly feed on children. Indeed, during our early days at Panyido, the whole sleeping crowd of boys would wake up at night and set off running towards where the teacher or caretaker was taking his rest, to run away from the *Nyanjuan*. None of the boys could swear they saw Nyanjuan but they would always say they saw something like it; that it looked like a dog. It was probably a stray dog from the nearby Anywak village. We kept no dogs.

Chan, the original Camp Manager, would make rounds at night to make sure that no child was scared. One time I was left asleep while the whole crowd ran for their lives. After the head count, the caretaker came to check on me only to find me still soundly asleep. If Nyanjuan was real and was actually the cause for that commotion, and if it was determined to have a meal that night, perhaps I would have ended up as its dinner. So, it simply was not there, but perhaps it was the regular lion or an Anywak stray dog that was scaring the hell out of us. A large stray dog could actually attack, maim, and even kill and eat a young boy. Maybe it was a thief, or terrors and mysteries. Anything could be prowling in the dark night.

And these menacing creatures weren't the only purported child-eaters that threatened us. There was even the belief among some unaccompanied minors that the native Tigrinya, who might have been supporters of the Tigrinya Peoples Liberation Front, TPLF, were, clandestinely, cannibals. It was said that a boy had accused a Tigrinya of having visited the boys housing at night to try to kill and eat one of them. The boys rose in commotion and one Tigrinya, who was found in the market, was beaten by a mob of the boys. It was said that he actually did vomit a human being's tongue! I never believed such tales, not because I had a better sense of reality than the rest, but because I never had anything to associate it with. Back home in the village of Wunlit, there was a belief that there were some human beings who feasted on human flesh. Some people reported that they had escaped being eaten by those man-eaters, and there would be elaborate descriptions of the cannibals, including that they looked exactly like human beings, but with more hair and with arms that never bend. Still, nothing was ever substantiated. I never saw physical proof, or heard a confession.

* * *

A good friend of mine died. He wasn't the victim of a disease, or murder, or starvation, but rather died in a tragic accident involving a bed. The beds in the camp were made from wood, with very little care given to safety. The four corners of the bed had sharpened tips, which made for safety problems. It usually was not a problem if the bed was in use, because unless someone tried to sit down on the bed without checking where to sit, the odds for an injury were slim. However, it was not to be so for a very good friend of mine, Mayor.

The hut that he lived in had no door, which was common at Panyido. Because of the fear of thieves, rodents, reptiles and perhaps some larger carnivores like the lion coming into the hut at night, the door to the hut my friend was using had one of those wooden beds to cover the entrance. In the middle of the night, Mayor decided, in a slumber that he was going to go outside. He rolled the bed away from the door by pushing it to the side, leaving just a part of the bed jutting into the doorway. But, when he returned to enter the hut, with it being so pitch dark that he could not see the doorway, he went feeling his way towards the direction he came from and by the time he had found the door, he was writhing in pain, impaled by the sharpened tip of a leg of the bed.

His stomach was gored. His roommates woke up to the groans, and in the middle of the night, went to fetch the caretaker who arranged for Mayor to be taken to the Panyido Hospital, whereupon it was deemed that he had internal bleeding and that it was best to remove him to nearby Gambella where he could get surgery to stop the bleeding. He didn't reach Gambella alive. It was devastating. Mayor was my church friend!

* * *

The boys at Panyido lacked such basic commodities as soap and shoes. This condition caused some boys to suffer jiggers called *tuktuk*. The *tuktuk* bug was actually a larva of some mite that bore into the skin of the victim, specifically the hands, feet, and buttocks where it laid eggs. The larva would then feed, becoming engorged upon the flesh and the bloodstream of the host. It would grow to the size of a corn grain, and have the same color. The engorged larva would then explode to rupture the skin, draining it out. At that point, the tiny mite, which was too small to see, would begin life anew, leaving the area smelly and prone to infections.

The best action to implement if one had larvae already, and some boys had them by the loads so that they almost couldn't walk or sit, was to go to the sandy beach of the river and spend time there in the water. After a while the skin around the mouth of the burrowed parasite is softened. Then, a faithful friend can use a sharp needle or a thorn to pry off the larvae one by one, a feat which could take days, and become quite a mess. The really smart solution was to stay clean and to try to use soap, if one could afford it, to wash clothes and to bathe with. The older folks, who could afford soap, were rarely touched by tuktuk. It was said that the bug was particularly bad in the *Dima* Camp. Maybe the information was a case of refugee camp propaganda.

I am glad to say that tuktuk never got to me because the moment I would feel numbness in an area of my skin, I knew to look there for the bug, which would be displaced immediately. The parasitic infection was akin to the gony, a skin lesion called scabies, which we had seen while we were living in Southern Sudan.

Gony was new and rare at that time, but once it had infected the skin, it was sure to cause havoc. The most affected parts would be the hands and the buttocks, and for some folks, staying dry would be the answer-both to keep the gony away and to speed up the healing. The patient would use any sharp object to scratch himself with, because he likely would have already worn down his fingernails from scratching. The scratching itself would cause the skin to break at the itchy spot, with further scratching increasing the opening leading to more infections.

How that epidemic ended I never knew, but while at Panyido some two years later, faced with the tuktuk issue, I kept thinking back to the village and the skin disease, *gony*. The village folks hated it and sang songs to encourage people to stay gony-free. For the Dinka, if something was feared, they would sing songs to shame or to scare the person away from the threat. The *gony* songs would be agonizing for the gony patients.

Also at the camp was a very popular *diktor* or the medical assistant. He manned the clinic where most boys were treated for ailments. His mode of diagnosing would be to look at the patient and then to listen to answers as he asked questions about how the patient felt, what kind of pain they were in, and where the pain was concentrated. He would ask, "How do you feel today? Do you have a headache? Do you have a stomachache? Are you constipated?" This questioning would end up with a prescription of a few tablets, often for pain and malaria. The medicine was not particularly potent, though, so the boys who were faking sickness to avoid manual work, especially *tulba*, could safely take the medicine. Faking sickness was common among the boys when they wished to avoid heavy work like hauling timber, cutting down trees or digging ditches.

The level of maturity, or immaturity, of our group was sometimes revealed by altercations. One such incident occurred at a busy water pump near our Group II compound one afternoon. The boys were fetching water for bathing, and for use at their huts, while people from the nearby non-minor communities made up of women and their young children, were also fetching water at the same water pump. That afternoon, an altercation broke out between an older minor, full of mischief, and an older gentleman. The older man was of fighting age, yet wasn't in the army. Nor was he a camp teacher, caretaker or other staff, nor was he on a family visit. The minors often held these adult camp residents in scorn.

The boys saw themselves as being in the camp simply because they were too young to fight. In any case, the SPLA high command wanted the boys to study and, if they so wished, to join the war in the future or to rebuild the country that was going to be destroyed in the war. Any man of fighting age at camp seemed like an AWOL, a deserter from the war front, and so they were never treated nicely. And woe betide them if they stepped foot near, or inside, the boys compound without being introduced.

The boy had picked a fight with the stranger, thinking he could easily beat up the older man. Commotion ensued and everyone gathered around to watch the fight. However, the situation changed all of a sudden. Had the man simply tried to attack the boy, the rest of the boys would've joined in the fight to beat up the man with terrible consequences, like being attacked by a mob. Instead, the man started demonstrating his karate skills, shouting while throwing punches, jabs and kicks in the air. "Hie, yah!" he shouted. And if none was convinced of his ferociousness, the gentleman did land on his bottom with his legs spread out wide, as could only be done by a practiced athlete. Needless to say, the boys converged on the foolish boy to recant, "*Duk ran ben jol, wamath! Jo mol!*" ("Don't aggravate the man, further, brother"), but he wouldn't listen.

Furthermore, the boy thought that having a club would help him deter the fighter and therefore, ignoring the warnings, he continued insulting the apparent karate fighter. This caused further shouts of anger and obvious pain. The pain I refer to is heartache. The man never wanted to harm just a boy because he would be considered a coward who had left a real fight to come back to beat up young boys. He was in heartache because he was grossly insulted, and immensely disrespected while his threats ignored by the offending juvenile. The fighter seemed like he didn't want to harm the boy. Yet the boy was emboldened by the presence of so many of his close friends from his group that he was willing to make sure that he had won the showdown. So, while the boy challenger saw no sense in the warnings, and resisted, the fighter continued his karate demonstration with the other boys milling around him to encourage him to show more. It was a raucous crowd that afternoon.

Rather than the situation ending in a disaster for the boy and for the man, who would later be sentenced by the Camp Administration to a bad jail from which he might never return, the boy finally backed down and the worst was averted. The boy finally saw some sense, because the charade had turned into entertainment. The karate demonstrator had become a hero and a showman, demonstrating his karate skills all the way to the river south of our compound, where most of the boys were swimming that afternoon.

When the situation had calmed down, another older gentleman, a well-dressed man named Mr. Abdala, who was watching the whole drama, approached a boy who was fetching water from the tap to fill the water container, a 2-liter container called a jerrican the boy was carrying, with water. The boy obliged. After Mr. Abdala had had his drink, another boy approached to ask to drink from the same container. I was watching the scene, thinking that maybe there was going to be another showdown. But when the boy was done, the man, expecting a thank you from the boy, seemed disappointed when he heard nothing.

This bemused Mr. Abdala, who took the container from the boy. He asked in Arabic, "Where is my 'thank you'?" The boy simply smiled. "I thought your only vice was disrespect, but you also have no shred of good manners," Mr. Abdala added. "Please, I want you to say 'Thank You' to me," he demanded quite nonchalantly. Anticipating another embarrassing debacle, we quickly prevailed upon the boy to say *shukran* ("thank you", in Arabic). "Now watch me say thank you, '*shukran*' to the owner of this jerrican," Mr. Abdala said. We quickly showed him our approval.

What Mr. Abdala didn't realize was that it was not that we had no manners, it was that the manners which we had were quite different from the manners of the folks like him. For us, doing something good to someone near you was an expected virtue, and something for which none expected commendation. Acts of kindness were duties expected of everybody. Indeed, if a person was in a position to provide such an act of kindness and didn't render it, that person was more often than not vilified. So it would seem pandering for someone to say 'thank you' to somebody for being given a chance to drink water! Such is the Dinka culture, to which Mr. Abdala must have never been privy. But we were being educated for a better Sudan and he was right to expect us to be better, or at least different. We needed to learn new manners.

* * *

Life was on the move at Panyido. One day, my friends and I were playing soccer in a field running through the camp that used to be an airfield. A helicopter appeared from nowhere, being piloted by a Sudanese, a southerner, who asked, "Where is Pochalla?" How in the world would a helicopter pilot not know where his destination was? We pointed southward in the direction we knew Pochalla to be, after stopping our game of football, briefly.

* * *

CHAPTER 16

PANYIDO WE BUILD

"You must guard these registration cards like you guard your own lives," the registration clerk told us. "And remember to come to vote on January 9th."

Surrounded by the Anywak community, the relations with them were always testy. The Anywak felt that their land was being taken from them. This led them to sometimes kill a few children quietly and then hide their bodies. The Sudanese Government infiltrated the area too and used Anywak elements to spy on the refugees and the SPLA passing or basing in the area. At some point, the Anywak decided to attack our camp. It was feared that the unarmed boys and women would be massacred, so the few SPLA soldiers in the area, along with our teachers, went in to fight the Anywak.

When the battle was over, the surrounding community was razed to the ground, and the minors went in for a look at the houses and shops. I would say that the most important loot was the corn flour. We kept it in sacks so that whenever our turn came to grind your share of corn for the public table on your day of duty, you had ready-made flour and you didn't have to work hard. The rest of the SPLA soldiers went on a campaign on the outskirts of Panyido, a punitive expedition to make sure that the Anywak never threatened us again.

During that campaign, the place was swarming with SPLA soldiers. An SPLA soldier came to me and gave me his bag for safe keeping, and to keep it for my own should he not make it back alive. "Keep this bag for me. I will get it when I return, but if I shall never return, you can keep it for yourself," he told me. I promised to keep it safe for him. However, I felt bad about what he was saying, and so I kept praying. Luckily, he came back safe and sound, days after a successful campaign. Needless to say, the Anywak never touched us again until we left Panyido. I think they were badly punished.

It was announced in the camp one evening that everyone was to attend a *Mahadhara* (a public rally) the following morning. It was emphasized that a very important meeting was going to take place that morning, and that it was mandatory for everyone to attend. The impression was that something extraordinary was going to transpire. Some imagined it would be a chance to be picked to go to school in Cuba, a very desirable opportunity. Other fancies were floated about. It was left to us to speculate.

So, the following day, we came to the *Mahadhara* venue. The venue was west of the camp, almost on the outskirts. The southwestern part of the camp was were the schools were located-twelve schools for twelve groups of unaccompanied minors and the accompanied minors of the family groups. So, the venue was just westward. It was a cleared field, cleared of shrubs and grass and generally a bare ground. It measured approximately 100 meters by 100 meters. Just west of the field is the edge of the woods. An SPLA Commander, a major, arrayed with the *sugur* (insignia), red for *shurtha*, (military police), was giving a speech. He lectured about how the people in the camp behaved. "There are thieves, adulterers, rapists, cowards, and spies among you!" he declared. "Criminals will never be spared," he said. "We have a few people who we have caught acting with criminality. You will see what will be done to them today!" he said. Being familiar with punishment from the stroke of the cane, I thought the prisoners were going to be beaten and then let go. So, when there was a call to the people handling the wrongdoers to bring them forward, I thought they were going to be beaten in front of the whole crowd, and I was curious to see how they were going to handle it.

Some soldiers were sent out to clear people out from the direction of the woods, where boys had gone to relieve themselves. A group of soldiers were assembled and the criminals stationed a little to the left of the field. "Bring them over here," the Commander at the microphone called out. The condemned looked very dull, and frightful. Their skins looked so dry like people who have never taken a bath for a long time. There was a sense that maybe they were going to be let go after being scared.

The charges were read out, there were some quick movements, and then the criminals were shot, executed, with only one spared by being cut away from the rest of the condemned. Their crimes had varied from adultery and rape of a woman and her daughter by one culprit, to charges of spying for the Khartoum government by another, to simple theft. When it was all over, you could see smoke rising over the bodies and there was a doctor who went to check their pulses to make sure they were really dead. At that point, all hell broke loose. The women and children ran, to church or home, to get away or to pray to God. It was a lesson none would ever forget.

Sometime after the two executions at the camp,[58] there appeared an SPLA commander, Achol, one of the very few SPLA female commanders. Even though these women never really commanded battalions to war, they were a huge moral force within the movement. Achol was a very respected leader in her own right, not only within the movement but also throughout the entire Sudanese community, because she was a member of the first Anya Nya war. So, it was with a great respect that Cdr. Achol was welcomed to give a speech at the Episcopal Church's service one Sunday afternoon at their compound in Panyido. What Achol spoke about must have shocked the women assembled, and warmed the hearts of the men, as well as the scared boys who were in attendance.

---

[58] A week after the first execution, there was a call out for another *Mahadhara*, which I failed to turn up for the following morning but which also ended in another execution, of one more prisoner accused of spying for Khartoum

It so had happened that the camp executions, purportedly demonstrating SPLA justice, a machinery which we had come to value and respect, now began to seem brutal and senseless. People had begun fearing the SPLA, the champion of the poor and the weak. In fact, the most brutal treatment of a person by the SPLA, to my mind, was that incident at Pibor when one within their own ranks was stripped of everything, being left behind with nothing but literally the skin on his back. Therefore, this new brutality by the SPLA against its own people needed an explanation, and Achol's speech was quite overdue.

Until this time, the executions were explained away as punishment to atone for intolerable crimes against individuals and the community, and the demonstration was carried out to warn other would-be criminals against attempting such crimes. But, we never understood ourselves as capable of such crimes, especially the young boys who made up the majority of the spectators, but whose center of attention was games. How could a young boy imagine himself raping a woman, along with her daughter, or passing on secrets against the SPLA to its enemies? We all thought that the punishment was not befitting of the crime; we never even understood the veracity of the crime. Still, an explanation was overdue.

Achol took to the stage to explain her position, condemning the executions that were carried out at the camp. "I have heard of what was done at this camp last year," she began. "If I was here then, it would have been those women who would have been executed, not the men. There is no way a man can sleep with a woman and her daughter at the same time without that woman's consent!" she declared. The congregation murmured, perhaps agreeing or disagreeing. Someone of her caliber was putting some sense into what made no sense for some of the assembled people. Akuol went on, "The case of the woman and her daughter is quite questionable. Were they raped or were they willing participants with the accused?" she posed. "Was it adultery? I don't believe their story; more investigation should have been done" she stressed. "You men don't know how women are," she confided. There were quite murmurs, perhaps discussing her comments. "You can't continue to kill men. They are fighting the war. Those who carried out the execution have erred," she concluded.

For half the audience, her speech was well received, albeit with some reservation, but perhaps not everyone agreed. In a sense, her speech was a way to assuage the fears of the camp population. Except for the witnessed executions, the details of the crimes were not clear to half the execution witnesses. What the Commander Akuol speech did was calm the nerves of the people and to make them believe in the SPLA fairness again. She was simply doing damage control—a counselor she had become. Her speech gave the SPLA a humane character, seeing that a prominent leader amongst it ranks was protesting an action some of the population was opposed to.

* * *

At some point, it was decided by the camp authorities that the area on the banks of the Gilo River, just south of the camp, was fertile enough to produce ample vegetables to support the nutritional requirements of most of the refugee population, especially the unaccompanied minors. That piece of land used to be farmed by some Anywak families up to the time that the minors arrived at the camp, and the Anywak crops began to be involuntarily shared with the hungry minors. The land, however, had overgrown with tough grass over the years, growing worse since 1988 when it was decided that the land could be used for refugee farming. The Anywak had abandoned farming it after being frustrated by the unaccompanied minors who would steal their fresh green corn.

To clear the land, the minors were rounded up and given various tools like cutlass, machetes, pangas, mattocks and so forth to clear the grass and the reeds on the banks of the river. The minors went to work in the tall, tough grass and before long, the grass was all cut down and the new farmland was ready for planting. Tractors were brought in to clear, and to start plowing, the field. It was something to marvel at. An area the size of about 100 hectares was cleared for farming in a matter of days.

The crops and vegetable seedlings were germinated and transplanted. They included tomatoes, okra, kale, and more. Then, a water pump was brought to water the crops, since it was in the dry season. In a few months, the refugees were enjoying the fruits of their labors. This was common-sense work and a smart investment by the UN, who was kind enough to help fund and organize the service. The camp management was active in finding ways to improve the lives of the refugees. For instance, they tried to produce crops like groundnuts on grounds outside the camp. Some of the refugees would be surprised during the harvest when these food sources sprouted up, and ask, "Who produced these groundnuts?"

During that time at Panyido, I made the decision that I should undergo a circumcision operation because it was simply the time. Circumcision is a custom for the Dinka of Northern Bhar el Gazel and every young boy before adolescence was expected to undergo this operation. In fact, the boys would be reminded about circumcision almost every day by relatives, or by anyone who happened to see the boy naked. Those reminders were seemingly given to scare the boys, since this operation is quite pain-inducing, and to steel the boys in expectation of this pain. It became a rite of passage, and a test of courage, for the boys.

While such an operation could be performed in towns, within a hospital setting, it was in fact expected that boys undergo the operation within their villages, for everyone to see who could endure it, and to collectively witness that this boy had undergone the operation successfully. This is because if a boy never had the operation at the village, the people of the village would start to question if perhaps this person never underwent the operation at all.

Recently, while I was at the village, I was reminded that perhaps some of my relatives thought that I never underwent the operation after all, and that my male relatives, who underwent the operation at the village, were manlier than I. Little do they know that after having ended up in Ethiopia without the operation done, I felt that I could never claim to be a Dinka unless I received circumcision there. I worked hard on my own to raise the necessary funds from the sale of a rudimentary piece of furniture, carefully made by my owns hands and sold to an Ethiopian restaurateur. Proceeds were used to contract the services of a physician assistant, who conducted the operation in secret behind the hospital compound with blades, syringes and anesthesia, probably removed from the hospital storage.

Perhaps the fact that I underwent the operation with some anesthesia does indeed water down the impact of the operation in the minds of my relatives, who would have wanted to see what kind of a man I might become by enduring the pain in front of their eyes. But, I might say that by taking the initiative to go ahead with the operation on my own, by planning it and undergoing my own healing by myself, that this deserves the respect of my relatives. I went through this like an adolescent going through puberty, without the benefits of advice about what was happening from an authority. I am much more than they think.

From time to time at the camp, the SPLA, in their march from Ethiopia to the Sudan would pass through Panyido. One battalion that I saw in all its glory was the *Intifada*.[59] The SPLA *Intifada* ('Uprising') battalion was on its way from their training camp at Bongo, to Southern Sudan for military operations. This SPLA group had camped at the Gilo river banks, our favorite swimming locale, to spend the night before heading out to southern Sudan, via the river, and then through Pochalla. Many things distinguished this batallion, including their numbers, their morale and their military uniforms.

---

[59] The SPLA adopted the Arabic word *Intifada* to name one of its battalions because though the SPLA is largely a Christian Organization, it tended to espouse secular democratic ideals free of any ethnicity or religion. It therefore could never shy away from using Arabic words or even allow Muslims to join its ranks. Some of its prominent commanders were Muslims and even some were Arabs. Arabic was one of its operating languages. In fact, the operational language for its military operations and of instructions was Arabic. Most of its lower ranks spoke mostly Arabic among themselves.

The immaculate uniforms were bright green as opposed to the dark green of the *Bunia* ('Boxing') Battalion, who we had seen at Pochalla on our way in from Southern Sudan. My friends and I decided to go look at the army along the shore. The whole area was swarming with troops, with officers of various ranks here and there. The whole place was a beehive of activity, with groups of senior officers passing from one group of soldiers to another, inspecting them and being saluted everywhere. The sight of the activity was simply amazing, to say the least. The officers' ranks were designated by stars. Second lieutenants had a single yellow star, while Captains had three stars each. The troop's morale was obviously quite high and it was evident that they were ready to face the enemy.

The troops were given rations of biscuits and other provisions. These donations certainly came from our camp, although this was a hushed situation, even though one could argue that it was just a token of support to the fighting men. The members of the Intifada were actually former civilians, who had traveled with us to Ethiopia and had lived briefly at the Panyido camp, before they moved on to be trained for the army. I am pretty sure that some members of our group could recognize a few people. The mission of the Intifada was different from that of the Bunia Battalion, and the morale was also different. The Intifada seemed stronger. It could probably be that the Intifada were trained during better times, in a better training location, and by better training instructors.

The Bunia were graduates of the Dima military training camp. While there, they had become quite emaciated, either owing to poor provisions at the camp, or just because the training commander was simply too brutal towards them. The commander was a captured army officer from the Sudan Armed Forces. How this fellow ended up training the SPLA soldiers at Dima is something that only the highest echelon of the SPLA could answer. But, as we all knew, the SPLA wanted an inclusive movement whose aim was to liberate the whole country and to turn it into a democratic and socialist state. Therefore, bringing in more northern Sudanese was a required advantage and this must have given the brilliant SAF commander the chance to become the trainer of the Bunia Battalion, whose job it was to face the Murahilin raiders. The commander would have had valuable skills and knowledge about the government militia, knowledge he could impart to the trainees. In fact, even the skill of how to fire the standard SAF issue G3 would be a rare asset.

So, after graduating from Dima, the Bunia Battalion trudged for three months, into Bhar el Gazel, where it was finally able to rid the region of the Murahilin incursions once and for all. And even though the Bunia Battalion commander did defect to the government side afterwards, he succeeded in training a superior force that outmatched the feared Murahilin.

When we arrived at Panyido, it seemed to us that it was simply a forested area with no dwellings, except for a small trading center and a school for the Anywak children, taught in Amharic. Apparently it was only the educated Anywak, and a few Amharic from the Ethiopian highlands, who made Panyido their home. However, during our continued stay, someone suggested that Panyido was used years before as a rest camp by the SPLA recruits on their way to the training center at Bilpam, and by SPLA soldiers returning to the Sudan. It was also mentioned that there were some graves in the area. But, knowing that the SPLA only started in 1983 and our group made Panyido a home by 1988, that proposition seemed quite incredible. There seemed to be no traces of a recent settlement by the SPLA, and no sign of a graveyard.

Or perhaps there was some truth to the proposition. On certain excursions into the woods, while performing the manual work of tulba, we sometimes stumbled upon potential evidence. While out fetching wood for fires, or for making fences or beds, sometimes a tempting piece of dried plank jutting from the ground would appear to have actually been a pole supporting some crumbled structure. Perhaps the strongest evidence we found of a settlement during those excursions in the thicket, was when we found a mound that would crumble in if stepped on, as if it was some sort of a pit latrine. For me, I believed that the area was inhabited by the Tigrinya people.

To be sure, there were Tigrinya petty traders plying their wares around the camp every day. They would call out *"mil-le, mil-le, mil-le* (salt, salt, salt)", advertising their salt. They also sold such staples as onions and garlic. But where they came from, none of us had been able to discover. So, it seems that the area must have been inhabited by the Tigrinya people sometime back. The connection of the area to the SPLA could be that the area was earlier used by the Tigrinya rebel groups or their supporters. Indeed, those petty traders were quite peculiar in that they seemed to be hiding some sort of a secret.

Maybe the boys had sensed some prying eyes and thought that the fearful Tigrinya were looking to eat them, not realizing that the traders were actually spying for the Tigrinya rebels. Indeed, when the Mengistu regime fell, Panyido was a rallying station for the conquering rebels. The traders might have told the rebels something about the camp, or maybe the traders were rebels themselves. The SPLA was also capable of this duplicitous feat, as it had sent spies into the garrison towns in the Sudan, posing as simple village farmers and cattle herders trying to sell their livestock and goods, while actually they would be SPLA soldiers, gathering intelligence for the SPLA command and also buying goods for the SPLA.

While the SPLA would try to remove children from its ranks, it would never shy away from welcoming the young adults. Boys aged 16 and above would be welcomed, and the SPLA would go as far as penetrating the refugee camps in Ethiopia to remove them clandestinely. Some boys would already be more than willing to join the SPLA, but others would be resistant. Education became more important to some boys than the war, knowing that at their young age, their contribution in the field would not amount to much. They needed to learn, so that they could join the army later, when they were more educated, wiser and stronger.

Being at the camp for a while, the boys saw more value in education than in joining the army, and so every time that the SPLA came calling for recruits to join the fight, boys, or their guardians, would prevent them from joining. On one occasion, the SPLA announced, through its representatives, that older boys were to be picked out and sent to Kenya for further education. Many boys were enthusiastic about the news. It was like the popular SPLA student shipment to Cuba. However, those

Walking Boys

in the know realized that the proposition was simply a trick to send the older boys to the eastern part of Southern Sudan for further military training, and then to fight on that side of the Southern front. Some boys were luckily warned in time. They immediately sought and received medical referrals that kept them from being sent with the recruits going to Eastern Equatoria.

Eventually, it was decided that the Anywak and the refugee communities must be reconciled and made to live together. So, some Anywak children, from the local community, were brought to stay with the minors. Our group happened to have an Omot, a tiny Anywak boy, who became our friend, very fast. Apparently, he must have been very well informed by his community to tell us of the 'dangers' of touching the Anywak property. He said that the Anywak God would punish anyone who climbed a mango tree to eat the fruits, without permission. A few boys had fallen from the branches of the mango trees. This could be attributed to the very weak branches of the tree. Even in places like Wau, it was known that a mango branch would fail to support even the weight of a boy. However, the work of the Anywak God and the structural attributes of the mango tree seemed to have coalesced. Needless to say, the boys continued to take the fruits of the mango of the Anywak, but more cautiously.

And to create even more reconciliation, some days began to be set aside for the women in the refugee community to cook food for all of the minor boys. This program was extended to the Anywak, who would bring their food along as well. It was noticeable that the minors didn't really enjoy the food of the Anywak. They pretended that they did, but the way the food was cooked seemed to have removed most of the nutrients, making it nutritionally dry. For instance, the Anywak would roast fish before boiling it. But though the food may have been dry, it made for a cohesive community. I think it was a brilliant idea to create reconciliation between the two communities. The camp managers were almost always brilliant in their plans, so that the boys would protest when it was time for the managers to be rotated.

We learned that our long time Camp Manager, Mr. Chan, would be leaving. He had been more than an exemplary leader, beloved by the boys, and by the rest of the camp population. The boys decided that Mr. Chan couldn't be permitted to leave. There were plans for demonstrations to have him reinstated. Perhaps the camp authorities got wind of this. They either decided to downplay the move, or they kept quiet about the particular time when Chan was going to leave. It so happened that by the time we realized he had left the camp; it was too late to mount any objection.

His replacement was loathed and derided, because immediately upon the new Camp Manager's ascension, the *tulba*, or manual work for the boys, increased in intensity, scope and frequency. All of a sudden, there was no longer a kind camp leader making sure that no unaccompanied minor was being forced to shoulder an unfair workload, nor was there a voice advocating or implementing best solutions. For instance, under the new camp manager, pounding corn became the order of the day rather than the exception, whereas during Chan's tenure, the camp had more prepared flour and other goods.

Something happened at the camp once that was quite as comical as it was tragic. We woke up one morning to find a cow groaning next to our Group II compound, with one of its hind legs cleanly chopped off right at the thigh socket, and missing! Who had done it, and where the beef was stewing, no one knew.

We all believed that nobody from our group of minors was capable of wrestling a cow to the ground, cleanly chopping off a part of it and leaving it alive. While the feat might have been possible for a group of boys, a group activity at night near our compound would have aroused other boys to the struggle taking place. Perhaps there were very few strong men who could have accomplished such a feat alone. It certainly wasn't done by any individual from our group, or even if it could've been, the traces of a stew would've been found in short order. In any case, the cow was groaning and lying on its side just a few meters from our compound. I never knew what happened to the cow after that. It looked like it belonged to the cattle camp, owned and administered by the camp authorities, and they might have returned to pick up the cow. Either way, it was amazing how the erstwhile Dinka cattle keepers, who treated cows as God's gift that should never be slaughtered in such a manner, had turned into some kind of monsters. Or maybe the culprit was not a Dinka.

The UN brought clothing for all of the boys, but the clothing faded easily, never lasting more than a month. This led the UN to bring clothing every year. In fact, the issue of clothing was a major one. For those enterprising enough to have gained some money, buying durable clothing was possible. The Catholic Church also brought many items including shoes and clothing for the camp population, and especially it's Catholic Church members. While this was known to all, getting hands on this clothing was like climbing a steep hill.

It so happened that our subgroup caretaker, Mr. Mabor, chose me to be the custodian of the schoolbooks at our School Number II. The books ranged from stationery to world atlases. The job kept me away from being picked to go on work expeditions which all the minors would go on every dry season, gathering materials for the buildings for that year. This situation gave me a chance to actually read some books, including the atlas which was the beginning for me liking geography and traveling. Even though I was a hunter by heart, and liked to travel, the huge circles around the globe, and some of the pictures and names of the faraway places, led me to think about those places. The thing that never occurred to me, even while looking at those atlases, was the fact that the world was actually round, rather than flat, as it seemed to a hunter.

I only learned about that at class six in Raja Primary School in Kakuma Refugee camp, years later. When this concept was introduced in class, I was dizzy with incomprehension and the load of data, struggling to imagine a world that was round. It took me back to a view that I found quite troubling one night outside our Group II compound. Group II, under Mr. Kuol, was the most clean in all of the Panyido Refugee Camp, all owing to the effort of Mr. Kuol. That evening, outside the compound at Panyido Camp, the trash was heaped in one spot and then set afire. While the trash was burning, lighting a large area which would ordinarily be under darkness at that time of night given the lack of electricity, looking beyond the fire towards the sky and beyond, provided a great contrast to someone not used to bright lighting at night. It looked foreboding because, while the background towards the compound was lit and looked solid, the space beyond the fire and all the way into the sky looked like an abyss and fearful. I stopped visualizing the image. It was like when they covered the horrors of the war from soldiers yet uninitiated into combat, to avoid scaring them.

Once I was among a group of boys sent to another camp in the jungle, to cut wooden poles for our huts. This was a seasonal job, in order to keep building new huts and renovating the crumbling ones, because during every rainy season, if your hut was a crumbled mess, you would have no place dwelling in which to stay dry. It so happened that during those pole expeditions, certain boys fashioned some beds, chairs and so forth for their use, or for clandestine sale when they returned to the camp. Enterprise was not encouraged. Yet, while we were cutting wood during that time, I decided to make my own bed. I soon found out, though, that it required too many poles, forcing me to carry an added load, beyond the pole quota expected of me. Those poles were too heavy and it would have been impossible for me to carry, even if I was successful in cutting them down in the first place. So, I decided to make the next best item: a bamber (a small chair with no particular use in mind). I used a friend's bamber as a reference in constructing my own. Later, when we returned to our camp, the chair fetched me the sum of the Ethiopian Birr 5. In present U.S. dollars, it would have been $50! That was a pretty sum for an unaccompanied minor with nothing resembling an income. I was surprised and quite proud at my resourcefulness.

Cutting poles during those expeditions was not easy. We would leave very early in the morning to escape the diurnal heat, and then we would begin felling trees once we reached the Ethiopian highlands' dense jungle forests. For about two to three hours, we would cut down trees, swinging axes, and it was the sound of the axe striking the wood that was heard throughout the jungle forest. Then it would all go silent, as we returned to our camp. The jungle was so thick, that at those moments, taking a few steps in any wrong direction could cause you to become lost and vulnerable to being killed by any mountain lion, or to ultimately succumbing to exhaustion or starvation.

On those occasions, the heavy pole loads, the distance, and the exhaustion would take their toll for young fellows like us. One day while we were cutting trees in one of those jungles, after the usual two to three hours of work, the axes went silent and it was time to go. I had made sure that my one pole was cut and squared away, ready to pound the road back to escape the heat. A group of fellows came passing by my work buddies and I. We were not in a hurry. But there was a particular guy who was older, and he thought he could carry more than four very long and heavy poles bundled together. He probably was going to sell some, or he was planning on having four days' worth of poles so that he wouldn't have to come back the following day.

The load might have been too heavy for him because as he passed by us, the front of his tied load got stuck in the underbrush, probably because he couldn't see very well where he was going. Taking a pause to pull the load back while it was still on his shoulders, he took a deep breath before attempting to push through again. But the load would not budge. So, he tried to push it forward once more, but again it wouldn't budge. The back and forth pushing and pulling rendered his load stuck, both ways. The crowd arrayed behind kept passing him in a single file, one by one, with no one stopping to relieve him. He kept trying, and nobody was stopping to help. I was so exhausted already from cutting down my tree that I was in no mood for humor, and the same went for everyone else. Not that I could have been able to offer any help even if I wanted to. No one was up for any jokes, sad or comical. So, we loaded up and simply began to pass him as well. We were among the last groups leaving the jungle that afternoon.

Seeing that he was being left behind, he simply started to cry, to which none responded. Nobody laughed. Nobody stopped to help. Perhaps everyone wished he would take just one or two poles and leave the rest, but he was obstinate. We all wanted the extra poles, but we hadn't the strength to transport them. Yet, the moron kept crying, and he was older than most other boys walking by him, so we didn't sympathize. The interesting thing was that nobody had the stomach to laugh. For me, I thought it was bizarre and I wanted to laugh, but I was not in the mood to laugh. Someone finally rescued him by forcing him to abandon his load and leave with the rest, carrying just one pole. Later at the base camp, when everyone had had a bite to eat, water to quench their thirst and had relaxed the bones and muscles a bit, it was time to laugh. We could not contain it anymore. The guy had the audacity to cry, as if he was being forced to carry the whole load, when he could have just reduced the load. It was simply incredible. It was not like he was in any danger.

One of the most euphoric and memorable happenings at the camp was when we were visited by the famous, late Sudanese singer, Muhammad Wardi, known simply as Wardi to most Sudanese. The visit of Muhammad Wardi was rumored for a while and the camp was abuzz with preparations for his coming. This was in 1990, after the beloved camp manager Chan had left. A big dais was built at the former sports competition ground, northwest of the camp. The singer was finally set to make his appearance, after waiting on preparations which lasted many months. With his musical instruments, including the large microphones arrayed, everyone was simply waiting for him to sing. Our camp's leading musician, Fanan, though, was allowed to sing first with his Afirka band, made up of some minors. Even Wardi joined with the audience in dancing! But we had soon had enough of Mr. Fanan, and wanted the master Wardi to sing.

When it was his turn to sing, just the twang of one of his instruments was enough to cause the crowd that was familiar with his songs to go wild. It was the first time for me seeing Wardi, and I was waiting to enjoy the show, more than anything else. Already, I had forgotten how the Arabs in the Sudan looked like, and I was not too impressed when Mr. Wardi emerged with the same look as the Ethiopian Amharic we had seen around. I had expected him to look a little different from the every-day person in my surrounding which included the Ethiopians and the Southern Sudanese. Appearing like the ordinary average Ethiopian Amhara took away the expectations of the extraordinary. I later learned that Mr. Wardi is actually not an Arab. In fact, most Northern Sudanese aren't Arab either, though they all confess to be. Rather, Mr. Wardi, who has admitted this fact, is a descendant of the Sudanese Nubians and the Arab Islamic invaders. He sang one song, then another, and there were soon people in tears, in trance, dancing about or flailing on the ground. Women were jumping on the dais to shower Mr. Wardi with money and expensive gold jewelry. For sure he could sing and he could make one cry, but for me it was simply a wonderful music festival, one of the most memorable musical events I had ever attended.

The camp administration thought it was an important part of its policy to have the people of Southern Sudan, and those from the larger Sudan, remain in harmony with each other in the refugee camp. Ethnic conflicts and divisions were to remain at a minimum. The first step in this policy was gathering all of the young unaccompanied minors, who were largely from Southern Sudan, but also from all over the Sudan and from every ethnicity and region, and to indiscriminately combine them into groups numbering from I through XII. Each boys group united boys from all over.

Moreover, the families that came to the refugee camp intact were placed within blocks or villages that housed families regardless of their ethnicity or region. The whole camp was mixed to the point that members of the same ethnic community would spend months, even years, within the same camp without gaining the knowledge of each other's presence, meeting only through a chance encounter or having to pay visits at each other's homes. The camp management would have it no other way. Without a doubt, this strategy did actually minimize ethnic conflicts and rivalries, evils which were manifest in Southern Sudan during peacetime. Indeed, ethnic animosity finally showed its head at Lokichogio and in Kakuma, after the refugees moved to Kenya, when they were asked to settle within the camps based on their regional, district and ethnic groupings back home.

At Kakuma, this arrangement immediately started fomenting ethnic strife in the camp, which plagued the camp for its entire life. In fact, this led to at least one major episode of ethnic violence in the camp every year, with at least one human life being claimed. Such a phenomenon, ethnic strife ending in violence on such a scale, was unheard of at Panyido camp. The Sudanese were so united there that we would share in each other's stories, folklore, songs, dances and other human experiences peculiar to our particular ethnic community. One such sharing was the Sunday dances arranged by the camp management to foster cultural exchange and ethnic peace.

The members of a particular ethnic grouping would seek each other out at the camp to organize dances that could only have been performed back home, at happier times. The times at the camps were actually happier, except for missing family members and being cut off from the communities back in Southern Sudan. On Sundays, the huge field at the center of the camp, just adjacent to our Group II dwelling, became a cacophony of dancing ethnic communities, where every community tried to display their best dancing techniques and songs as only could have been hatched back home in their ethnic locales. One such dance that I went to every Sunday was the Nuer ethnic dance. And even though I could never understand the meaning of the songs being sung, the dances, as well as the beats of the songs, were simply too entertaining for me to miss. But perhaps my enjoyment of the Nuer Gajak dance was based more on one-woman dancer's appearance.

That particular dancer was simply beautiful and was certainly the center of my attention, she with her girlfriend dancers singing away happily in Nuer, songs that I could never understand but which warmed my heart, so that I would end up running after their dancing group around the field. It could be said that I enjoyed the Nuer woman's singing and dancing moves for the same reason that the SPLA military personnel, if not the entire South Sudanese community, admires Eritrean singer, Helen Meles as a singing sensation. While none understands her language or the meaning of the songs, nobody would suffer the banning of her songs from South Sudan without protest. This is the same reason one can enjoy all Ethiopian songs without understanding a single word.

But I was happily entertained, and I can testify that at Panyido camp, the Sudanese community had actually become a single community.

While there were several camp administrators, the two most commonly known were the camp manager and also the long serving camp logistician, Mayol. Mayol was famous for his trademark fast, even furious, scribbling on his notebook, scribbling that could earn the lucky observer bales of clothing or packs of refugee foodstuffs. We sometimes would stand to gawk at Mayol scribbling away, probably not caring about who else was nearby, gawking or otherwise. Having Mayol hastily write you a note was not something easily earned. The order to write a note for someone might come from the camp manager himself, in which case a young boy was never going to be the recipient. The other way was for an aspiring beneficiary to be in the good graces of Mr. Mayol, but this also never seemed possible for a young boy of our caliber, given that even though we stood by Mayol, witnessing him at his game, we never received an acknowledgement or a nod. Mayol was the camp administrator everyone was sure he or she knew, yet he was never known to have given a speech, or even to have been seen talking to anyone for any length of time.

It was so that the best way to get Mayol to allow someone to share from the goods from the stores controlled by him, at least at the level of those having notes quickly written in their names, without him having to write any notes would be to pay a visit, unannounced, to one of his stores and to take without being noticed. If caught, this could earn the culprit some jail time but more often than not, the culprit was simply released after punishment with painful lashes. While stealing was certainly frowned upon, the communist system in Ethiopia then rendered this course of action morally ambiguous. If everything was held in common, as it sure was, sometimes taking without asking was the equivalent of having due share, given the inefficiency and the inequality in the distribution system. Getting caught in the act was an embarrassment for the wrongdoer and punishment would likely follow. But, sometimes the guards would just allow the theft to continue in their presence, if the loss was not substantial enough to rile the boss, including the smart Mr. Mayol. However, the most cautious and prudent, and the morally timid, never tried this route even if it would have been surely workable, albeit with minor risks. Mr. Mayol surely never condoned the theft but the loses from the stores this way were minimal, given the strength and skill of the young culprits. Bigger thieves would get in huge trouble, including almost being shot.

When it came to health matters, the camp health system was certainly much better than the average health system inside the southern Sudan countryside at that time. While the local dispensaries were the places to go when someone was suffering with fever, commonly malaria, the Panyido hospital was the central health point where the major cases would end up. Even though I never really toured the hospital to discover its inner workings, I remember the peculiar smell that emanated from it. It was the smell of the laundry detergent, jik, which was used to wash the clothes of the patients and perhaps the floors. Or maybe it was another chemical that smelled like jik, but the smell was so foul, and would travel so far out of the hospital, that being nearby, and downwind from, the hospital could give someone a nauseous sense that they needed to vomit.

Panyido camp had a town crier. Makuei was the comical character who made announcements affecting people in the camp. He would travel on foot with a loudspeaker from block to block and group to group with his announcements, punctuated with his jumping dance, and accompanied by a song.

> *"Makuen Gok anong chok Majek awet, ken ngen a*
> *nong chok Majang-rial awet.*
> *Jabona a roc cuot e nhial aroc.*
> *Jabona a roc cuot e nhial aroc.*
> *Jabona a roc cuot e nhial aroc.*
> *Kene menh kene menh aroc, cuot e nhial a roc."*
> **(Makuen Gok wears bangles. Can't you see he has**
> **got bangles?)**

Makuei would sing, with the hastily gathered, curious onlookers singing along with him. Then, he would say, *"Aywa el iquo al Mawotonin..."* (To you fellow town dwellers...) adding whatever message he wished to announce to the camp inhabitants that day. His announcements were always well received on account of that song.

At Panyido, our group of boys generally tried to observe the rules, but sometimes there was misbehavior, and mischief. The boys, who composed the majority of the camp residents, were confined mostly to their groups. A boy was permitted to travel outside of the group only with the consent of the immediate leaders, made up of other boys, and with the ultimate authority, which rested with the caretaker. However, there would always be some boys who would decide to break the rules, perhaps believing that rules were made to be broken. For instance, those boys who ventured to, and were found at, the Ethiopian marketplace, would be placed in the hands Mathou. His job, aided by a few tough boys, was to maintain discipline by striking fear into the boys, whether it was directed at those who broke the rules against being at the Ethiopian market, or those who broke any laws including stealing, or acts of violence.

The boys found at the Ethiopian market would usually be held overnight at the Mathou detention *tukul* (hut) where the overnight bed would be the bare sandy floor, and the dinner would be boiled *Dura* (Sorghum), sprinkled with traces of grains of sand, just enough to be felt when chewing. Refusing to partake of such a 'feast' was usually quite impossible because the intrepid and apparently sadistic *shurtha* (public safety boys) would make sure that you had the best means of coercion to make you 'enjoy' the dinner. And overnight, the elements of cold and dew would chill you to the bone. Only the hardened offending juveniles would be found at the Ethiopian market subsequently. Those wiser would never even attempt to go to the Ethiopian market for any reason, except when given a written permission to purchase something for the relatively richer caretakers. However, some could be there briefly to fulfill their pressing business needs without detection.

Harsher treatments awaited those boys, though, who would be so courageous and criminally minded to continue to commit acts considered offensive to the public good. In such situations, the repeat offenders, invariably guilty of theft, petty or otherwise, would have writings about their crimes taped on their backs. They would then be led by the shurtha boys from group to group, stopping at every group to state their crimes in front of every crowd of boys that came out to investigate. Such a display of shaming was too much for those mindful of themselves. Making the boys aware of the punishments that awaited them should any of them violate the rules, was enough to make them think twice, even though nobody really wished to become a thief.

* * *

I went to grade one through four before Mengistu Haile Mariam's regime collapsed in 1991, whereupon we had to leave and return to the Sudan. Mengistu's security must have been very active in Panyido Refugee Camp because there was an aid worker, a Tigrinya, who was quite liked by many people, until he vanished one day, believed to have been eliminated by Mengistu's forces. He was overweight which to us in the camp was remarkable because almost everyone else had very little weight. He was a medical worker and he helped many children through his service. He would chat with anybody, including the children he was treating. But, it so happened that he just disappeared. People who knew him were asking about his whereabouts but the little information we got, which was quietly whispered, was that he had been picked up by the ruthless Mengistu security and never came back.

It was further said that the Mengistu henchmen took him to Addis Ababa, after they had informed the good medical worker that Mengistu himself had become aware of his good deeds to the young Sudanese refugees, and that he wanted to meet him personally to thank him right at the seat of the government in the capital city. The medical worker ended up in a furnace, the favored form of execution by the Mengistu regime, or so it was said. Whether this was the full truth, cannot be ascertained. The crime was that the good medical worker was actually a channel through which some of the medical aid that was meant for the refugees found its way to the Tigrinya Rebels,[60] of which he was a sympathizer and active supporter, clandestinely.

* * *

---

[60] Or TPLF-Tigray People's Liberation Front

CHAPTER 17

END GAME

We had registered to vote, and now each of us held in our hands the papers that would allow us to cast our vote in the Referendum. That was the end of one road and the beginning of another. At Panyido, during our youth, we knew that we were only at the beginning, but we knew also that the Sudan would be peaceful again. Times in the camp were times of preparation for a great future.

As children at Panyido, we were always busy. We went to school, built huts and participated in sports. The camp administration created an Olympic-like sports competition among all the Sudanese settlements in Ethiopia, played at Panyido Refugee camp. Sports was a big part of life at the camp, with the most ubiquitous being football, called soccer in the United States. For lack of resources, our soccer balls were made from worn-out socks, stuffed with worn-out pieces of clothing, tied on one end, then turned inside out and tied again on the other end. A good ball would involve sewing. The hand-tied soccer balls were more common and were pretty much the standard for the unaccompanied minors.

During the evening hours when there was no major work expedition, the camp, especially the unaccompanied minors' groups, would erupt in small clique soccer games which you would never get to play in unless you knew someone on the teams, and they allowed a spot for you. These scrimmages were where skills were honed. But, in the real competitions between groups, or in this case between settlements, it was mostly only the experienced older boys who played. Many of these boys were already champions, and were already in high school in Rumbek or Wau, before leaving for the bush. They formed the bulk of the team members, whether in volleyball, soccer, running, throwing the javelin, or other competitions.

The intergroup competitions, between Groups I, II, III, all the way to Group XII, were always won by Group I, with Group II always placing second. This was because the most skilled athletes, specifically those from Rumbek, were concentrated in those two groups. The two most talented soccer players, Seth, the striker in Group II, and Makuac, the goalkeeper in Group I, tilted the games in favor of their teams, and against all the rest. Although Seth could never score against Makuac, he would always score against the other keepers, and he was peerless as a striker. But in the intercamp games, when Makuac and Seth played together, along with the best of the rest at Panyido, Panyido won most of their games. The intercamp games brought teams from all over, including the SPLA team from Bongo. It was the whole Rebel Sudan participating in those games, people from every ethnicity and part of the Sudan.

One particular sportsman was remarkable for his strength in the sport of javelin throwing. This huge Nuba fellow, from the Nuba Mountains, must have weighed more than 250 pounds. He would pick up the heavy instrument and hurl it over a large distance, further than any other on his practicing team. It was simply something to just behold by us wiry Dinkas. I never had a chance to watch him in the real competition, but I can vouch that there would have been no challenger for him.

There was a member of the Ethiopian Anywak soccer team who was also very good, and was someone to watch when our teams would play against their teams. This fellow found his way to New York in the 1990s and was murdered because he got into an altercation with someone about a girlfriend. This happened while I was still in Kenya. It became a cautionary tale, something to avoid when one came to the US: Never get into an argument with an American about his girlfriend. This was one of the tidbits of information one would do well to remember the moment one sets foot in the US.

In 1989, the camp management decided to clandestinely take the caretakers and administrators to a military training in a nearby SPLA training camp. The camp itself was about 60 minutes' walk away from the Panyido Refugee camp. The aim was to introduce discipline and the ability for the teachers, caretakers and administrators to protect the minors in case of trouble. Also, there was a policy that all Sudanese affiliated with the SPLM/SPLA were to have a military training. Even the minors wanted to be trained as well. It didn't take long for the teachers to be done with training. Shortly after, it became our turn to start our military training.

Every group was divided into six subgroups. The first three subgroups from every group were to be taken for training. My subgroup being the sixth in Group II, I didn't have a chance to be among the first batch. Still, being able to go to training was a desired end and I sought to get myself through no matter the effort. It was tentatively hoped that the remaining three subgroups would have their own chance later on. I was impatient, though, as I waited for the select subgroups to be called to travel to the training camp. When the call was given, I slipped myself in among with the selected travelers. That evening, we were brought together in one larger group and then dispersed into new groups leaving me to feel that it was a done deal. However, the following day, it was found that the number expected was too high. Apparently, there were a substantial number like me who were not supposed to have been there so the trainers decided to regroup everyone into their subgroups.

Being that my subgroup was not to be part of the training, I and a few others were left to sit under a tree while the rest of the exercise was going on. It not only looked like a lost cause, but we were likely to be punished, not only at the military training camp but also back at the refugee camp after we returned. Each of us was left to imagine for himself what such punishments would be. We were scared and it seems that was the purpose. The instructors wanted to lead us to feel ashamed for cheating the system. After about an hour, another trainer, whom we were told was related to Dr. John Garang, the head of the SPLM/SPLA, and who almost commanded the process, came passing by and was overheard to have said "You will see today. Who told you to come here? Trying to game the system?" he fumed. We knew we were in hot soup.

Another hour and there appeared another instructor, older, obviously an officer, who inquired quite nicely, "Why are you under a tree here when all of the exercises are going on? Don't you want to be a part of the army? Whom do you think is going to fight the war?" Upon learning our predicament, he immediately took us to the exercise area and personally made sure that we were distributed among the new groups forming. Thus was averted a certain humiliation and pain. After the exercise, with everyone separated and assigned into new groups, we were ordered to build our own houses before starting our training, as was the standard SPLA training procedure. The younger crowd was grouped together and given lighter tasks while the older boys were assigned the heavy manual labor of felling trees for timber and gathering grasses for the roofs of the huts. I was among those given the lighter tasks, something I was glad about.

As the rainy season began, the older boys were ordered to establish an emergency shelter for the younger folks. Being forced to do work on such a shelter knowing that they would never be able to use it, the builders did a very shoddy job. Before the shelter was ready for occupancy, however, it started raining one evening with a downpour. We rushed into the new, hastily constructed hut made of grass and heavy timber. I was assigned a spot right in the middle of the shelter. The wind blew and the rain poured shaking the shelter to its foundation but we were glad to have somewhere out of the rain, wind and cold. However, in a few minutes, the shelter could not hold against the wind and rain, and it simply gave way. I felt a jolt like something bad had happened and it was all blackness with some heavy and huge void engulfing me for some minutes—I don't know how long.

When I came to, I could hear other boys trapped under the timber and grass groaning in pain. I had passed out. However, I found that I could breathe, but barely. There was a large beam right on my back, pinning me down, with my nose pressed into the still dry dust, with excruciating pain, and my feet also pinned down by another beam. I tried to call for help as I heard rescuers talking urgently, finding boys trapped underneath the rubble and fishing them out. Luckily, someone called out to the others to have me rescued as well as he heard breathing and muffled calls. "Another one is here!" he called out. After getting out from under the heavy timber and grass, I could think neither of my bedspread nor my bag. I left them all under the rain soaked heap. We were allowed to shelter inside the huts of the guards of the camp. The following morning, the order came to us that everyone, even the younger crowd, was to be ready to go to the forest to cut timber and grass in order to make shelters before the rain increased in intensity. None was going to be exempt; not even those who might fake illnesses to avoid *tulba*, the manual work.

I was very badly injured on my insteps and ankle, though internally so that it could not be seen. But I knew from the pain that the injuries were bad. I went to the parade (military assembly) seeking permission, a written note, to go to the dispensary. My group leader allowed me to seek permission from the medical officer. However, the moment the officer saw me, he ordered me to go to work with the others. He flatly refused to listen to my pleas to go to the dispensary and instead called over the military police made of fellow boys. "Take him away! You must go to work!" he ordered. But when he saw that I was merely walking in front of the *shurtha*, he ordered that I be made to run, even beaten. He ordered that I be beaten until I ran to join the members of my group to go to work. "*Dugu! Kali ye jiri!*" he ordered ("Beat him! Let him run!"). But, knowing that I was right, I refused to run. They kept beating me but also urged me to run, as if to assuage the pride of the medical officer. "Run please!" they begged me, but I refused. I never wanted to be so humiliated. Even my tormentors hesitated a little bit after realizing that I was not going to be forced to run.

Upon reaching my group leader, he told me to remain behind to do the lighter work. I remained behind. Around midday, my feet were so swollen that I could not walk. And then there was a storm. Everyone ran to seek shelter, while I had to crawl all the way to the guards' huts we had used the night before. I crawled under one of the beds on the ground, with nothing to spread on the floor or use to cover myself from the cold. The whole night, I was in tremendous pain and everyone in the room knew about it because I was groaning in pain. The following day, the guards went secretly to report about my condition. During the parade time, it took me a little longer, crawling, to get to the parade. If one were sick, unless you were carried, you had to go to the parade[61] to get permission to be sick. These military parades were carried on a daily basis at the military training camp for purposes of accountability. These parades were daily in the mornings, strict and mandatory.

From a distance, the whole parade crowd saw me crawling, so my group leader, along with a few friends, rushed to pick me up and carried me to the parade. The officer who refused to let me go to the clinic the day before was beside himself with rage. "Why wasn't I informed? Why didn't you bring him to me in time? How could you wait for another day when the accident happened yesterday? Who is responsible for this?" he fumed. So, he was quietly informed that I was the one he had ordered the *shurtha* to beat the day before. I had to be carried to the clinic and was admitted immediately. Seven days after, I was feeling much better, but I probably was internally injured in ways I would never know until later. When our training was over, we went back to our camp to return to learning, now more disciplined, proud and confident of being a big part of the Movement.

There at Panyido, the boys would do most of the manual work. The work included gathering wood and grass for building big huts and compounds for the boys and for some families of the camp powerful, and to also build school classrooms and fences. The manual labor also included clearing tracts of land for compounds and for other uses. One particular tract, running northeast through the length of our Group II camp, right through the middle, was the landing airstrip. All of the groups of boys were brought to clear the grounds with cutlass and pangas and axes for the few trees. The grass was higher than the tallest boy, and it was our duty to cut it all down to make the landing strip. The

---

[61] The parades talked about here are not the typical festive celebrations reminiscent of the 4th of July marches, with people in costumes, dancing music, pomp and performance.

place was being reclaimed after having been used as public dumping ground, and it looked and smelled the part.

Religion was an important aspect of life for the Sudanese refugee community in Panyido. On Sundays most of us would attend one of the three churches that predominated in the Sudan and were transplanted into the camp by the pastors and priests who had joined the refugee community. Those churches were the Episcopal Church, the Catholic Church and the Presbyterian Church. During that time, a friend, Malok, got me to go to the Episcopal, or protestant church, as we called it. As a member of that church, he would go every Sunday.

I was also searching for that Church to which my sister used to take me in Wau. So Malok and I made a pact that we would go to their church every Sunday. I tried to remember if the church I was attending was the same church that I went to with my sister in Wau, but I couldn't. I continued going to that church anyway and I enrolled in what is known as catechumenate, in preparation for baptism. I learned songs, teachings about God and the rules concerning the Episcopal Church. One thing I learned to like was the preaching rendered by both the pastors and their helpers. They made the Bible readings and songs meaningful. They always talked of how to live well in the community and how to maintain a worshipful communication with God. My religious development reached the point where I was to be baptized. I still remember a part of the incantation by the pastor which meant that I had become a child of God and that I had an added power to fight the devil- "*ba heed ke durieth*" ("to struggle against the devil and win").

The words were powerful and I knew that something really important was being said. After the baptism, I came away very happy, telling everyone about it, but I was informed by some relatives that we the people from Bhar el Gazel of Southern Sudan go to the Catholic Church, and not the Episcopal Church. "We are Catholics and we go to the Catholic Church!" a cousin told me quite disdainfully when I told him enthusiastically about my baptism. I thought the advice was annoying since it seemed to devalue my joy that day. However, I decided to be led to that other church. The moment that I entered the

Catholic Church under the tree, I saw people genuflecting and making the sign of the cross. So, there and then, I knew that was the church I went to with my sister, and I enrolled in catechumenate ready to be baptized again. The teachings, in recited form, from the catechism of the Catholic Church, translated into the Dinka language, were not as similar as those I went through at the Episcopal Church, but I was glad to be back home in my own church.

Three months later, I was baptized once again and became a catholic. One thing that I missed, though, from attending the Episcopal service, was their ability to interpret the Sunday Bible readings, amply illustrated with everyday stories, much better than the catholic priestly preachers. Also, I thought that the Episcopalians worship was quite triumphant, with how they began their service with "*Yin lo Jik Nhialiny dit, Rier ye Rir ke dhie Wor*" ("You are Holy Almighty God, power above all powers"). I finally remembered that indeed my Father and Sister were Christians and not pagans. The catholic priest there didn't really like the Episcopal Church, and he didn't hide his dislike. I later discovered that the seeming animosity was apparently created way back during the Anglo-Egyptian Condominium in the Sudan, when Southern Sudan's three provinces were assigned to three different denominations, so that Bhar el Gazel was given to the Catholic Church, the Upper Nile given to the Episcopal and Presbyterian Churches, while the greater Equatoria was given to the Catholic Church.

The Priest at the Parish left the Panyido camp and went on a trip. It was said that he had gone back to Southern Sudan, to the areas of Kapoeta and Torit. He was gone for months, but when he returned, he brought back property for the church. Among these was a white Toyota landcruiser, making the Catholic Church more appealing. On the day that the priest, Fr. Akot arrived, the young men and boys who frequented the church came to welcome him and were entertained with the priest's new boombox. That evening, prayers were more solemn than usual.

Sometime after that, catholic nuns were brought in to become part of the church. The nuns, Daughters of Charity of Mother Teresa of Calcutta, brought a sense of service and community into the Parish.

Before long, the Catholic Church's parish at Panyido became a sprawling complex of tents, tent stores full of items, and grass thatch huts. The catechumenates swelled in ranks and the church became quite vibrant. One thing, though, that the church could never bring itself to do was to build a house of worship. This could have been done relatively cheaply and by the faithful, as was done by the Episcopal Church without any outside help. The people continued to pray under the trees, with this becoming particularly treacherous during the rainy season.

The Catholic Church's teachings on the value of work were not known to most churchgoers until Father Akot decided that it was time to build a compound around the sprawling dwellings of the catholic nuns, the priests and the catechists who taught the catechumens. The priest asked the church community, especially the young men who were the majority in the church membership, to start bringing grass and poles to construct a fence, on a voluntary basis. The Church was doing so much for the community as it was. While that was just a plea, and the church members were free to contribute to the effort or not, the priest was quietly making a list of those who were doing work. Every Sunday, there would be a report of the work done gathering the fence materials, favoring those who were helping. Some people decided that perhaps the work was progressing fine, and to not bother really contributing until the fence was ready to be built.

When it was completed, the priest was so happy that he decided to throw a fence-opening party. He was actually quiet on the particulars of the attendance, and simply announced at the church that "there is a party today to celebrate the completion of the fence in record time, and it will be a joyous moment." I don't believe an open invitation was extended. Yet it was assumed by most people that the party, being a church party, was open to everyone, including those who never contributed to the building of the fence. Unfortunately, at the entrance gate of the sturdy fence, those whose names weren't on the party list were simply turned away. Such was an act unheard of in the Dinka culture, and it seemed to run against the charity mandate of the Christian church. In the Dinka culture, it is alright to carry the workload of others at times, knowing full well that when it is your turn to rest, and it always comes, that the others will carry the workload for you. It is part of the common wealth of the community: You work today, so that we all enjoy; I work tomorrow, so that we all enjoy. Only, the catholic Dinka priest didn't think that way, or perhaps he was simply abandoning his culture.[62]

The other catholic priest whom we came to know, at Pochalla, was Fr. Matong. Fr. Matong did the same, turning away those who hadn't contributed work from enjoying the labors of others. Under Fr. Matong at Pochalla, the Catholic Church finally came around to build a huge church structure with timber and grass, utilizing the labors of the simple parishioners. When the church building materials were being collected, and the church was being built, some members of the community never contributed. Finally, when the church was up, and the congregation was celebrating, the priest got a shipment of some church goodies from Lokichogio in Kenya, by way of some good western aid worker, and the distribution of the goodies went according to who had participated in building the fence around the church. I always liked this because it showed that the church was teaching her people to be hard working. I thought it was actually a good thing.

However, the stay at Panyido was not to be long-lived. For, just as the Catholic Church was establishing itself, and it had become peerless by 1990, it was only a few months later, May of 1991 that the Panyido refugees were to leave to go back to the Sudan. The church property went to waste, along with all the shoes and clothing that the boys never got to wear, but remained in storage at the catholic parish in Panyido. It was said that the SPLA soldiers, who were evacuating their Ethiopian bases at Bongo, Bilpam and elsewhere, took some items, and then placed landmines around the rest, when they retreated, after the refugees were gone. The Uyana (Ethiopian) rebels were blown up by the landmines and suffered many causalities around the site of the former Panyido Catholic Church and around the other refugee stores that were

---

[62] From the viewpoint of the Dinka Culture, I don't support the exclusion of those who never participated in the work-we should all share even if all of us never sweated. However, in order to support hard work, reduce the issue of heavy reliance on others, as well as banish creeping laziness among the refugees, a lesson of exclusion as shown by the priest should be effected.

also mined inside Panyido. This contributed to the madness of the Ethiopian Uyana rebels, during the Gilo Crossing, and the subsequent cooperation of the new Ethiopian regime with the Anywak Militia and the government of Sudan Army in attacking and capturing Pochalla in the dry season of 1992.

In May of 1991, it gradually became clear that the refugees were going to have to leave Ethiopia and head back to the Sudan, whether they wanted to or not. We knew that there would be a lack of education and other pertinent services awaiting us, which we had become used to at the refugee camps in Ethiopia. And we also knew that there would be rampant insecurity and that the situation would be nearly the same as when we had left it. Nevertheless, we were happy because we were going back to the Sudan where there was going to be a greater chance for family reunions. We were also happy because of the fact that some refugees who had grown insulated from the pain of war going on in the Sudan, where mostly men were prosecuting it, would be able to come back to the reality that the Sudan was still suffering.

Over time, some people at the camps became too accustomed to their privileges, and lost connection to the suffering back home. It was said that some women in the Itang Camp would refuse to prepare beans or corn for food because their stomachs or mouths couldn't handle it! Moreover, it was said that some women would sometimes claim, "I wish I had the mouth of an SPLA soldier to come eat this food for me." The beans and corn which she didn't like were supposedly too coarse. We were quite indignant to hear such stories. However, to be fair, those were mere rumors passed along to pass time or to create villains of some groups of people, but there must have been some truth to it. On the other hand, the unaccompanied minors, growing up away from family care and only taken care of by the caretakers, were becoming lost and almost hopeless. Whether their family members were left intact back home in Southern Sudan or not, they were clearly orphans and had the problems of all the orphans. So, going back to the Sudan would bring our group back into contact with the reality. Panyido was like a camp for prisoners, as all camps are. So, everyone looked forward to returning to the Sudan.

It was the rainy season when we finally were to leave. It was decided that the 16 groups of boys would be the first to leave Ethiopia, to be followed by women and children and the rest of the bulk of the refugees. This was because the unaccompanied minors were the responsibility of the caretakers who were the administrators, while the rest of the population, whose vast majority were women and their children, would make the choice for themselves, or they would go slower. Those Ethiopians who were Mengistu supporters, and who were sympathetic to the Southern Sudanese refugees, told the Sudanese to take anything they wanted, including trucks, bulldozers and cars. However, due to muddy roads and the rains leading to the impassibility of the roads, no vehicle or property could be taken by us. Moreover, we wouldn't have had enough drivers, owing to our lack of training and education. If it were this time, we would have driven every vehicle in that area to South Sudan. Our trouble would only be gasoline, or petrol as it is called in those parts.

The Mengistu Government had just collapsed and the new government, formed by the victorious rebels who were backed by Khartoum, wanted the Sudanese refugees and the SPLM/SPLA out, by force if necessary. Apparently they also wanted to capture and bring to Khartoum the famous unaccompanied minors, the present lost boys. Khartoum saw this group as being trained to be the soldiers and rulers of tomorrow who would help transform the entire Sudan into the SPLM New Sudan vision. If brought to Khartoum, the alternative education would be forced islamization and arabization. The belief would be instilled that Islam is the only true religion, and that unless you were a Muslim, you were simply an infidel and not worthy of even being a citizen. And also the belief that unless you saw yourself as an Arab, spoke Arabic, had Arabic culture and an Arabic name, that you were not a worthy human being would also feature. We never appreciated these notions. The Unaccompanied Minors would get ahead of the pursuing combatants.

CHAPTER 18

HOMEWARD BOUND

"Southerners are already leaving Khartoum. Soon we can be proud of our new country. Finally, there is a place we shall call home," Deng told me when we spoke again days after registration.

We started on our return journey back into the Sudan. It was May, 1991. We would enter the Sudan through the town of Pochalla. Our group took three days to reach the Gilo River, which is considered to be where the border lies, with only a few belongings on our backs, trudging through thick muddy paths and on rainy days. We took the circuitous way to avoid the marshes on the shorter route which would have taken us but a day's walk in the dry season. The Gilo River had three encampments: two on the Ethiopian side and one on the Sudanese side, all manned by Sudanese SPLA soldiers. We crossed the river to the Sudanese side on the first day we arrived. We used little dugout boats brought to us by the camp guards and after all of our groups had crossed, we settled up to await the rest of the unaccompanied minors still on the way from Panyido. We stayed in Gilo for some two weeks, before we moved over to Pochalla, the border town of the Sudan.

In those days we spent at Gilo, we were crammed in with no chance to go for a swim because the area was soaked by rain and the river was bursting its banks, with water rushing so fast that someone unfortunate enough to fall into the river would be gone too far downstream before any rescuers could arrive. We spent our days sleeping and talking. On one of those days, on a clear sky, we saw several airplanes, white in color, coming from Ethiopia, flying south to a place we never knew. The convoy of airplanes, plying the sky from Ethiopia southwards and then returning to Ethiopia, as if they were transporting something, was simply amazing for us to witness. Was it Col. Mengistu leaving the country?

On another of the mundane days, a group of soldiers came into the encampment which we then shared with the beloved SPLA guards. The soldiers were chaperoning a very interesting group of ragtag combatants, Arab mujahedeen, among them a colonel, whom we later learned to have been captured from Nasser by the SPLA. This was the famous Abdel Majub. It was quite humid that afternoon. The prisoners proceeded to pray in their Islamic way, under the shade of the large tree at the center of the SPLA Guard's compound. It was a shock to us that they had been allowed to pray, not in the usual way of us Christians, but in their Islamic way, which we all abhorred! I personally thought that something was really wrong with the SPLA, but I later came to realize that the SPLA was there and then showing a shining example of its own ideals: Freedom of religion was a guarded right for anybody, including the SPLA prisoners of war.

I was seeing Arabic people once again, but it seemed as though it was the first time. This is because I had been removed from my childhood days in Wau for so long. In those days, I would see Arabs in their jalabias in the marketplace or as soldiers, even up close when the security personnel would come to our house to search for ammunitions, guns or anything that smelled of the SPLA. Yet I had forgotten what an Arabic person looked like after such an absence from the Sudan. I had even forgotten what my mother looked like. We were all gawking at the Arab el Majub, praying with his comrades, a proud man! He seemed too proud, even looking down upon the SPLA guards, but they didn't care. El Majub was a grumpy prisoner.

A few days later, we were finally ready to leave the Gilo encampment to go to Pochalla. However, because we could not carry enough supplies on our backs, we came to Pochalla with only very few belongings. Pochalla was a desolate town, soaked in rain and mud, when we reached it. It was inhabited by a few SPLA soldiers, some families and by the Anywak farming community. The town was composed of tukuls, grass-thatched huts, and we believed that we were going to be staying in some of the tukuls to keep away from the elements, but it was not to be.

We were not sure if Pochalla was going to be our new permanent encampment, but we got to work securing an area for our new shelters. We cleared a patch of grassy, water-soaked knoll, among the trees south of the main center of town. It was always raining so we had to use plastic sheets to cover ourselves, not to mention that we were wading through soggy mud. The ground was cleared and the soggy earth was heaped together to make mounds. This was done to raise the area above the water level to avoid being soaked. We slept under mosquito nets, which were each covered with a sheet of plastic. This system kept people protected both from the mosquitoes and the rain. However, sometimes when it rained at night, the water would rise and then we still got soaked. And sometimes the mosquito net would get soaked, become heavy, break and allow mosquitoes in. In any case, we were always prepared for any eventuality. For example, when it had rained at night, raising the water level high and submerging the rest area, it was always good to continue lying on your side because turning would expose your body to more cold and loss of body heat. Staying on one side ensured that the body heat was conserved. As I lay in my makeshift bed, I wondered how long we would stay at Pochalla, where our next stop will be or when the pounding rains would stop. It rained and rained and rained. The country was covered with water, the croaking frogs and the twittering crickets. Near dawn, monkeys would then hype the noise.

The worst part of being so close to the river at Pochalla was the morning cacophony of the troop of monkeys on the other bank. It was suggested that the monkeys made wild noises near dawn, or sometimes during the night, because they were trying to scare away night hunters, especially the leopard. It was said that the monkeys would sleep in hierarchy, with the very young at the top of the tree, followed by the little ones, then the young adults, all the way down to the big male of the troop, sitting close to the trunk, getting only a wink of sleep, while guarding everyone. Upon sensing danger, he would give a warning, and then the whole troop would sing out their cacophonous sounds to scare the predator. It seems that it actually worked, though there was no way of knowing.

CHAPTER 19

AID FROM THE AIR

The registration had gone on smoothly and was completed successfully. We hoped that the Referendum would go on smoothly and end well. Our fingers were crossed.

In Pochalla, it was a surprise to us to find out in the very first few days how rainy the God-forsaken land was. We were faced with a rainy hardship and empty stomachs. Shelter was an acute problem, as there were few dry places for any of us to stay. The few huts owned by the town dwellers were too few to accommodate everyone. And what could we do with the biting hunger? We could not carry enough food supplies from Ethiopia during our evacuation, being that there was no way to transport enough supplies because the road was impassable. There were enough rations in Panyido to feed our refugee community, even for a year, but the supplies couldn't reach us. Even though the local Anywak community was willing to pay with grain for some of the non-food items we carried like blankets, mosquito nets, jerry cans, and plastic sheets, there wasn't enough grain to go around to keep everyone from starving. This condition led some to trek back to Panyido, Ethiopia, a situation which increased the total number of refugees still remaining in Ethiopia, so that by the time they were forcefully removed by the Ethiopian Army, in just about a month, a lot of lives were lost at the Gilo River.

When most of the refugees and the SPLM/SPLA[63] main body were already out of Ethiopia, Salva Kiir, the current leader[64] of the SPLM, Commander-in-Chief of the SPLA and President of the Republic of South Sudan decided to leave Pochalla for other areas of Southern Sudan. That afternoon, he boarded a dingy little airplane, an SPLA aircraft, no doubt. The plane was so much in disrepair that when it was in the air, it promptly lost the function of one of its rotors and had to return for a landing to repair the rotor. Those SPLA liberators trusted in God to protect them at all times. The tougher we were, the better for everyone else and for the country. We knew that God was going to save the South, the Sudan, and all of us until the storm passed.

While the SPLA was quite effective in prosecuting the civil war, it did so under very strenuous conditions. The distances the SPLA soldiers had to cover, both during the trek to the training camps and after the training, traveling towards their operational corridors, were long and treacherous. Supplies of material for clothing and arming, movement and sustenance were quite limited. However, the SPLA would always find ways to fulfill those needs while on the move.

Traveling through the communities of Southern Sudan, and through the rest of the Sudan, the soldiers would share what the communities along the way were able to supply them with, whether voluntarily or, sometimes, forced. The SPLA soldiers were only as bad off as the communities they were traveling in, or operating among. Furthermore, by attacking garrison towns, the SPLA soldiers would capture and make use of the supplies of their enemies. This was one way to gain another set of uniforms, after the single pair given during graduation at the training camps. Indeed, after successful operations, the SPLA would gain a lot of material including ammunitions, guns and even transport vehicles.

Vehicles were quite limited for the SPLA, which is why they traveled on foot most of the time, for up to three months sometimes, to attack a

---

[63] Salva Kiir oversaw the evacuation of the SPLA/M main headquarters and bases from Ethiopia

[64] President Kiir was at that time the third man in the SPLA/M line-up, after Garang and William Nyuon-Kerubino Kuanyin was already under detention

town. However, there were at least two very enduring and famous trucks that were used for the first divisions of the SPLA, and continued to be used subsequently for a long time. The two trucks were Man Koryom and Ok Aboc. Man Koryom belonged to the Koryom Division of the SPLA, when it was used to ferry the troops between their training base and their operational areas, and it became quite popular, so that it was like a mother to them. Man Koryom means mother of Koryom, even though the original word on the truck, MAN, is actually the stand-alone brand name of the truck series, MAN. Koryom was simply added to complete the enduring meaning, to proclaim the wonderful saving grace and service offered by the sturdy trucks.

Furthermore, and never to be left out, the other very famous SPLA Division, the Mormor, used the ok aboc truck. The phrase, ok aboc, means "we are struggling". Those two trucks, Man Koryom and Ok Aboc, were tended to very well, and even though sometimes the electric system might fail, the trucks could still be on their mission overnight, driven around with the aid of a pair of torchlights, carried by officers sitting on either side of the truck, while it lumbered through the night from one little dingy outpost to the next. Ok Aboc and Man Koryom indeed fulfilled their service to the SPLA troops.

I didn't know at the time how sophisticated the Sudan Air Force was, but their Antonov plane was a feared machine, even if it didn't cause many causalities among the civilians. The MIG plane and the gunships attacking the soldiers around Juba, and at other SPLA operational areas, were much more gruesome and destructive. The Antonov was milder by comparison. Its main goal was to terrorize the civilian population. The fear that it caused was so effective that before we removed ourselves from Pochalla to travel to the Kenyan border, where it was used every day among the Sudanese population there, we knew we were getting into hell. There was going to be Antonov from the air, and there was the ethnic militia on the ground, not to mention the arid conditions and the other elements. However, the closest I ever came in contact with the Antonov was at Pochalla.

Everyone knew there would be Antonov bombings someday at Pochalla. It was a matter of time. It was said that the pilot was a Dinka

Agar named Machwei, who felt it would be nice to keep terrorizing and bombing his fellow ethnic people just for the money. And the people composed songs in his name, chiding him for unleashing such a weapon of death on his own people. These songs were usually composed and sung amidst light conversation, in the absence of the Antonov. The Machwei, as was the name that the Dinka SAF bomber went by, was almost a legend. His name was so pervasive that every time an Antonov was bombing, or was said to have passed through, Machwei was said to be piloting it.

And it was not long before we had our encounter with Machwei. It happened soon after we had arrived from Ethiopia, and were just settling in at Pochalla. One afternoon, as I was having a haircut, we heard the sound of an aircraft. The sounds of the SAF death machines usually had deathly fearful whining sounds, whether it was from the German made Magirus trucks at Wau or the Antonov, it was that whining fearful sound, and we sort of knew there was trouble afoot. Certainly, we were not expecting any aircraft over the Pochalla airspace at that time unless it was an Antonov bomber. And sure enough, it was.

And so, when we heard the sounds, everyone craned the necks to hear, and see, what was happening. The whining stopped for just a moment. Then, all hell broke loose, as there were loud whooshing sounds and bombs falling. Some people fell on their stomachs right where they were, a move which was the smartest thing to do, as every trained soldier knew. The moment there is a sound of some aggressive gunfire, lying flat on the ground is the first thing to do. Then you listen for where the shots are emanating from, making necessary decisions after that. Others ran for their dear lives, into their huts or to hide behind trees.

However, the Antonov, after dropping its payload, circled briefly and then was off to the west, towards Jonglei. Everyone breathed a sigh of relief when the sound was audibly far off. The bombs aimed at the nearby cattle camp fell far off and nobody was harmed, but we had begun to know what an Antonov was and what it could do.

At Pochalla, with biting hunger and nowhere to find enough sustenance, everyone knew it was only a matter of time before starvation would set in. The way to Ethiopia was finally closed shut, and the proposition to return there could be fatal, even for the intrepid. The new Ethiopian regime was angry for the way its army was humiliated by the SPLA booby-traps and minefields. Ethiopia was therefore a no-go. Furthermore, the way west, towards home in Jonglei or Bhar el Gazel, was fraught with treacherous forests, soaked grasslands teeming with lions, and muddy paths, patrolled by hostile ethnic communities like the Murle. It was therefore not the right time to attempt such a move, even though some people did actually go through.

The best approach was to gather whatever few articles of value one had, mostly clothing, and then go looking for Anywak families willing to barter their grain for such articles. The enterprise was quite workable and it did save a lot of people who were able to bring their clothing with them from Ethiopia. The other way to stay alive was to forage in the forests and shrubberies nearby for any edible leaves or berries, and then to consume large amounts of water just to fill the stomach and to hydrate the body. Otherwise, the moment someone drank water on an empty stomach, one would immediately vomit it out, hastening starvation. It was always advisable to be out there (in the woods or out and about looking for anything to stay alive. Staying in the shadow hastened starvation because it was the beginning of hopelessness). We had not yet made contact with the UN, and the International Red Cross (ICRC) was not available in town.

A french anthropologist, Mr. Kwashkwara, would eventually bring the ICRC to Pochalla, and proceeded to champion its work there, until the Red Cross moved, along with the rest of us, to Narus, and later to Lokichoggio. But at this time, the ICRC had yet to arrive. Kwashkwara was in the area because he was studying the cultural ways of the community. Eventually, the International Committee of the Red Cross, the ICRC, brought in grain with a single engine airplane from Lokichoggio to Pochalla, flying at least 16 times a day. While those airlifts never provided enough for everybody, the most vulnerable were saved.

A mosquito net was also useful for fishing, especially if it was a real net and not one made from clothing. This contraption would be used to scour for small fishes in the fast running river water, which was always quite rewarding. The only caveats were to make sure that the netting was not cut on any side, and to stop fishing early enough, before the sun went down, so that the net could dry during the night's sleep. Otherwise, the mosquitoes would have a night feast, a fearful thought given the fact that the little fish one got from using the mosquito net would never be enough to compensate for the blood lost, or the itch of the mosquito needles.

However, the real rescue was two-fold. We were aided by the UN, through the ICRC, and also by Manute Bol, the former NBA player. First, it was Manute, the 7 1/2-foot-tall basketball giant and humanitarian. He arrived at the camp to find a welcoming party at the little airstrip, some of whom were personal acquaintances from back home. Manute began to shed tears upon the sight of the suffering, emaciated, starving refugees. Upon recognizing someone among the crowd, he asked, "What do you want me to do for you?"

Manute had addressed his question to a man named Dut, who responded, "Give us nets and fishing hooks and we shall be alright." Skeptical but willing, Manute left for Kenya. Before long, he returned, and everyone who cared at Pochalla now received the thread needed to make the nets, and a great supply of hooks. Starvation was averted, almost overnight. The UN also provided airdrops of grain, like sorghum and wheat. Sturdy bread, made from the pounded whole wheat grain, was always good to take for the road to the fishing ground.

To increase the size of the landing strip to allow for larger aircraft to land, the ICRC, in conjunction with the Pochalla SPLA administration, decided to ask people to clear the land. It would be nearly impossible for the refugees to do this manual work, though, especially cutting trees, on empty stomachs. The agencies, therefore, asked those willing to work to come forward, to be given a measured strip to clear for an allotted portion of grain and beans. Though doing manual work while weak was not appealing, it was much more enticing due to the lucrative reward at the end.

While clearing the airfield, one of our diggers managed to dig up an old landmine, which, thankfully, never exploded! The mine was collected by the agencies, but our group was a little shaken. We were warned about such mines before digging. It was a general warning about the possibility of the presence of some old landmines in the field we were about to start digging on, but never about a particular area. Mines were known to be at the southwestern end of the town, but not on the eastern side-we were digging on the eastern side, just next to the river. This mine was probably laid back in 1984, when a battle occurred between the SPLA and the government army, and the town fell into SPLA hands. Now, seven years later, the land mine was an old one. Yet it would still have exploded if the digger was not careful with it.

Throughout the months of starvation at Pochalla, the greatest obstacle was not that the UN was not there to help. The same refugees who had arrived at Pochalla, were the ones who the UN cared for in Ethiopia. But the UN was never sure how to help at Pochalla, given the insecurity and the lack of infrastructure, namely, inadequate landing facilities. The huge cargo planes could never land anywhere at Pochalla, since even the small planes had trouble landing. Also, land transport was impossible through the rainy season, due to the instability of the road.

The idea was hatched to drop grain from the air, without the aircraft having to land. Huge, lumbering planes, called Hercules', would circle over Pochalla, making arcs, turning for a direct drop at the dropping zone. It was like the Antonov's flying over the area to drop their cargo, only the Hercules's cargo was lifesaving, while the Antonov's was a death drop. Several bags of grain would be tied onto a plank, with heavy belts, and then dropped from quite a high altitude onto the drop zone, which was just north of the main town center. The drop height was low enough to prevent any load landing outside the drop zone and harming people. The UN always let the medium-sized aircraft airlift other food items, like cooking oil. The whole exercise brought plenty for the poor refugees.

Bishop Paride Taban, the then Catholic Bishop of the Torit Diocese, was a man we knew nothing about. In fact, even for those of us who began to be observant of religion in Ethiopia, we mostly hadn't been previously exposed to seeing Bishops in the Sudan. We could assume that a Sudanese Bishop would look very much like the Priests we had come to know, Fathers Akot and Matong, yet we couldn't know for sure. However, when the Bishop landed at Pochalla, people instinctively ran towards the airstrip to see him. We had just arrived from Panyido, and I guess he must have heard about the refugees, or he must have met Fr. Akot during his trip to Kenya, or possibly through the Eastern Equatoria. Moreover, the refugee settlements in Ethiopia were no secret to the general Sudanese public and the SPLM/SPLA hierarchy. It was where some of their families were. Whatever the aim of the visit, it was said by those who attended his short speech at the airstrip that he was just passing by to say hello to the newly arrived refugees. The Bishop would be pivotal during our travel out of Pochalla, just eight months after his visit. We complained to him about our situation anyway.

At Pochalla, at the local Catholic Church, Fr. Matong, was the center of attention and representative of Christ, as all priests are. Everybody knew him, even if not all of the congregation was known by him. I came to know Fr. Matong for the first time at our Panyido Catholic church. He was friendly to almost everyone and was well liked. Fr. Akot, on the other hand, was a no nonsense man, known to beat boys if they were found to have been trying to court the few girls who came to church and danced on Sundays in what were called 'Crusades'. But Fr. Matong called every young person *'menh wa math'* ("Child of my brother") and this endeared him to every young man who came to church. Fr. Matong had gone to Rome, and had met the Pope, John Paul II. He told the Pope about the tribulations in the Sudan, upon which the Pope urged him to ask the Sudanese Christians to pray, through the intercession of the Blessed Virgin Mary, to bring the cause of the oppressed people of the Sudan to God. The Pope told Fr. Matong that that was how the Pope's home country, Poland, was saved.

Fr. Matong was given a large statue of the Virgin by the Pope himself. The statue was displayed one Sunday at the Episcopal Church, during an ecumenical combined prayer. I wonder what the Episcopalians thought about the statue and the Pope's message, but the good priest must have created a very good impression on the Christian congregation, for he preached with zeal for unity of purpose and prayer for the Sudan, which every Christian at the gathering rallied to.

It was said that Fr. Matong would have been appointed the Bishop of the Diocese of Wau were it not for the political maneuverings of the then Bishop at Wau. That Bishop never liked the idea of appointing Matong. He resented that Matong was such an advocate of the Dinka language and culture, and that he was among the first to advance the concept of inculturation as the best way to evangelize the Dinka and the rest of the Africans. When Fr. Matong died in 1993, it was said that the Dinka haters, who were everywhere, including in the church, poisoned him. No investigation has ever been conducted.

Fr. Matong reminded me, when I had a chance to meet with him under the tree at the Parish, about my mother. He had met my mother and I years before, at our home in Twic County. I didn't remember encountering him before at the village, but it was such a nice thought. Up until then, the thought of parents had evaporated from my memory, and I often felt as though I never had any parents. When some boys would announce that they were going to see their mothers or going to their families, I would feel like I was never in the same category. It felt weird to be thinking of a parent. I had forgotten about my parents, and I couldn't even recall what they looked like. The picture offered me by the priest was of a caring parent, and a very important one, who would remain in my mind. I left that meeting a happy man, and not just some boy who felt like he was an orphan. For, even though my parents were still alive, I had the trappings of all orphans.

CHAPTER 20

AT DAYBREAK

In the days leading up to the January vote, I spoke regularly with Deng about the process. We counted down the days to the vote. We also monitored the situation in the Sudan. Our hope for a free homeland was absolute. The day we had been waiting for was near.

Long ago, at Pochalla, we knew that God was near, but the two catholic Dinka priests, Father Akot and the late Father Matong, also sustained our hopes at the camp. As a reverend, Father Matong was a great and powerful preacher who made sure that his listeners understood the Christian message. The Christian message that he taught was not foreign to Dinka customs and beliefs, but rather, dovetailed with it. It was not a surprise, therefore, to see that every Dinka, educated or not, would troop to the church on Sundays to hear Fr. Matong speak. He had organized to have a large church built of wood and thatched with grass by the people themselves, and the church started to become a center of learning and prayer. Every Sunday after mass, he would have the elders remain, to debate with him about the Dinka language and beliefs, and about how they correlate with the catholic faith. If he were alive, I strongly believe that every Dinka would become a Christian overnight.

While Fr. Akot aspired to have the rules of the church followed to the hilt, Fr. Matong was more lenient in the sense of what Jesus said about Sabbath,[65] Matthew 12:1-8: "The son of man is the Lord of Sabbath-Jesus allowed his disciples to pick the ears of wheat to eat on Saturday because the Sabbath was made for the man, not the man for the Sabbath-meaning that there is a time when a rule could be broken when life is at stake." Our lives were at stake all the times during the civil war.

The refugees were divided into two groups. Most of the unaccompanied minors were placed east of Pochalla at Golkur, while the rest of the general population was near the main town of Pochalla, in what one might call the suburbs. The Catholic Church was at the south end of Pochalla, just next to the river and by the main road which led to Golkur and then on to Pakok and Boma. The Golkur unaccompanied minors had what you might call a government-styled school system. In Pochalla, however, Fr. Matong built a school at the Catholic Parish. The church school was modeled after the Catholic School fashion, and especially after the Comboni Missionary School system in the Sudan. In Pochalla, some unaccompanied minors, who had found families they knew or who were attached to the Catholic Church, stayed near the church and attended the church school. The Church school was by far the best in terms of the quality of teachers, and the quality of teaching. I was one of those fortunate to attend the Church School. I stayed at Pochalla with a friendly family and attended the Church School only, rather than attend the Golkur School. I began to delve into biology by learning about chlorophyll from that school, when such learning was not usually started until Standard Five. We were in Standard Four. We were also taught religion by Fr. Matong himself, and English by Mr. Baruch, a Nuba gentleman who became a great role model for us and someone we all aspired to be like.

Mr. Baruch was our church's choirmaster. He was so good at it that the choir membership swelled. A boastful member of the choir once bragged to me that he would rather remain a choir member than accept a chance to attend a seminary. "I just want to be a singer. I would choose being in a choir over priesthood!" he said. The thought was that he

---

[65] King James Version

liked singing better, but the real reason was that the Choirmaster was excellent at teaching songs and organizing singing. Priesthood was the best choice, given the standing of the priests then, so anybody choosing choir over priesthood must have actually been joking.

Mr. Baruch was outstanding with English. On Sundays after church, and on Saturdays during choir practice, his voice would ring out distinctively, intoning the hymn to be practiced, or calling out the names on the choir membership roll, "Lawrence Ring ..." Though I was never a choir member, because I felt that I couldn't really sing well, I usually would come by the church. The church building was thatched-roof, large, but with sides built of small trunks of wood that had spaces in between. Through the openings, I could hear the voices and see the people inside, as well as be seen. Mr. Baruch must have noticed me, for once he approached me and asked, "Why are you not in the choir?" Perhaps he also observed me in the English or the Biology class. He taught several classes, for he was the main teacher. In any case, I decided to join the choir after all.

I felt grateful when I could be useful at church, now that I was a member of the choir, I learned some of the songs, yet I didn't attend any extra practice sessions. So when a fellow member learned that I was now in the choir, he made it a point to criticize me every time I attempted to sing one of the songs outside of church service. He never criticized me before! But, added to that, I also became a leader of the rosary recitations, on Saturdays, and I made great use of it by intoning very clearly the prayer decades for the congregation to follow. I became better liked by the church membership and by Mr. Baruch compared to my jealous fellow choir member who never stood out. Mr. Baruch was so well liked that I now believe that it is regretful that people like Mr. Baruch, a great Christian, and the great Yusuf Kuwa Mekki, a Muslim, are seen as foreigners. Having South Sudan independent, without the people of Nuba, is a painful pill. They were truly Sudanese, and what the whole Sudan should have been, but now they are foreigners!

There was also Peter. Peter was an exemplary young man whom we took for our role model. He was a great choir member, and an altar boy, and when he was set to make announcements or lead members of the church in any public exercise, like during prayer excursions to other churches for interfaith purposes, Peter did well. He was also quite resourceful. By the river banks in Pochalla, just across the road from the Church, he was among some fellows who planted a little garden of tomatoes, and they would be there in the morning to water them.

Another important person with us was Father Matong's driver, Issa. Issa once claimed that he could cross streets in a busy city by walking on top of the cars, from one side of the road to the other. When I heard it the first time, I thought it could be possible because Issa seemed like he was capable of doing it. But, when I came to New York City, such a thought evaporated from my mind, since it is actually impossible, or even if possible, the NYPD would never approve of it. The stuntman, Issa, would either end up in jail, or in a battle with one of the drivers on whose car roof he was climbing over. Issa must have been watching some Spiderman movies.

Fr. Matong taught right out of the Bible. He taught about Abraham, his nephew Lot, and about their contemporaries like Chadarlaomar and Melchizedek, the high priest of Salem and the model for all the Christian high priests. Fr. Matong taught that even though Melchizedek was not a Christian, that his priesthood was God-given, and that it is not unlike what the Dinka have. So, rather than make our culture feel pagan or primitive, Fr. Matong taught us to respect our culture, and showed us that it was not in conflict with Christianity, and that we were not evil people nor did we worship the evil one. In fact, he would encourage those who knew, by heart, some of the prayers and blessing incantations sung or recited by traditional Dinka priests, to sing them at church. He would even bless the congregation with water on Sundays, just like it would be done in a Dinka prayer ceremony.

Knowing that we might make a dash to go back home across the Nile, those among us who had found the Catholic faith were worried about reconnecting with our parents, who would immerse us in the "pagan" Dinka culture. For instance, they would have us eat foods sacrificed in the traditional way, sprinkle us with water, and so forth. To this, Fr. Matong told us to know that none of those practices were evil at all, and that we should even ask for such blessings when we went home because it was all done in the name of God, Nhialic, and it was all a prayer to God. Such was how a Dinka priest reconciled the young with the old, and made Christianity and our Culture compatible.

At church one Sunday, Father Matong made an odd request to the members of the congregation. "I need a chameleon," he said. "Anybody who will bring a chameleon next Sunday, will receive a reward. But please don't let yourselves be bitten by the chameleon; the cows are far away!" The congregation laughed in unison. Father Matong made his request without telling the people as to why he wanted them to comply. This kept people guessing as to what he was going to do with a chameleon, but being the priest, none was too keen on pressing him on the reasons. A bite from the chameleon, as the belief among the Dinka goes, would require hearing the mooing of a cow by the victim to keep him or her alive. And being in an area where cattle were scarce, except for the cattle camp kept by the SPLA, which was miles away, no one was ready to test the belief. Yet I am not sure if there was any chameleon found and brought to church. By the following Sunday, though, we found out why capturing a chameleon was required by the priest.

He wanted to show people who had never seen a chameleon before, how the creature changes color to suit its surroundings at a given time. And while the reasons for the chameleon were clear, to avoid the predators, the example of the chameleon was for a different purpose. The priest told the congregation, "Christ is like a chameleon, taking the likeness of the people who have accepted him. Christ is the lord of all ethnicities and peoples," he preached. This was in answer to a widespread but quiet questioning about how the Crucifix likeness of Jesus, and the pictures of Mary, were all of people who were not black.

So, the question among the Sudanese faithful was how Christ became like us Dinka, but never appears like us in human features. The capture, and contemplation, of a chameleon was meant to dispel the doubts and questions. Christ was a chameleon. Christ was in all and for all. This was inculturation, a term that I didn't know at the time. Here we were shown the relevance shared between the indigenous cultures and the Christian faith. Fr. Matong was a pioneer in bringing Christianity to the Dinka.

Later, in Kenya, the Bishop Caesar Mazzolari, in his homilies and teachings about Christ, taught inculturation. He taught not only that Christ was a Dinka for the Dinka, but that the Christian culture, and the strong unbreakable Dinka culture that had become an obstacle to full immersion in the life of the church, would merge to become a single Christian Dinka culture through inculturation, putting the best of both together to become one. There was even a painting of Jesus, as a black Dinka, at the well with some Dinka women fetching water, and with girls smiling.

At this time, Fr. Akot, then the junior pastor at the church in Pochalla, started teaching some Anywak people the catechism of the Catholic Church, preparing to have them baptized so that they would become the nucleus of the Catholic Church in the town when we left. However, Fr. Akot failed to inform the senior priest, Fr. Matong, about the scheduled baptism of the group at the church one Sunday. It was a well-known fact that Fr. Akot was always trying to scuttle the authority of Fr. Matong, and so it went without saying that scheduling the baptism of a major group without consultation was a way to subvert leadership. None knew what would happen, but on the day the Anywak were going to be baptized, Fr. Matong was surprised after the Sunday mass when Fr. Akot announced the baptism. Sensing schism, Fr. Matong decided to stop the baptism, and got into a very clear disagreement with Fr. Akot.

Fr. Akot had asked a group of young men and women who were confirmed at Panyido, and acted as the Christian role models for young men and women, to remain after the church service to act as Godfathers and Godmothers for the Anywak group. But, Fr. Matong, having the final authority, ordered, "Disperse now! Go to your homes. There will be no baptism today!" It looked like they had heard the command and did leave, but they were secretly ordered back by Fr. Akot. Fr. Matong had gone back to his tukul. Those young men and women were loyal to Fr. Akot, for he was the one who taught them through, but Fr. Matong was older, senior, well-educated and a powerful priest, and was held in reverence. He was also popular, so the young men and women were torn between the two.

After most parishioners had gone home, someone went to inform Fr. Matong that his order was disobeyed, and that Fr. Akot had reassembled the Anywak group, the young men and women Christians, and was proceeding with baptism. This brought Fr. Matong back to the Church. Upon seeing the group assembled, with Fr. Akot present, he repeated his order, "Everyone, disperse right now. Go home, I said 'No baptism'! Didn't you hear?" he shouted. The crowd dispersed, disobeying Fr. Akot's interjections to stay.

"Don't leave! We are proceeding with the baptism," said Fr. Akot. The two priests almost fought. It was like they were two were senior army commanders fighting in front of their adoring soldiers. I believe that I lost interest in their fight after that, because it was trivial. Seeing men whom we followed displaying their differences like that, I don't quite know how it ended, but I was bemused, not by the behavior of the two priests who should have known better, but by the behavior of the Christian Godfathers- and Godmothers-to-be. They should have picked the side of the overall leader, Fr. Matong and then pack up and go; remaining undecided made them indecisive and not any different from the two priests. When leaders fight, the followers should take over and bring some sense and order. There was clearly an institutional breakdown, and Rome was so far away.

A Cow Grazing in Twic County

Akurnear Wunlit

Author & Children @Wunlit2010

Author & Current Bishop of Wau Deng Majak

Author at Bakhita Center with Fellow Seminarians
1999 2nd Third Rowing lasses

Boys @Wunlit2010

Catholic Cathedral in Wau

Eagle on River Lol

Hippo Nile Shore

Kerubino 1980s

Photo of the author at Panyido 1989

Ripening Mangos

Ripening Sorghum

The Kind of Dugout Canoes we used to cross the Nile

WomenDancers@WunlitWelcomingtheAuthor2010

CHAPTER 21

THE LONG MARCH OUT OF POCHALLA

"It seems to me that Dr. John Garang was a unionist, but on the other hand, he seemed to have favored the overwhelming Southern Sudanese resolve for secession. What do you think?" Deng asked me one day. I didn't know Dr. Garang's particular personal view, but I know that his strategy of a united Sudan, on a new democratic basis, made the self-determination vote possible, though that strategy also caused a great loss of life. If seceded, Southern Sudan would be a landlocked country, at the mercy of the very nation up north who it had fought. Southern Sudanese all seemed well aware of what their decision would bring, but they were ready for the consequences.

Sometime during August of 1991,[66] Dr. Riek Machar Teny, a member of the SPLM/SPLA high command, attempted to wrestle control of the movement from Dr. Garang. It was not clear what would happen next. Being that I was too young and far away from the SPLM movement and the liberation war, I cared little what happened in the movement, and so I lost track of what Riek Machar and the rest of the SPLM high command were up to.

---

[66] See also Human Rights Watch, "CIVILIAN DEVASTATION: Abuses by All Parties in the War in Southern Sudan," (New York: Human Rights Watch, June 1994), p.32 for the description of Riek's 1991 Coup.

Some friends decided to go on a hunting trip. These friends were SPLA soldiers who were living at Pochalla, not in the active army, yet in possession of their guns. I decided to tag along. We set out in the morning, from near the Ajwara River, southwest of Pochalla, and headed toward Pibor. The game in the area was large in numbers and it was the season when the migration back to the watering area, the Ajwara River, increased in earnest. Before the sun was high overhead, the area from the river to the savanna forests was full of wild herbivores as far as the eye could see. It was another Serengeti. When we had caught up with the animals, our group hunters started shooting randomly at the animals that ran by us in large herds. I swear that I could have caught one of them if I was fast enough, but surprisingly, no shot even struck a single animal.

By the time the guns had gone silent, there was no animal to be seen! It had been a frenzy of movement and shooting, but with nothing to show for it. An Anywak shooter would have killed several animals by just finding a nice place to hide and then picking them off one by one, like a sort of sharpshooting, rather than using AK47 assault rifles. Not that the rifles couldn't kill in such a situation, it was that the shooters got confused in the frenzy, with every chaotic shot fired at the galloping hooved herbivores missing the mark.

We ended up traveling the whole day in the forest, trying to find any stray animals to shoot, but to no avail. That evening, when we were traveling back, we discovered that we had traveled too far from the camp pursuing the animals, and that we had lost track of the camp. We kept traveling until it was decided that the group should find some spot to spend the night. It grew very cold without fire. So a tracer bullet was used to light a fire. The bullet point was taken off, and then put to the mouth of the barrel of the gun, and then a bundle of dry grass was put close to it and struck with a piece of metal. That yielded fire, and soon we were enjoying enough warmth. The bullet end was returned to the casing and then fired off, whooshing as it flew, for it had lost a lot of its power. Also that evening we had no bedding materials, so we had to make do sleeping in our clothing, a very bad proposition. The following morning, traveling east for a short while brought us into view of our camp. We packed up and went back to the main Pochalla Internally Displaced Camp.

In December, 1991, the local Anywak Militia, backed by the Anywak of Ethiopia, the Sudanese Army and the Ethiopian army, invaded Pochalla.[67] The news of an imminent attack circulated around Pochalla for several days before it actually happened. One morning, at around 2am, the attackers targeted the Unaccompanied Minors camp east of Pochalla at Golkur. The gunshots went on until around dawn, when the main assault on Pochalla started.

The assault came from east of town, from across the Tierkodhi River. The fight went on for about an hour, with heavy machine guns and AK47s exchanging fire, resulting in several causalities on both sides, though more causalities on the side of the attackers. The morning mist was lit up with tracer bullets, but they were too high on our side to cause us any damage. The attack was successfully repelled for good. The enemy took a thrashing. The hospital was full of the very seriously wounded, when we went to see the damage done. Those wounded were bleeding profusely. Some were regular SPLA soldiers, while others were women and children and other civilians caught in the crossfire. One could not look at the gunshot wounds twice. A favorite teacher of mine was injured very badly and was taken to Lokichogio, in Kenya, by the ICRC, via airlift. The plane was a World War II style fighter-bomber, in disuse of course, but it probably sent the message to the attackers. It came from Lokichogio, with its door removed and painted red.

After that incident, every day we spent at Pochalla was on borrowed time. We needed to leave the area, and fast. Some unfortunate incidents continued to happen, however. There was someone who was in the SPLA army, but had taken leave from his unit to spend time with us. He had a rifle, which he would leave inside the hut sometimes when he was out and about. For me, though I knew that the gun knew not its owner,

---

[67] See also Human Rights Watch, "CIVILIAN DEVASTATION: Abuses by All Parties in the War in Southern Sudan, "(New York: Human Rights Watch, June 1994), p.45 for the description of the Government of the Sudan 1992 Dry Season offensive that forced us out of Pochalla.

I would leave it alone, but a friend decided differently. After looking over the gun, he decided to pull the trigger. The shooting shocked people in the neighborhood and they came rushing to investigate, fearing that perhaps there was someone who was attacking people. What they found was a shocked someone, shaking, and a gaping bullet hole through the strung cloth and grass wall, with its path blackened. The bullet would have done a lot of damage if someone was in its path as it left the hut. Luckily, none was hurt, but there were a whole lot of shaken people, with the visibly sorry shooter the worst off.

In February of 1992, it was said that the Sudanese army, backed by the Ethiopian army, and the Anywak militia, were planning another combined attack on Pochalla. Nobody was playing a joke. We had to leave in a hurry. Some refugees left to go back to their villages in the rest of Southern Sudan, but we set off for Eastern Equatoria, close to the Kenyan border. It was decided that the safest bet was to go to the better secured Eastern Equatoria where the SPLA was much more in control, and where the other neighbor, Kenya, was willing to take in the refugees. The journey out of Pochalla was quite anticipated, given the rumors of attacks and the fact that during the dry season, the government of the Sudan's offensive against the SPLA-held areas would begin in earnest. Our journey south would begin one evening.

That evening, we began leaving Pochalla. It was decided that the town should be evacuated, except for the SPLA soldiers. We were headed for Kapoeta, close to the Kenyan border. It was clear to us that we would have to cross the eastern desert (the Sahara Tikling) of South Sudan before getting there, and that there were dangers, including lack of drinking water and potential attacks from the local tribal militias. One consequence of the Sudanese civil war was the many ethnic militias it had spawned and arrayed against the SPLA whenever the government of the Sudan provided them a better alliance. We were prepared for the long haul. It was said that the local Toposa militiamen, trained and armed right in the government-held garrison town of Juba, the largest city in South Sudan, were then sent to the Toposa countryside to prowl and to fight the SPLA using guerilla tactics. The Toposa would probably be lying in wait to attack us. It was said that a lone gunman could pick off members of a group of travelers by constantly firing from either the rear, the front or the side, and then instantly melting away into the Toposa thicket, known as achab. It was also said that if a traveler were to leave the confines and the safety of his group to travel alone, even a few meters to the bush, that there would be a Toposa militiaman waiting, unseen by the wanderer, and then there would be a gunshot sound and that would be the end of it.

To make matters worse, there was also the desert itself, the Sahara Tikling, popularized in the SPLA songs. This is a desert area between Boma and Kapoeta. And as with all desert lands in Southern Sudan, there was an acute lack of quenching water. In the Sahara Tikling, the major problem was that, even though there was enough vegetation to have crickets, and their noisy sounds which could be heard for miles around, there was no water. Having been told how tough the distance was going to be, many people decided to find other ways to hitch a ride.

Some found ways to hurt themselves physically, so they would be airlifted to Lokichogio and then by road to Eastern Equatoria! There was one such fellow who somehow got himself a gun and shot himself, literally, in the foot, on one foot. The young man was quite popular, so we were sorry for the way he decided to avoid the walk out of Pochalla.

When we set out, we traveled that evening and then spent the night at the lost boys' camp outpost at Golkur. Early the next morning, we were traveling before daybreak, so that at about 10am, when the Sun was up and it was really getting hot, we had reached an Anywak village. Months earlier, rumors had reached Pochalla that around this Anywak village, many travelers from the Pakok camp, the next major South Sudanese refugee settlement, on their way to Pochalla, were massacred. But given that the SPLA was near us, we were steeled, knowing full well that the Anywak would never attempt to hurt the children in broad daylight. When our elders were conversing with the Anywak elders, you could see the mutual distrust, even though each side would clearly try to show how peaceful and trustworthy they were. It was seen as a very elaborate trap, leading to a massacre for both sides. But at that Anywak village, we were only to spend the daylight hours, until the mid afternoon, when we would leave the feared village for the safety of the road, where we could never be trapped. We were free to roam around the village, just making sure, however, that we watched our backs.

Beyond the grassy field around the village, we found seared grass, burned off, leaving an open field with blackened ashes all around. A few friends and I took leave to go to the river nearby, strolling across the burned field. It was never a surprise for us to happen upon an entire burned skeleton of a human being. Here we had found another. The height of the bones, and the structure, told us that it was either a Dinka or a Nuer. We had found the unfortunate end of a human being traveling without enough caution. This sight was such a constant occurrence that none was surprised when we informed the elders back under the shade at the village. That afternoon, we went our way.

In the region of eastern Africa, all the way from Ethiopia to Kenya and through to the Great Lakes of Africa, lies one very important geographical feature: The Rift Valley. The valley runs all the way from the Dead Sea in Israel, across the Red Sea, all the way to Tanzania. The first time that I saw this geographical wonder was when we were traveling in this area, between Pochalla and Pakok. In the afternoon, as we marched in long lines of walking boys and families as far as the eye could see, with our few belongings slung over our shoulders or carried on our heads, I climbed a part of the hilly landscape and was struck by the sight behind us, as I tried to look back to see how far ahead I was from the end of the line. The hills and valleys formed a series of cascading waves. The hills formed a surrounding barrier that seemed to surround the countryside. However, at that time, I didn't know how to describe the sight, only to stand in awe. The hill formations reminded me of both Wau and Panyido.

During my time at Kakuma Camp in Kenya about four years later, I learned in my school classes something about the Great Rift Valley. The Great Rift Valley runs all the way from the Dead Sea across the Red Sea, across Ethiopia, parts of Eastern South Sudan, into Kenya and up to Tanzania. It was formed from plate tectonics moving and splitting away from each other. Traveling further into Kenya, from Lodwar, or Kitale, to Nairobi, similar views can be witnessed again.

CHAPTER 22

STAYING ONE STEP AHEAD

The world community would support the Southern Sudanese in their decision, whatever it would be, whether secession or unity. In New York, at the UN, in September 2010, I was among a group of Southern Sudanese demonstrators calling for Southern Sudan separation, when a prominent African Union diplomat broke away from the group of other UN diplomats to whisper to us "Go home and vote!" Right there and then, it was clear to us that the UN and the African Union were ready to accept what the choice of the people of Southern Sudan was.

We traveled to Pakok, another Sudanese settlement, where there were Ugandan refugees who were farmers. There were also Sudanese refugees from the Dima Camp in Ethiopia, who had relocated to Pakok. We spent the day there. The following day, we headed to Boma. We had to keep moving.

We stayed for a few days at Khor Nyalongar, where we were met by some ICRC truck drivers. It was interesting to find someone who called water akipi in his mother tongue. The Dinka called water piu. All of the Nilotes, I later learned, have 'pi' as the root in the word for water in their various languages. The man we had met who said akipi was a Turkana, I believe, with two lower teeth missing! The ICRC were on their way delivering food to the refugees at Pakok.

There was a fellow who left us flabbergasted with how he perfected an uncanny technique to produce corn flour from corn. He would dig a hole, smear the inside with mud and let it dry. He would then put in grass and twigs, and then burned them inside the hole to make the inside of the hole rock hard. Then he would cut a branch of a small tree and fashion a pestle with it to grind the corn! I thought he was a genius until I learned, in 2010, at the village, that that was the way that folks at the cattle camp would survive.

Drinking milk every day is so boring that everyone would crave warm asida, or bread, but carrying around a mortar and pestle would be out of the question. Using bulls and strong cows to carry some belongings, as done by some cattle keepers like the Fulani of Nigeria, was also out of the question! Such an act would be abominable and a sacrilege not worthy of a cattle keeper! Only a lazy man would do such a thing, and God would be unhappy. Such a person would become a pauper. So, you would carry both the mortar and pestle from one cattle camp to the next, which could be hundreds of miles' distance, or you just had to improvise like my friend did. We were also able to find a pond connected to a creek running down from the mountains of Boma, but there were no fishing nets to use.

It took us seven days to reach the town of Boma, only to be informed that the town of Pochalla was occupied by a combined force of the Sudan Army, tribal militias, and supported by the Ethiopian Army and that those same forces were moving very fast towards Boma. There was an imminent possibility of them capturing Boma. We had to leave in a hurry. We also heard that the sick and disabled refugees in Pochalla, among them the walking boys, including my friend Makoi, who were awaiting a transport to be arranged by the ICRC, were then captured by the combined forces. If Mr. Makoi was lucky, having had the nasty ratuba, or arthritis, he would have been taken to Khartoum, and maybe become a Muslim!

Upon entering Boma, we found that the resourceful SPLA commanders wanted to make sure that the arriving refugees, and particularly the young men who were largely grown up and sturdy, would have to join the army war effort. There was a selection process where we marched under the watchful eyes of the dynamic soldiers who would occasionally pick out a fellow to step aside, while the rest who they deemed still too young, below sixteen, kept moving along. Some folks were inducted into the SPLA that way, while others who could have been inducted as well sailed through, either because of their luck or because someone in the army spotted them and pulled some strings to have them move back to the main group of the walking boys.

We spent the day at Boma Fok, Upper Boma, on a mountaintop, where the only water to drink was infested with parasitic leeches. From the mountaintop, you could see the blackened water running along the creek. We expected, at first, that the water was clean and only appeared black because it was under the shade of a tree. But it was all flukes! One had to get a scoop in a container, and then drain the water into another container, while making sure that no more leeches got into the next container. Killing them was out of the question because you would have so much blood on your hands, or at least a lot of blackened debris. It was safe to just return them back into the creek. I don't know what they fed on; perhaps there were some fish they attached to, or something else containing blood.

At this time there was a radio announcement out of Khartoum that was of interest to us fleeing the government offensive. Omar Hassan El Bashir, the Sudan strongman whose army had just captured Pochalla and was then headed towards Boma and Kapoeta, was offering an amnesty to those who would surrender. El Bashir was telling the soldiers of the SPLA to put down their arms, and the civilians to enter the nearest town to surrender and be treated well. "You will be pardoned if you lay down your arms," Radio Omdurman announced. "Report yourself to the nearest garrison town." So, there was a general offer of amnesty, but perhaps what El Bashir didn't realize was that nobody would heed the message even if we were on the losing end because we were so fed up with the rule from Khartoum that anything else was better than that amnesty, including just fighting back. Indeed, while the boys were going the direction of Kapoeta, the SPLA soldiers were going the opposite direction for a military attempt to recapture the town. Indeed, before the dry season was over, the town of Pochalla was in the SPLA's hands again, but with causalities.

191

One such SPLA soldier who died there was a former head boy of our Group I at Panyido. Being among the literate and older, Bol Madut joined the SPLA early on and was among the soldiers who went to recapture Pochalla. Bol was a fellow I would have hoped to stand next to, giving the SAF soldiers a hell of a fight. Known to me personally, people like him made the war personal to me. Indeed, many older boys who were in our groups at Panyido joined the army, among them were my friends Aher, Malak, Diangbar and others. It is apparent that many of them didn't make it through alive. I am aware of the situation of Diangbar because his unit was among the group of SPLA soldiers who were sent to fight the advancing rebels overrunning Ethiopia, leading to the collapse of the Mengistu regime. Indeed, even after Mengistu was overthrown and had fled already, Diangbar's unit was still actively engaging the enemy in the Ethiopian mountains, a terrain they knew little about. He was lost with a few of his fellow soldiers, never to be heard from again. This is as it was narrated to me by our friend, Kuot.

After our night at Boma Fok, we left very early the following morning and arrived around mid-day at a place called Khor Agaref, "the Stream of the Scorpion", named after the Scorpion Battalion of the SPLA. This was the staging point into the Tikling Desert towards Kapoeta. At that point, before crossing the desert, the traveler had to make sure that water and food supplies were ample for the desert crossing, and that traveler had the strength and determination to make it through. Lacking those vital requirements led to death from thirst and maybe hunger, assuming that a militia attack was successfully avoided. It was here that we discovered a technique to have clean water! There was a root of a small shrub that could be crushed and mixed with the really muddy water, which was the only water we had, and then the mixture could be left to stand for a few hours. Eventually the mud, and any other sediments, would all settle to the bottom of the container, leaving the water all fine and clear as a crystal! However, there were three caveats.

First, was the smell. There was this sweet smell that could make you quickly become nauseous if you neglected to totally concentrate on quenching your thirst by gulping down the water in mouthfuls. If you breathed in the aroma, you could almost throw up. The second trouble with the water was the taste. It tasted slimy and sweet, sickly sweet, though it was bearable. The final trouble was the time involved! Never let that water stand in the container unused for later use, because in more than eight hours, it would get rotten! Clean rotten. Yet, even considering these caveats, we preferred to drink the water. The only real alternatives were to drink your own urine, which would run out in short order, even if you could withstand the taste and the smell, or to drink the muddy, untreated, water, which felt like drinking porridge made of clay.

CHAPTER 23

THE LAUNCH

On January 8th, we assembled in Syracuse, NY, at the apartment of Deng, ready to travel to Boston to be at the voting station at 7 the following morning. We would be the first to cast our votes in North America. Due to international time differences, the first votes would have actually been cast in Australia, before we started our voting at Boston. But, we were unfazed. We went by local time, and we would still be the first. "I can't wait to vote tomorrow, man," Deng declared. We all were quite elated for it to come to pass.

We were all set to cross the Tikling Desert. The loss of Pochalla was bad for the SPLA morale, and the post of Boma was in danger of being overrun in short order, but we were safely away in Khor Agaref, planning to launch into the desert. How the exhausted boys, children-the fewer girls present were with their families and so they are counted with the families. There were no unaccompanied girls-and women were going to cross over to Kapoeta was anyone's guess. Luckily for us, the Sudanese Catholic Bishop of Torit, Paride Taban, sent over the empty trucks from Kenya that had brought food for the internally displaced in Kapoeta and Torit. It was a joy for us, but the trucks were few, and we were great in number.

However, being aware that individuals could try to cling to all sides of the trucks, the authorities ordered that no truck was to carry more than a certain number determined by them. It was decided by the authorities that only the really sick among us, who could not make it through walking, were to be carried in trucks, while the rest of us were to trudge it to a point in the middle of the desert where we would be picked up in groups and ferried across to Kapoeta. It was up to us to find any individual chances to get on the trucks, if we were not sick.

As for me, I could not convince my group authorities that I was sick and needed to have a comfortable, if bumpy, ride into Kapoeta, and so I set to work to find another way. I decided to befriend one of the Kenyan drivers using my broken, halting English. A group of boys milled around his truck and we were all clamoring to talk to him and his busboy, as a way to catch a ride. But, we all had trouble with the English language. So, the driver, Mwendwa, asked, "Who loves Jesus?"

"Me!" I replied right there. So, I had started a conversation, in halting English, that won me a good friend who drove a very badly needed truck. Surprisingly, the driver offered me a ride and everything was set, only to have the authorities sabotage the whole plan. Nobody was going to use the trucks, after all, not even the sick, because the authorities could not figure out who was sick and needed a ride, and who would have to cross into the middle of the desert on foot. But, a friendship with the Kenyan drivers, which included a Musa, was made. Mwendwa promised to pick me up first at the point in middle of the desert. So, we trudged along overnight while the trucks drove back empty!

At 10am the following morning, after having trudged throughout the night and reaching the clearing in the thicket in the middle of the barren waterless desert, the first group of us was picked up by the trucks. We boarded the trucks and traveled through the Toposa countryside the whole day, until we reached the little village of Magos by late evening. My Kenyan friend was nowhere to be found, but I was happy to board a truck, any truck. We found the first groups settling in and making a lot of commotion. Throughout the day on the road, we had worried about the Toposa gunmen, but not too much, since at that point, everything was still hearsay.

We spent the first two or three nights at Magos without any incident. But one fateful night, the Toposa shot at us while we were asleep. That night, after the commotion, I realized that I was spared. I suffered no injury, except for a shaken spirit. I had become adept at escaping these situations so often, even barely, that I found myself asking God as to why I had been spared. How many such escapes had I gone through, and how many more would I go through? Was there a purpose for me?

I closed my eyes and went back to an uneasy sleep. Despite the tragedy, there was nothing else that I could do, however troubled I was. I knew that we would leave the post in just a few days, if we could spend that long without getting shot at again.

The following day, we found out that there were nine boys shot, with four of them dead, and our guard, posted at the edge of the shrubs, also dead. He was the first person shot, in the head, ambushed by a gunmen emerging from the shrubs, in the darkest of the night! Was he possibly in a slumber when he was never to have done so? Did he contribute to his own demise, and that of the other four boys? The answers were never easy to come by, even though there was sure to be much speculation about the incident, once the noise had died down. Time would tell.

Meanwhile, the rest of the victims were taken to the nearby SPLA-held town of Kapoeta, the main urban center in that corridor, and therefore a friendly town. I never learned how they fared. That day, the little encampment smelled of death everywhere. Every tree or shrub seemed like it would shoot forth a bullet. In the afternoon, I walked to the dry riverbed near the main center of the post, daring the shooters, since we never had a choice, the riverbed being where we dug to get water, however unclean. Was there a Toposa gunman lurking under the huge trees out there, taking aim right then? What would I do if I had a gun?

Remarkably, there was no appearance of any Toposa around town that day. The town was empty of those who were there a day earlier. Where were they? Were they told to stay off the post, or had they heard that there had been a killing? I couldn't wait to get out of that encampment.

My Kenyan driver friends were a little worried for their safety and kept asking me for particular news about causalities and who was responsible. They were at the encampment by their trucks in the middle of the clearing that night, but they were never in danger. They escaped unscathed but their fears remained. I did my best to reassure them in my halting English about everything I had picked up about the incident.

However, they knew the kinds of dangers they rode through in the Toposa countryside, with their trucks ferrying foodstuffs to hungry refugees and internally displaced persons in the far-flung Southern Sudan. There was even an attack on a Western aid worker, to which the Toposa made songs in their dances. It was the Wild West, for the Toposa, and anecdotes that would rival the American Cowboy and Indian stories abounded.

A few days later, we were ready to move on again. The boys who were deemed sickly would be given a ride on the trucks, but anyone else was to make the walk to Kapoeta. I got to work talking to my Kenyan driver friends. They were still curious to know about the shooting since they themselves were also frequent victims of robberies and shootings on the roads in Toposa land. My English helped me get a spot on the trucks, in exchange for looking after the dozens of jerry cans of Mr. Mwendwa. What he was going to do with them, I never asked. Thus in a few hours, we were in Kapoeta, but passed right through, heading to Narus at the Kenyan border, which was going to be our camp. Everywhere on the road to Narus, there were Toposa gunmen emerging from the shrubbery, staring at us, with their AK47's at the ready. We anticipated bullets out of the shrubs at any minute, on any part of the road, but luckily, no guns were fired.

It was later said that after the shooting at Magos, the Toposa community was informed that shooting at us was never in their best interest, since our continued presence in the area would bring to their region schools and development. The trigger-happy Toposa were obliged, for there was no more shooting of a young person after that.

When we reached Narus, my Kenyan friend was beside himself to discover that his jerry cans were smashed beyond repair during the commotion, when the throngs of the so-called sick boys got on his truck. "You didn't save my jerry cans. Why?" he lamented. "You should have called me," he said. He couldn't believe that I could not have done anything to save his jerry cans in such a crowded truck, and that I could not call down to him in his driver seat while the truck was on the move. "If this is the way you are going to Kenya, you will be forced to return," he said bitterly. So, I began to believe that perhaps he knew that we were going to Kenya, because we were all anxious and wondering if we would ever get to see our families.

Going to Kenya was prolonging the absence of such a meeting. Later, at Kakuma Refugee Camp, when the 'lost boys' were being selected to go to the U.S., I saw one friend sulking after his name was put on the board. I asked him why he was so unhappy, pointing out the anomaly that a chance to live in the U.S. should be a joyous moment. The situation there is much better than the situation at Kakuma, or being back home in the insecurity of Southern Sudan under the raging civil war. "I am contemplating whether the move to the U.S.A. is any better than not seeing my family after so long. My relocation would only increase my absence from home," he had said. So, we were always torn between seeking safety for ourselves, and the need to be with the members of our families.

When we were finally in Narus, we were informed that someone we knew at Pochalla was killed while the group he was traveling with was passing through the same village- in a village between Pochalla and Narus, about a week after our party passed through. It seems that the Anywak were surprised, unaware that the Pochalla camp was emptying, and they took their time to make a kill. Near the village is the locally famous *Jebel Giza* ("the mountain of stories").

In April of 1992, our whole group was centered in Narus. We got down to building structures before the coming rainy season. The ICRC provided a few tents to act as group dwellings until we built thatched roof houses. It was decided that we were to camp in Narus indefinitely, assuming that the government was not going to recapture Kapoeta to threaten our location. Moreover, the Antonov bombers who had terrorized Kapoeta were generally afraid to bomb at Narus because Narus is so close to the Kenyan border, and there was a risk of a fly-over into the Kenyan airspace, a fact which Kenya would not have appreciated and might have resulted in a loss of the Antonov, or an international debacle. In fact, one such Antonov was later sequestered at the airport at the Kenyan border town of Lokichogio, Loki for short, for flying into the Kenyan airspace on a bombing sortie.

One night, shortly after we arrived at Narus, I was woken from a sound sleep to be informed that there was a boy who was in pain. I was asked to go fetch the caretaker, because I was the only one who knew where the caretaker was. I asked if it could wait until morning, but it was an emergency. I went to wake up the caretaker, who was not too amused about it. When he arrived, he found that the boy had already passed away-the boy died of exhaustion since he was physically weak after having been through an illness-the journey from Pochalla to Narus was too much tasking. That was one of the saddest moments of our stay in Narus, or anywhere else.

Narus was also where the SPLA had some prisoners of war stationed. One day, the SPLA were bringing a group of guards, freshly trained, to come replace the guards who had been watching over the prisoners. The young graduates from Kapoeta were loaded onto a truck, with no ammunition but with guns all right. On the way from Kapoeta to Narus, Toposa gunmen killed one by firing shots into the truck, while the driver sped to get out of the shooting range. When the group arrived at Narus, the rest of the soldiers disembarked while a body bag was unloaded. It was one of the saddest moments to witness. Some weeks later, the same group of soldiers was being returned to the frontline, to fight the Sudan Army. One soldier who I had befriended, and who hailed from our home area, knew what he was getting into, and he clearly seemed lost for words. As they say in the army, a low morale for a soldier is a very bad thing. The group was very low on morale.

There was a fear of the Toposa militia in Narus. It was evident that they were being placated by the local administration, the ICRC, the Catholic Church and our very own caretakers, so as not to harm us. Those agencies and organizations were doing a good job at keeping the Toposa militiamen peaceful, because the Toposa militiamen in Magos had made an attack on our group, and we were subsequently in fear of another such attack, yet we were mostly spared. The militiamen, armed in Kapoeta and Juba by the Sudan Army, generally shied away from attacking us in Narus during the three months we were there.

Even though, here and there, there would be isolated incidents of Toposa militiamen shooting or killing some unlucky camper, the militias were generally well peaceful. There was a Toposa militiaman named Lino who frequented our group. He carried a rifle at all times. One day, we were sharing a joke with him, when he challenged one of us to go to the bush with him if this friend was brave enough. "*Kede namshi fi ghaba, inaaka!*" ("Let us go to the nearby bushes and you will see"), he said, laughing. We all laughed, but each of us understood the point: The danger was closer than the nose. Sometimes, it would just be mere robbery or night thievery- all were isolated incidents.

Indeed, it was very likely that I could have been a victim of such an attack one day, if the militiamen I found had acted adversely. Very early one morning, to escape the daytime heat, I went into the bush to cut sticks used in building huts. I was there along with a bunch of other fellows, but my work gathering sticks took me longer than the others, and I was the last to leave the bush. I happened upon two Toposa gunmen, who had been herding their cattle. They were paused, seated under a shrub. The minute that it took me to pass them completely, felt like an eternity. So, one could go looking for the Toposa, or stumble upon them, but they always posed a potential threat, day or night.

One such night, I was sleeping next to our tent, with members of my subgroup, in the open. Then in the dead of the night, a Toposa gunman appeared, stood over my friend and me and proceeded to take some luggage and disappear. It happened so quietly that I remained sound asleep, but my friend saw him. My friend managed to keep quiet because had he uttered a sound, the gunman would have panicked, taken a shot at my friend or me, or at any other sleeping head, and then would have just vanished, leaving disaster in his wake. Moments later, we were all woken up by a gunshot into the air, nearby. We didn't know what to make of it- was it an imminent attack, or just some angry or happy Toposa gunman? It was known that a Toposa gunman would never shoot to get nothing. If you heard the gunshot, and you were not dead already, then of course the danger was passed. They are sharpshooters. Single, or several quick shots, were all it took for the tribesmen and it was all over, and then they would just melt away into the feared Achab shrubbery.

My friend's missing bag was found the following morning, just beyond our camp, at the place where that night shooting occurred, with a shell and spare clothing spread around. There was definitely a happy robber.

Years later, in Kenya, a friend who had been a member of the SPLA, stationed in the Toposa country, narrated to me his experiences. Biar told me, "Most members of my unit were slaughtered one by one by the Toposa gunmen, who would shoot suddenly and then disappear as quietly as they had taken aim and felled a victim. At times, they would ambush a whole squad and then would massacre them all. When this happened, we would pursue the gunmen to the point where they would try to mingle with the Toposa civilians at cattle camps. This caused trouble identifying the gunmen involved, because we couldn't distinguish who was a civilian and who was among the culprit militia." All in all, the gunmen trained and armed in Juba became a great nuisance, not only for the SPLA, but also for all of the displaced people, and, like the Anywak, the Toposa saw the displaced and the SPLA as having come to take over their land.

There were happy moments in Narus as well, while we whiled away our time. For instance, I was just walking around the camp one day when I was called over by two men. One man was a Sudanese who was official looking and certainly not one of our teachers or caretakers, whom we all knew, and the other man a UNICEF officer. It was obvious that I was being called for something important. Thus, I went into an interview that took about three hours, centered on my life experiences running around in Ethiopia and Southern Sudan. The UN officer gave me his card at the end of the interview, and told me he lived in New York. I had heard of the U.S.A. but not N.Y. He lived on 10 Waterside Plaza, N.Y., N.Y. and his name was Varindra Tarzie Vittachi. He was probably in his 50's or 60's, and looked to be of Southeast Asian origin, though I didn't know how they looked at the time. He gave me a writing pad and pen, and told me to write to him in N.Y. about anything I needed while he was gone, and that he would help me.

I showed the card to some of our caretakers who admired it like schoolboys. They knew where N.Y. was, and they seemed pleased of the fact. I placed the card in the safekeeping hands of a friend who was known to keep such small items very safely. I then proceeded to use my notepad to copy hymns from a hymnal. God and singing were more important! When we arrived later in Kenya, and I had become wiser about sending letters, I went over to my good friend to fish out the address so that I could ask my N.Y. friend to do me a few favors. I presumed that the card had been kept so safely for such a long time, yet, my keeper had lost the card. I later thought that perhaps I had angered him somehow along the way, and he had consequently intentionally 'lost' my card as a form of retaliation. He was known to be absolutely reliable, and to have never lost such simple items, so I had reason to be suspicious.

At Narus, we were without our beloved former Pochalla choirmaster, Baruch. He probably must have gone to the Nuba Mountains, or elsewhere. Pochalla was a place in transition, and even Fr. Matong had left, for Bhar el Gazel. So, in Narus, it fell to Karlo to become the choirmaster, a role that he sometimes performed at Panyido, in the absence of the urbane Baruch. Karlo was also a counselor, who talked about maintaining hope and faith in God, and that no matter what happened, everyone would be fine. Teaching hymns and passing on life lessons, buttressed by the word of God, Karlo became quite indispensable once again. At this time at Narus, though, I personally began to feel forlorn, for it seemed that the desolate land we were to call home had none of the blessings we had come to take for granted at Panyido. Little did I know that in just about three months, I would end up in another, even worse land, that was even more arid and as hot as can be, with dusty winds abounding every day. But, my thoughts were of the home I was never getting to, and of a closer to home place we had left behind; Panyido.

For Panyido reminded us of home in many ways, especially the land, climate and vegetation. Not so for Narus. At Narus, the only standing body of water, stagnant as could be, was the pool at the center of the little settlement. Everywhere else was crisscrossed with dry streambeds and dry riverbeds which just carried water in large, swift volumes during the rainy season, only to dry up in less than five hours flat. Moreover, there were no trees to speak of, except the ubiquitous shrub, the Achab. The Toposa countryside was quite unforgiving. The only vegetation for miles around was the Achab, which had no particular use except to perhaps maintain the soil cover and to prevent soil erosion.

Not that anyone was farming the soil, but the Achab maintained the land from becoming a desert of some sort. For sure, the places to get water were few, and only known to the Toposa people in the surrounding, scattered village settlements. But there were watering points like the pool at Narus that never lost its water, no matter the time of year, and the Toposa tended to use such watering points, a sort of oases to water their goats, sheep, dogs, cattle and donkeys. I am not sure if people drank from them.

The Toposa countryside lacked any wildlife of note, except for the little dikdik. However, it was said that there was gold in the hills and in the riverbeds, so that when it would rain, someone walking in the dry riverbeds could find gold nuggets of some value. To be sure, there was truth to this, because the SPLA administration often traded for gold nuggets collected by the Toposa people. The SPLA would gain some more value when such raw gold was sold in Kenya. In fact, while I was in Nairobi, a woman member of the SPLM bragged about how they were able to smuggle 15 tins[68] full of gold nuggets for the then Kenyan president, Daniel Moi. Whether there was truth to this or not, is something else altogether. In any case, it wasn't worth the risk to go prospecting for gold. The Toposa gunmen plied the countryside looking for something to shoot at, so that it was never advisable to wander out of the camp.

In June of 1992, the Sudan Army marched into Kapoeta and captured it from the SPLA, leaving no other escape route back into the rest of Southern Sudan from Narus. When Kapoeta was captured, there was virtually no other way to go back west to the rest of Southern

---

[68] A tin has the capacity of .02 cubic meters, equivalent of 20 Liters)

Sudan, nor was there any other Sudanese town beyond Narus towards the Kenyan border. We had to make do with Kenya.

Moreover, the presence of the Sudan Army in Kapoeta completely threatened our stay in Narus. It was just a day's drive away, and the proximity of the Sudan Army in Kapoeta would have increased the accuracy with which the Antonov bombers could have targeted Narus. The militias would have become uncooperative as well. And soon, the Sudan Army would have stormed Narus, to get a hold of us, the Jesh el Amar, the Red Army, as we were being fondly called, even though we were not a standing army. It was decided that we would finally have to go to Kenya, as refugees one more time.

CHAPTER 24

LIFE IN LOKI

At midnight, we roused ourselves, got into our convoy of cars, and off we went towards Boston. Nothing would stop us that night. That journey was not unlike any of the others we had been taking for Southern Sudan. Only, it was the final one. At daybreak, we pulled into the parking lot of the voting station in Boston. Snow had fallen that morning, and there were a few journalists with TV cameras, interviewing a few people. We were among the first, and the first to cast our votes. The energy in the station, and the support for secession, was unmistakable. The day we had all yearned for had finally arrived. Even though we could recognize factions within the station, we all wanted Southern Sudan to be free; we could fight or politick later on. There was no use fighting over something yet in the bush.

Years ago, in Narus, none of us knew that we would end up in Kenya. One evening, it was just declared that we needed to leave Narus, or be left behind. The SPLA was going nowhere, of course. At first, our destination was unclear. It looked like we would be going someplace southeast, or back north towards Boma from where we had come, or southwest towards the Ugandan border, before finding another way to travel the routes to return to our home area, west across the Nile. But, shortly before dusk, at Narus, we set off towards Kenya. I think that the reason for not communicating where we were going yet, was perhaps because we were awaiting a decision from Kenya. It would have taken awhile for the Kenyan authorities to accept the influx of refugees from the Sudan. However, we were glad there was somewhere to go before it was too late.

We traveled overnight, without alerting the local Toposa community, whose militiamen would have had a field day or worse, called in an attack via an Antonov. At midday the following day, our first group had already entered Kenya, through the town of Lokichogio. We found the Kenyans sophisticated and flamboyant. They searched our luggage for dangerous weapons, and then allowed us into Kenya. A Kenyan trader at one of Lokichoggio's shops told me, "You Sudanese are really poor. Look, you don't even have shoes; not even sugar." He said this when a group of us went to tour the town. But, we could not converse with him because of our poverty with the English language, though we could understand what he was saying. Little did he know that some of the sugar he was selling might actually have been farmed and processed in the Sudan's Kenana Sugar Plantations, in North Sudan. Perhaps our condition had informed him of very bad circumstances back in the Sudan.

Within the span of a month, the whole refugee community was in Loki, and the border was sealed. None would go back, or come in, from the Sudan. I guess this was to keep the peace at the Kenyan border. Some Sudanese who could not make it in time to Loki, and who remained in Narus, would find ways to get to Loki through other means.

I met a Kenyan soldier, by the name of Joseph, who befriended me. I learned to use the phrase 'I see', to punctuate my conversations with him. Though I could not understand him well in English, due to my own very halting English, and due to the problems of accent, the Kenyan accent being a little different from the clear, familiar Sudanese English accent we were accustomed to, I kind of understood the major parts of our conversation. The Kenyans, even if they are wearing skins and are far into the very rural countryside, like the Turkana villagers, still spoke English. It is like the national language, even though it is merely the official language in use in official government, and private corporate circles. Kenyans are well educated in English.

While my new friend, Joseph, and his army unit, were on the move at the border with Southern Sudan, I bumped into him a few times. The last time I met him, traveling in a file with his unit, he said "We will meet in heaven, if we don't ever meet again." Such was the faith of a Kenyan soldier, a faith shared in Christianity, and that is one reason we became friends. I never saw Joseph again. For the remainder of my time in Loki, until our refugee community relocated to Kakuma, a few kilometers inside Kenya, I never saw him.

The Kenyan Armed Forces, after the 1982 air force coup against President Moi, were revamped and made to be very loyal to the presidency, and it was evident how that loyalty was secured. Apart from retraining, and recruitment, they were clearly pampered. For instance, at the Army barracks, including Joseph's mobile tent barracks, everything was subsidized. When they saw me barefooted, they offered me several nice pairs of shoes, some of which didn't fit me, so I made a trade with some lost boys for other items I required, leaving a pair of shoes for myself.

At Lokichogio, the Radda Barnen team from Ethiopia, led by Mr. Alibela, arrived one day. Radda Barnen is an organization dedicated to protecting the welfare of children and their caretakers, and they had arrived to pay our teachers their arrears, incentives they never received in Ethiopia, while we were on the move. Such integrity is what makes Ethiopians particularly respected in the region. Any other East African nation could have made great use of the cash. Our teachers and caretakers were so thankful for this token of respectability, and were happy to receive what was their due.

One such teacher got his pay and decided to go do some shopping at a shop in Loki. While there, he had in tow a nephew by his side. The teacher had been informed of the widespread pickpocketing rampant in that part, so he was quite aware of the possibility of theft. But perhaps his nephew was more aware, and the child delivered a quick warning, in Dinka, to his uncle who was purchasing something from the shopkeeper. His nephew warned, "Uncle, there is a pickpocket standing right next to you, and he is about to empty your pocket."

The pickpocket was among a troop of pickpockets, just lurking about, waiting for the pick, but they all seemed like genuine shoppers, milling around waiting for their friend to purchase something so they could get going. The uncle whispered back, in Dinka, "I know!" At the moment when the pickpocket had reached his hand inside the uncle's pocket, the uncle shot a quick elbow jab into the nose of the would-be pickpocket, and there was blood and a cry of "*woi thokoi!*" ("Mother," in Turkana). The whole troop ran off, with the bloody-nosed pickpocket in tow, and in pain.

Loki lacked water sources. It had no all-season rivers or streams, and water was only acquired from underground aquifers, so everyone at camp was thirsty. The ICRC would bring water in tankers, and then have it pumped into barrels, where it would be finally distributed into jerry cans for the refugees to take home. The thirst became so bad during that time that everyone was clamoring to get a drop of water. The crowd lurched forward to get to the barrels. Everyone who had a jerry can would put it into a barrel, to get even a drop, but nobody really got enough water, and often the barrels toppled, spilling the much needed water.

Then there were the shenanigans of the aid worker, Mr. Philip. This man thought it would be nice to a make demonstration. After succeeding in pushing everyone back, using the Kenya Police personnel, he washed his hair in the barrels of water, to everyone's chagrin! Mr. Philip was much hated after that. I believe that the aid group found a better way, afterwards, to provide water to the thirsty refugees, because water was never a problem after that incident.

God being important to us, Fr. Akot established a church under the trees at Lokichogio, and, as usual, we were happy to make the church the center of our lives. Some fellows in our group, who were confirmed in Panyido, started taking the reins and taught songs to the new choir at the church. It was particularly great to see that we could participate in the church in such a meaningful way. The Comboni missionaries in Nairobi became interested in our tree church at Loki, and there would be visitors, priests, nuns, journalists and well wishers coming to pay a visit.

I was still undergoing training with the catechism of the Catholic Church, through afternoon recitals in the Dinka language, in anticipation for confirmation. We had to recite the questions and answers and put them into memory. Those teachings of the church would be used during the recital tests, before being selected for confirmation, a step which we all craved because then you would be fulfilled in your faith, and be fully accepted as a member of the Catholic Church. For Fr. Akot's church, an unconfirmed among the faithful, even if baptized, was deficient in faith, and must strive to make the next step. In fact, the unconfirmed were never allowed the Holy Communion, which, though of bland taste, was the ultimate blessing we all sought every Sunday.

There was an Italian priest at Lokichoggio, Fr. Joseph Pellerino, who had been in Dinka country most of his priestly life, and he seemed to wear the same clothes every day, avowing to his priestly vows. We wondered how he could wear the same clothes every day, while the clothes always looked immaculate! Little did we know that he actually had several pairs of identical outfits. What a way for someone to maintain a vow!

The opposite was the case for "*Nyan a piin*" ("the wasp lady"), the Kikuyu Kiswahili teacher later on at Raja Primary school in Kakuma. She would come to school every day in a different outfit. One would never see her repeat wearing the same type, or same colored, dress, any day of her teaching career at the Raja Primary School. She taught from quite early on in 1993 until the time when I left the camp in 1997, and on no single day did anyone remember to have seen her repeat an outfit. She must have been rich to afford all that clothing, we thought. But that was not the case, as we later found out.

As the Kikuyu go, she was not only thrifty but she was also an entrepreneur who had a clothing line at the Kakuma town main market. There it was! But, she was a great Kiswahili teacher, and a very good friend to the lost boys who were students. Some of us passed the Kiswahili portion of the Kenya Certificate of Primary Education, KCPE, with her amazing teaching.

There was a European doctor at the camp in Loki, Dr. Paul, who was put in charge of the little tent hospital, taking care of the refugees at Loki. One day, he was making rounds and came to the maternity ward where he found a woman who had just given birth. When he looked at the baby, he was puzzled to find that the color was light red instead of black as he expected to see. Aren't black babies black like their black parents, he must have mused. The doctor didn't know that black babies only become black after a few weeks, changing from light red to dark brown until they get their particular complexion as they age. The good doctor was informed of this fact by his helpful assistants and nurses.

Near the end of August 1992, the UN decided to relocate the Sudanese refugees from the volatile hub of Lokichogio to the more secure Kakuma Refugee Camp. When the day arrived for our group to be transported, we all boarded the trucks very early in the morning. The UN coordinators made sure that nobody was skipping the line to confuse the staffers, and then get counted twice for personal economic benefits-by being counted twice and gaining the identities of two people, the recipient would receive the rations for two people-a very common practice for the refugees during headcounts. This practice resulted in inaccurate numbers, giving the UN agencies headaches.

But, while the truck was on the move, deliberately speeding up within the town to make it impossible for people to jump off easily to recycle themselves, a fellow named Mayuen, who was sitting in the back of the truck, attempted to jump off. He landed face down on the murram (gravel) road, rendering him briefly unconscious. Everyone in the truck thought that the truck was overturning. It was great to hear people in the truck calling to their particular God, from Jesus to their fathers. Mayuen survived. It was a lesson we would not repeat. Each one of us could have done the same, though, if we were half-daring.

Being in Kenya, everything was new. Dangers abounded in so many forms; dangers which were difficult to successfully navigate through without being harmed. There was the scourge of AIDS, which was now widespread. Contracting the disease could kill the victim in short order, and the most feared part of it was that it usually could not be treated, because we lacked access to treatment for it. While we were already racked with pains getting away from the Sudan, navigating through the scourge of a disease was something that we never bargained for. We did appreciate the warnings about the disease, though, spearheaded specifically by Fr. Akot.

And another immediate danger was brought to our attention; we were starkly warned against ever inhaling or ingesting the toxic cleaning agents used for the public latrines. The warning was so dire that I think none of us witnesses ever fell victim to the danger. The caretakers were much concerned that the boys might ignore the deathly odor and attempt to assuage their curiosity, given their bush background. They feared that someone among them might try to ingest the toxic substance, or try to directly inhale the deathly vapors, which would lead to immediate, possibly fatal, poisoning. To be a little dramatic, the head caretaker called everyone in our group to a gathering for a major announcement.

We assumed that the announcement would be nothing bad, and we casually strolled to the gathering point which was next to the newly dug latrines. The caretaker gave a speech about how valuable life was, as if we didn't know already. Caretaker Mel said, "Life is very important. If anyone of you thinks that life is not important, you are welcome to harm yourself. You all know toxic materials are bad for you. Well, there is a toxic material for cleaning the latrines that we have here." He lifted a can of a substance with strange drawings on it, which included a human skeleton. We all looked up at the shimmering tin can in the sunlight. "You must never taste it, nor ingest it, whether you are hungry or curious. You will die immediately. When you open it, don't stand directly over it, don't bring it close to your face and don't breathe in its vapors directly. The dangers of ingestion or inhalation from this toxin are real!" Mr. Mel continued, "I want one of you to come forward to smell or taste this substance right now." He gave a minute's pause. You could hear a pin drop. However, nobody was going to bring attention to himself in such a public place by displaying his stupidity, which was what Mr. Mel was driving at. The caretaker thought everyone had then understood the danger, and what never to do.

At that time, we heard about the government of the Sudan campaign in Southern Sudan against the SPLA soldiers, and how that campaign was leading the SPLA to concede a lot of territory they had already captured. The *Murahilin* and the Mujahedeen were co-involved in this effort to conquer the SPLA. While the Murahilin were an Arab nomadic outfit, trained and armed by the government of the Sudan to teach the locals in Bhar el Gazel a lesson never to support the SPLA, the larger Mujahedeen were a part and parcel of the Sudan Armed forces, with the aim to wipe out the SPLA, end the war, deliver the Sudan to Islam and bring Islam to the rest of Sub-Saharan Africa. To the Islamists in Khartoum, among whom where Hassan al-Turabi, the SPLA were the obstacle to the envisioned expansion of the fundamentalist Islam throughout the Sudan and the rest of Africa. Whereas the Murahilin were a creation of Nimeiri and, primarily ASadiq, the Mujahedeen were the work of al-Turabi.

The al-Turabi-Omar National Islamic Front, NIF, invited the fugitive Saudi Mujahedeen, Osama Bin Laden, to the Sudan after he caused the ire of the Saudi King and was expelled from the Kingdom of Saudi Arabia. Osama was offered a safe haven, training zones for his fighters, business opportunities and a chance to participate in the war to remove the SPLA. In 1992, when we were fleeing Pochalla, the Mujahedeen were being rushed through training, and carted to the front in Southern Sudan where they would battle the SPLA. The *Mujahedeen* were assured that, should they die in battle, they would go to paradise.

The SPLA was saved from certain demise for two very important reasons: thanks to the SPLA's own tenacity,[69] and to a decision of the Sudan government to finally discontinue support to Osama Bin Laden, leading to his expulsion from the Sudan due to US pressure. Of course, Dr. John Garang, the SPLA leader, was having his voice heard in the US about the intentions of Khartoum, and about their Islamic agenda.

---

[69] The SPLA was able to destroy and capture thousands of Mujahedeen fighters in the fields of South Sudan

CHAPTER 25

GONE TOO FAR

"Are Southern Sudanese biting off more than they can chew, by choosing independence?" Deng asked me as we stood in line, waiting to cast our separation vote. In seeking secession from the Sudan, rather than continuing the fight for a more inclusive society true to its multi-ethnic and multi-religious heritage, were we entering the unknown? It had been clear that unity, the way we wanted it, was going to be impossible, so it was better to get our independence, face the consequences and enjoy its blessings. But, we still had concerns for the future.

Kakuma was a hot, dusty, dry Kenyan town when we got to it. For the first time since leaving my home village and my family behind, I began to feel anxious that perhaps I had gone too far off into the completely unknown, and I really wanted to see my family again, after five years of being in the bush, and plenty of trouble. It was not fun anymore and it seemed that the trouble was abounding. Not only was the place so foreign, the administration of the camp was not fully in the hands of the Sudanese.

Whereas in Panyido Camp, it was reminiscent of home and it seemed that we were at a cattle camp or at a boarding school somewhere in Dinka country, Kakuma Camp was in a very arid region with no all-season stream or river, and nothing else to do except to sing your heart out at church, read some books, play sports or dance with your community on Sunday. In a way, we had no sense of our nationality to console us.

Arriving at Kakuma that afternoon, from Lokichogio, and after the scare of one of our group members falling from the vehicle, we wanted to get off the truck as fast as possible and to find out what had happened to him from the new camp manager who communicated with Loki. But, first, the Kenyan police frisked everybody and searched through our bags to remove any sharp objects, especially knives and clubs. Then we were shown places, invariably under trees, to start building the tukuls for our new dwellings.

Though Lokichogio was as hot and dusty-dry as was Kakuma, when I arrived at Kakuma after traveling in the truck towards a dusty unknown, it really began to unsettle me that we might have bitten off more than we could chew. I felt like I had completely crossed into the unknown, with no knowledge of when I would return home. The feeling was made worse after a few people who I knew, and who were brought to Kakuma from Lokichogio before us, were already found dead. It was said that one of them just never woke up one day.

Someone conversing, without any signs of illness during the day, could suddenly die overnight. It must have been largely due to the exhaustion of traveling, and to the lack of better nutrition. We were exhausted, physically and emotionally. For me, my hopes for a family reunion, conjured up upon arrival at Pochalla, were now a mirage, and I began preparing myself for the long haul. I was simply hopeless. But, going to church, and to school, and then participating in the sports which included football, were great pastimes that gave each of us something to help forget the immediate problems.

At Kakuma, there would occasionally be sudden, damaging floods, with water hurdling rapidly down, inundating the dry riverbed. The very first sign of an oncoming flood was when dark clouds appeared over a distant hill, especially south of Kakuma camp. There would then be a smell of rain in the cold air, coming down from the direction of the southern hills. A tumble of very fast running dirty water would pour into the erstwhile empty riverbed, carrying a freight of logs and uprooted trees, all sort of debris and even dead donkeys. Sometimes people drowned.

While the rushing water would wash away soil and trees, and sometimes kill hapless Turkana donkeys, the major damage to the camp was done to the riverbanks. The bends of the two rivers, running on opposite sides of camp, would widen after these flash flood episodes. The floods carried away chunks of the riverbanks, and also trees standing right along the banks. The camp management decided to start soil erosion measures to reduce such a danger.

Because we were refugees, *Wakimbizi* (runners) to the Kenyans, we could never participate in their national life, and they would never allow us to fully practice our Sudanese customs. Adjusting to the new camp life, I felt ill. Many people were dying every day of disease, fatigue and malnutrition. I reflected that a teacher of mine could be doing well today, teaching a class, and tomorrow he could be no more. Perhaps in Panyido Camp, I never realized the daily suffering because I was too young to take it in, but the two years it took us, from leaving Panyido to settling at Kakuma, gave me the insight that suffering was real, and that I was right there in it all.

When the refugees moved to Kakuma camp in 1992, Kakuma was an arid, desolate area with very few scattered Turkana *manyattas* (settlements). But, before long the area settled by the refugees had the beginnings of a town. The Sudanese refugees were settled into groups based on ethnicity, a management attempt that was a departure from the Panyido Refugee camp arrangement where the Sudanese were settled in no particular grouping, never ethnically for that matter. So, almost immediately, conflicts between the communities began to arise as they arose back home in Southern Sudan, with the Nasser faction defections and the war ensuing.

At this time, in 1993, the Nuer, who were settled within the larger Sudanese camp population, asked the UN to relocate their community farther away from the main Dinka settlement and closer to the UN compound. The only Nuer who remained deep in the main camp were those few boys who were catholic and were quite under the protection and safety offered by the powerful, at least morally, Catholic priests.

From one season to another the animosities between the two communities rose and fell, similar to the fluctuations with the faction rivalries back home. However, as one year led to another, there came a fight that would settle once and for all the simmering animosity. The Dinka Bor community, settled in groups closer to the UN compound, got into an altercation with some Nuer people whose dwellings were on the route between the UN compound and the town of Kakuma. So, for a Dinka person to travel to Kakuma on foot, the shortest distance was to pass through the Nuer camp. It was usually advisable to do so in groups, and at daytime. Moving in the area on foot, at night, was calling for certain trouble, including possible death. The fight was always a group fight with sticks, stones and even spears or knives, either against a hapless Dinka victim or between the Nuer group and Dinka group, or even among Dinka groups.

However, when the fight got out of hand, during the night, the Bor community members evacuated their women and children northward, to the rest of the Dinka groups. The men, young and old, remained to fight it out with the Nuer, with some aid from the other Dinka communities after the word was passed around that the Bor community was taking a beating. By morning, six young men and an older man were dead, with possibly no causalities on the Nuer side. This left the rest of the Dinka furious, as they felt that they had left the Bor community to be slaughtered by a superior fighting force. So, even though the Bor community was often fighting with the Gogrial community, leading to some deaths almost every year, and animosity was closer than the nose, ethnic rivalry against the Nuer now took over, and the word was passed around the Dinka communities to assemble under the huge acacia trees next to the streambeds. The war council was going to assemble, surely to compel the Dinka to fight, to bring sense to the Nuer community to never slaughter the Dinka Bor like that.

However, as the fighting Dinka men gathered together, a word was also quietly passed onto the Nuer about the Dinka intentions, and about the alliance forming. Sensing danger approaching, a very smart Nuer fellow went to inform the Kenya police, and the UN Camp management, about the trouble brewing.

Before long, the cool shaded area under the acacia trees, where a war council was forming an hour earlier that was planning to attack the Nuer, causing a possible massacre, was deserted. The fight was averted, thanks to Chec Kabur, the Nuer man who informed the camp management. Everyone trickled back to their communities as fast as they had appeared, and that was the end of the affair. One wonders why the camp management was never forthcoming, when such war councils would form all the time. Perhaps the camp management wanted the belligerent refugees, often remnants of the war, to revisit the atrocious situations they had left behind, if briefly. Indeed, those fights were brief. The police would be there before long.

The squabbles between the Sudanese refugees, through their local administration representatives, and the UN camp managers, were quite frequent and often ended up in a give-and-take, even though words of challenge would be exchanged that would leave anyone watching in stitches. While those managers were invariably either western Europeans or westernized Africans, their thinking was, more often than not, the same approaching the complaints of the Sudanese refugees. Usually, such complaints were based on the quality and level of services offered at the camp.

While water was abundant, clean, safe and potable, everything else was of limited supply, and the refugees had to fight for it, winning here and losing there. Interestingly, at Panyido, complaining about services would never suffice. There, even though the camp managers were Sudanese themselves, some of whom were great administrators and very well liked, such as Chan, or not so liked, such as the man who replaced Chan, they wouldn't yield to the refugees' complaints. This was partly because of the range of the terror of the Mengistu regime, which enforced certain rules about the services at Panyido. Under the communist system, complaints were not acceptable. You took what was there. Choices were limited and yet we felt we were free because we did most of our own stuff-we build huts and schools on our own and had our own teachers. We were self-reliant. In fact, it was so that any service offered at the refugee camp at Panyido was indeed a privilege and not a right. Since we were not directly under the U.N. system, whatever the

U.N. offered was a privilege not a right for us-we could not complain. At Panyido, it was as if we were within our own country.

Moreover, given the ferocity of the war effort, the great want of fighting men, and the stranglehold placed on the local populations back home by the Khartoum regime, a simple offer of a piece of cloth or a sack of corn grain was more than a blessing. Any amount of UN goodies was manna to be received with gratitude. Not so at Kakuma, however.

At Kakuma, the refugees had a right to complain, unadulterated by any other considerations. Was this a product of the Kenyan democracy? I never knew, but at Kakuma we became more aware that, whereas it was quite shameful for Dinka men to complain about their personal troubles, it was actually within our rights to complain and demand at camp, which is what we did. Complaining, even vocally, was the way to go at Kakuma.

We found that protesting was quite acceptable and relatively harmless. In fact, services might begin to get improved. Therefore, the moment we felt that the kind of grain being offered was simply too different, a complaint went up, and before long the Kenyan Luo lady, Margaret Amol, whose idea it was to offer some grain that was so tiny it looked like nothing we had ever seen before, was in trouble. Margaret Amol backed down after handwritten articles appeared, taped on the camp trees, bearing unprintable insults aimed at her.

At some point, our local Sudanese administrator, the equivalent of a camp manager at Panyido, squared off with the expatriate camp manager. At the war of words, the real camp manager had to reply with bellicosity, "You Sudanese, if you see fit, you can mobilize."

This was in reply to the challenge by the Sudanese camp manager who had said, "If the UN is not forthcoming with the changes we require and have advanced to you, we will be disappointed. Perhaps it would have been better to have stayed in the Sudan, to endure the situation as it is, without having to be in Kenya and be mistreated like this. We can go back to the Sudan. It is our country!" The comparison suggested that the UN, through the camp manager, was mistreating the refugees worse than the folks at Khartoum would have imagined.

Of course, this was a negotiating tactic, but the reply showed the resolve of the camp manager in calling the bluff. Perhaps the camp manager was just fighting, but there was something he could have done to bring better services to the refugees. It seemed that the Sudanese refugees were not really being treated fairly. For instance, it was whispered by those in the know, perhaps by some expatriates themselves who felt that they might have seen some injustices, that the Palestinian refugees would receive better services, even bottled water, whereas for the Sudanese refugees, the dream for such services would be a mirage.

And when the new camp manager, a Canadian citizen who was a native of east Africa', was appointed and issues came quickly to a head, as they often did, the reply to the eventual war of words between our local administrator and the new manager was something out of a comedy show. The new camp manager said, "I am white in the head," when he was chided that he was acting as if he was a white man. That was quite hilarious to some of my schoolmates.

From then on, when some refugees suffered from hunger, they would say that they are afflicted with 'Zakism', for Zak, the belligerent white in the head camp manager. I am quite sure that Mr. Zak was never informed about this, but that is what happens when the administration has no ears on the ground.

Something terrible happened at that time in the camp: the murder of Deng Machol. Deng Machol was a prominent Southern Sudanese intellectual, the sort who is so urbane and eloquent in English that whispers circulated among everyone about his immense education. I first came to know Deng Machol at Panyido. There, his eloquence and fluency in the English language were quickly recognized by the Parish priest at the Catholic Church. In our English-starved camp, Deng Machol became the man who was always there to talk directly on behalf of the church and the Sudanese whenever the church dignitaries from Rome, which included Archbishops and even at one time, a Cardinal, would pay a visit. With Deng Machol around, everyone was sure that the visitors would learn about all of our grievances in the best light. The church came to rely on him.

Deng Machol was an amiable man and quite respected, not only because of his education, but also because of his personality. We also noted that he had a very beautiful wife. Deng Machol was a major part of our lives, especially as part of the Catholic Church congregation. However, at Kakuma, his life was brought to an end by a man who was my Arabic teacher at Panyido. The two hailed from the same area of Southern Sudan, the Tonj District of Bhar el Gazel Province, from what is now the greater Tonj District of Warrap State in South Sudan. How they got into an altercation, or what the issue was about, was never communicated to us at the camp. His body lying in state at our camp hospital was the only absolute information we got about the tragedy. How could so a great man just end up like that? It was a mystery. I could not bring myself to believe that our teacher, whose name I have now forgotten, but who taught us so well in Arabic that I still remember his one lesson in class three Arabic and still can recite the short poem he read, could do something like that.

It was said that one evening, my former teacher got close to Deng Machol, stabbed him to death, and then did something out of character for a Dinka man- he fled the scene, never to be heard from again. It was later said that he had fled to the Sudan. One thing is for sure, if the SPLA were informed about his crime, and if the SPLA had any connection with Deng Machol, or if any SPLA brass had any personal knowledge of the dead man and the value he offered to the Sudanese community, the fugitive would be apprehended and, mostly likely, executed. But I never found out what happened next. Deng Machol's wife later went to New Zealand, the wonderful country of our great teacher at Bakhita, Brother Ben.

After returning to the Kakuma camp from Dadaab, I decided that I was done with ever thinking of going abroad. In September 1995, I had left Kakuma Refugee Camp and my schooling at Lopur Primary School to travel to Dadaab, Eastern Kenya, along with other refugees, to try to get abroad. It was unsuccessful. I was back at Kakuma the following year on January to catch school. After passing through Nairobi to Dadaab on my own, and then getting back to Kakuma through the lush

Mt. Kenya area, via a UN truck, I found that I had had enough with thinking of being somewhere else. Nairobi, and the rest of the Kenyan countryside, was as beautiful and as developed as the photographs of the places abroad, and yet I had not gained anything by being in Nairobi and Dadaab. I reckoned that I merely needed to study well. Education was going to be my goal.

However, a group of friends, some of whom were among those who traveled to Dadaab with me to seek resettlement, believed that there could be a way out of east Africa. These friends were still looking for ways to get abroad, and they succeeded in dragging me to the gates of the UN compound, where they informed me that there was a Ugandan national who had found a way to get many people abroad, but quietly. I was skeptical, but I decided to check it out. When we found the fellow, the only thing he did was lecture us on why staying in the dusty, hot conditions of the Kakuma camp was never going to increase anybody's life expectancy. "Look, after ten years in this dusty place, your life expectancy will shorten," he declared. He showed us immaculate, awesome pictures of the city of Melbourne, Australia and said, "It is within our rights to demand to be resettled in such a city." I quickly noticed that that was one of those squabbles, or tug-of-wars, between the camp managers and the refugees, and I decided that I never wanted anything to do with it, because nothing would come of it. He asked us to sign our names so that we could launch a petition to the UN administration for resettlement, and if the UN didn't respond positively, then we would hold demonstrations to block the gate of the compound. It was all workable, except that the Sudanese refugees were not known to hold protests. We fight our way in. And so, we trekked back to our camp, and I am quite sure that no one came back to join his plan to protest at the UN compound.

Later, I went to Bakhita center and did my four years of high school studies, completely forgetting about going abroad, even though some of my friends were finding chances at the camp to get abroad. I had found my path, and I was never going to be bothered again. However, when I came back to Kakuma in 2001, I was shocked to find the same Uganda national, then a changed man. Whereas he was formerly young, immaculately dressed and seemed quite the clean-shaven fellow who knew what he was talking about, the guy I saw now seemed utterly confused, in dreadlocks, carrying a bag that looked dirty, and he seemed to have gone quite crazy. Was he singled out to be shunned by the camp administration? I never knew the answers, but the man must have played his cards quite badly. That is how I knew never to play dice with anything to do with the United Nations.

When Manute Bol, the legendary tall Southern Sudanese man and famous NBA basketball player, came to Pochalla, he was met at the airstrip by many people, where it was later said that he shed tears and then brought fishing gear for everyone. I used some of the fishing gear, though I was unable to meet Manute then. Therefore, apart from using some of the fishing gear distributed to the displaced at Pochalla, and hearing the tales about his visit there, I never really knew who Manute Bol was, or how tall he really could be. And as one of those larger-than-life figures who appear once, but who the ordinary man can seemingly never hope to meet with face-to-face again, I felt that I would never, ever meet Manute.

However, sometime in 1994, at Kakuma, Manute Bol appeared at the camp. He was traveling via a bus to the camp, along with the SPLA Nuba commander, Yusuf Kuwa Mekki. While it was usually not encouraged by the UN to have the SPLA commanders in contact with the refugees, having Yusuf Kuwa at the camp, officially, must have been sanctioned by the UN, given that he was quite known. It used to be that Yusuf Kuwa was associated with good happenings within the SPLA movement, appointed to such situations by the Chairman who valued the presence of Commander Kuwa very highly. Having Kuwa traveling with Manute was certainly a sign of the graces Manut found himself in with the Chairman. It was later said that Manute Bol gave millions of dollars to the movement, and the movement must have been very grateful. However, at Kakuma, when I finally made sure that I was present to actually meet the legend, Manute Bol, in person, I was a little disappointed at first to be shown a man seated inside the bus, with his head at the same level as everyone else!

How was it possible that someone who everyone attested was taller than any other, would have his shoulders and head at the same level as everyone else in the bus? I had prepared myself to witness the tallest man who ever lived for I had heard so much about his height and his generosity, of course, which is why I wanted to finally see the legend with my own eyes.

Months earlier, an uncle of Manute Bol had arrived at Kakuma, from Nairobi, with a huge black bag that contained a lot of clothing for all the relatives of the tall man. The black bag had emblazoned on it the name of Manute Bol. To know that someone could have his name written on his own bag, that was sophistication for a Kakuma schoolboy.

Furthermore, there had also arrived t-shirts with the image of a tall basketball player shooting a ball into the hoop, with the name Manute Bol written on it. For us, the Kakuma young intelligentsia, the correct spelling was 'Manut Bol'. Spelling the name Manut with an added e was simply not right, but we were in Kakuma anyway and the writing came from the US! We still pronounced it Manut, but painfully aware of a misspelling. So, while I waited to see Manute Bol alight from the bus, knowing that rumormongers could never really be trusted with their tall tales, the bus door opened to allow the passengers to disembark. Before I could get closer to the door, though, the bus was swarmed with throngs of people trying to shake hands with the visitors, especially Manute. And when he did actually get off the bus, and stand up to his full height, I suddenly saw that the rumormongers were right after all. Manute was head and shoulders above everyone, including the tall administrator, Dau, the top of whose head was just below the shoulder level of Manute Bol.

Dau was among the tallest, if not the tallest at the camp, and to be shorter than the shoulder level of Manute Bol proved the tale-weavers truth. Due to the throng, I couldn't get close to the visitors, but I could see clearly that Manute was so tall mostly because of his long Dinka legs. The height was in the legs and not the torso. Later, when everyone had done enough gawking at him, he came to our Group 31, where he stood under the shade of the achuil tree, with the top of his head in the tree branches. He held onto the tree branches with long, spindly arms while delivering a short speech, given in English. "Education is very important," Manute began. "I have been told by the camp leaders that education is open to everyone here. Please take advantage of it. I am not educated, though I have been in the US since the 1980's," he stressed. We could not understand how he was never educated, and yet spoke good English. For us, knowledge was synonymous with the English language. Manute continued, "Where is Akuei, the fellow who asked me for nets and fish hooks at Pochalla?"

"He went home to Bhar el Gazel after we left Pochalla," someone in the crowd answered.

Manute said, "I must confess I was a little disappointed with the request Mr. Akuei made of me at Pochalla. Instead of asking for money and food, he asked for nets and fish hooks for fishing. However, what he asked for was actually much better. More refugees were saved that way. I wanted to thank him today for that. Also, I have learned that it is better to teach someone to fish for himself than to provide a fish for him.[70] Mr. Akuei had asked for the right thing." This brought applause. "Please study no matter your age. I wish I had done so," Manute concluded. Manute might have listened to some lectures by Dr. Garang, being that education was the number one piece of advice Dr. Garang wanted every southern Sudanese to have, as he would urge us to "Go to school." This was the advice given by almost every wise southern Sudanese anywhere. Kakuma was the center of education for Sudanese, supported by the UN and the Christian churches, especially the Catholic Church.

Prominent among the Catholics who supported education was Caesar Mazzolari, the Italian bishop of the diocese of Rumbek, who was an exceptional and very humble man of God. Those who became his acquaintances, came to easily revere him for what he did for all the Sudanese. The first time I met Mazzolari was during a church service at Kakuma. The new monsignor was expected at the Catholic Church at the camp and we were all lined up to welcome him at our under-the-tree church. However, when he arrived that afternoon, there was rain, at least a little drizzle for the first time that season. For the Sudanese, if a man of

---

[70] As the proverb says, "Give a man a fish, and he will eat for a day. Teach a man to fish, and he will eat for a lifetime."

God pays a visit to a place and there is rain upon his arrival, this is treated as God's acceptance of the man. It is as if God was saying, "This is my chosen servant, listen to him." It was seen as sort of an endorsement from God, the almighty. It was also something that made us pause for a bit.

However, the second meeting, and the time when I really began to respect the Monsignor who later became the bishop of the same diocese, was during one of the midnight Christmas vigils at the Catholic Church at Kakuma. The service was in the open, at the volleyball field south of the parish. At midnight, the service, as usual, was full of joy and solemnity, and all of us were dressed in our best, whatever few items of nice clothing we had. This was also the time when girls were at their best, and when scoring a smile from a girl was a heartwarming experience.

However, when the good bishop gave the homily, everything else paled in comparison. Homilies are the parts of worship which I had begun to enjoy for the life lessons that they imparted. The bishop narrated a story: "There was a man in the United States who had gone out to buy himself a motor vehicle, a Ford, and had excitedly gone on the road in the afternoon to test it out. However, during a long stretch of the road, and after having gone quite far at a very high speed, the car came to a stop suddenly. He pushed the car to the side of the road, out of the way. He then tried to restart the engine, but after each cranking, nothing would happen. All of the dials and indicators were fine. The motorist tried to flag down passing cars, but none of the speeding cars stopped to help him. He got frustrated, so he stopped trying to ask for help. He sat on the bumper of the car, watching the cars passing by, thoroughly frustrated. Minutes passed. Then, a car passed by him. This car was slower and the driver was an old man, white haired and kindly. The car passed and then stopped a few yards down the road. The driver drove backwards to stop next to the parked car. He spoke to the motorist, 'You seem a little frustrated. Is there a problem with your car?' the old man asked, stepping out as he parked his car just a few paces ahead of the parked car.

The motorist replied, 'Yes. I bought this car today. I brought it out to try it out, but it stopped on the road. I don't know what the problem is.' The motorist was thinking what can this old man do? The car was brand new and he could not find what the problem was. The old man asked the motorist to 'Pop the hood!'

Reluctantly, just out of courtesy, he popped the hood and the old man leaned in to check, searching about. He went back to his car, and then returned with a container of gas and proceeded to pour it into the tank of the car. He then asked the driver to crank the engine. Reluctantly, the driver jumped in and, voila, the engine was on again. The now happy driver could not believe what had just happened, and profusely kept thanking the old man. He asked the old man, 'How did you know what the problem was?'

'I am Henry Ford. I make these cars!' the old man replied quite simply, in a monotone."

The good bishop went on to say, "God is our master and, as in this story, if we find that we have insurmountable troubles, we should simply turn to God who will give us the healing touch we need." From then on, Mazzolari was seen as a great man of God, for anybody could easily see the kind of deep faith he had. Like Ford cars, so are we to God.

While armies the world over like to camouflage themselves and stay concealed, it is interesting how a Kenyan Army Barracks could sit within the confines of the Kakuma refugee camp and rarely did anybody ever even bother to talk about it. The signs of the barracks were the large barbed wire fenced compound, with several trees inside, screening the view so that nothing could ever be seen inside by anyone who was outside. Even though there was a huge water tank on stilts visible for miles around, refugees would pass by it and never even talk about it. It was the equivalent of avoiding a thorn tree. While the local camp population left the place alone, the occupants kept to themselves and would never even be seen around. Even during the troubles of fights in the camps, their presence would never be felt.

Kakuma was very arid, without enough rain throughout the year, yet the underground aquifer system provided enough water for drinking, watering trees and vegetable gardens, and for washing clothes for everyone in the camp. Though crystal clear, the water was further cleaned with the addition of chlorine bleach to kill any microscopic germs in the water. Pumped through an elaborate piping system throughout the camp, accessibility and potability was never a problem. There was a faucet at every group, and water could be procured any time, day or night. There were localized tank systems for zones of the camp. Those tanks would be filled to the brim for later use when the central pump was off. The water was pumped from underground by use of a powerful generator located within the central area of the camp, and the sound of it could be heard for miles around.

The pump was quite efficient, so that there was no day without water at the camp. The camp administration must have noticed early on that water was the most basic commodity of life, missing in the arid Kakuma area, and that unless there was a reliable source, the thousands of refugees would gradually die of thirst. So, water was properly sourced and made available reliably throughout the camp all year-round, twenty-four hours a day.

The whole of northern Kenya is arid and semi-desert. There is very little rainfall throughout the year. This climate is therefore not good for vegetation of any kind. The only vegetation that successfully grows there are the acacia trees that grow in the valleys of the seasonal dry rivers, given their tap root systems which go down to the underground aquifers. Consequently, the whole countryside lacks enough vegetation, with sunlight beating down very intensely, all year. This leaves the ground quite desiccated, and the soil completely uncovered. The soil is then often carried in the air by the high winds of the desert, causing dust storms which, once they start, can last for hours, carrying large amounts of solid material, and even altering the landscape, causing dunes.

These storms would last for hours, or even days, and for the people in the camp, it was simply time to hunker down and stay indoors, making sure to seal every part of the housing to avoid the swirling dust storm. Heads could be covered with scarves, and eyes shielded, but there would still be dust in everything, including food and water. Dust storms were the first things that I encountered at Kakuma that made me feel that I had gone into the unknown. It was a place of devastation.

The UN camp administration, given that the main focus of the refugees was education, decided to build a brick and concrete building, very large by camp standards, to house books and be a multipurpose resource center. They called it the Teacher Resource Center. I benefited by reading so many of the books stored there. I later translated this habit to the library at our High School at Bakhita, when I became the only student who would read the books on display there, while everyone else was just reading notes and the textbooks. The books that I read most were the English literature books, including the series of Hardy Boys books. The Resource Center was a place I could escape to, and emerge happy, after having just completed the reading of yet another book.

Being a multipurpose center, conferences and meetings were organized at the center for many groups, both within the UN and refugee communities. One such conference was the Human Rights conference spearheaded, quite vocally, by the sophisticated and educated refugees from the Great Lakes of Africa. It was at those conferences, with the singing of 'Human Rights are God Given' by the great Lakers, that our eyes were opened to the fact that one could complain to the international community to be heard, if one was under persecution.

For us Sudanese, complaining to anybody was not a route we wanted to follow. It was simply not our experience. We fought for our rights, but we never complained or made demonstrations to show our displeasure. During the 1980's in the Sudan, demonstrations were commonplace, spearheaded by students, but they were met with extreme brutality from police and security forces, causing deaths and destruction. School children were massacred, even when the security forces were under the command of the Southern Sudanese. That may have been another reason why we refused demonstrations. However, the great Lakers made complaining seem like it could be a passionate part of an afternoon's work.

CHAPTER 26

MAKE IT OUR TOWN

Outside the voting station, Deng said, "It is over, isn't?" It was. Truly. 50 years of pain was finally over. It was left to us to make the land we won our own. We were free. We were all shouting inside the center. There was no turning back.

At Kakuma, I enrolled in school, in Standard Four, like the rest of the so-called "lost boys". I soon found that I was not achieving highly, though. My results placed me in the 18th rank after the first exams, far behind the first three ranks in class. That result was significant in that I had never placed outside the first three ranks in all of my classes up to standard four in Ethiopia and Pochalla. It took me by surprise and, with it, gave me a renewed sense of purpose and the drive to do better in subsequent classes. To that end, I jumped classes, from Standard Four in term one to Standard Five in term two by a stroke of luck, broken English and a connection to the Ugandan Mr. Fred, the deputy inspector of the school district. I even acquired a bunch of books that the rest of the students in my class only dreamed of. This placed me at odds with them and they started trying to find out where I had come from, how I came to be in the class and what my connection with Mr. Fred was. I went along with answering their questions as far as their suggestions would allow. Satisfied, they went along believing I had been with them somewhere in the Sudan because, being snobbish, they didn't want someone who had been at Panyido to be with them in class, since the Panyido pupils were all lower by one class. They began to accept me. My friends had to share books while I had several of them to myself. I eventually ended up being number three in the class, to the chagrin of Mr. Fred who wanted his star student to be number one. After that point, Mr. Fred never talked to me again.

Learning was everything. But, sometime in 1994, when the government of Sudan offensive against the SPLA was at its strongest and the SPLA morale was really down, messages came that the SPLA was getting weaker and that the northern army would win the war, take over the country and rule it the way they had wanted to before Southerners took up arms. This proposition would render all the hard work and sacrifices that the SPLA soldiers, and really everyone else, had contributed to the cause just a waste. It was said that the few diehard soldiers still in the field thought that every man in the refugee camp was simply a coward. At that time, several young men decided to go to the front.

Those of us who still believed that we could contribute to the betterment of the Sudan through education, remained. But, the crowd on the expedition to go to the front, decided that they couldn't leave the camp without first taking from the goods so carefully stored inside the residential part of the camp. The store could have been placed inside the UN compound, where it would have been well protected by the Kenyan security and police, but it wasn't. One dark night, the gallant boys passed the word around to their friends. The camp store was going to be brazenly broken into and broken down. The looting would last into the early hours of the morning.

A friend who attended the sacking of the store later told me how it all went down: "The individual participants at the ransacking did well to avoid getting crushed by the throng, as well as by the goods being shoved and pulled around. It was a field night for all who felt it was the right thing to do. I did my best to get what I could and to avoid being crushed," he narrated. The following day, the looters were still sorting through the loot into the evening, at their hideouts, with the black market awash with blankets, plastic sheets and so forth.

After that, the UN made sure that the stores full of goods were safely placed within the impenetrable UN compounds. The vandalism was explained away by the Sudanese camp managers as the work of arsonists who could not be traced. I believe the arsonists, most of whom were answering the call for the motherland, didn't want to see a repeat of Panyido. There, the goods meant for the wellbeing of the boys never reached them, but instead remained stocked while the poor boys trooped back barefoot, naked and hungry, and never the richer. It served them well.

There were Turkana bandits at large, who would prowl the camp at night, looking for something to rob. Usually if somebody had bought a goat, or if the Turkana knew someone who was a petty trader and had some money, they would pay him a visit at night with their guns to rob. Sometimes there would be murders, which would never be investigated by the camp authorities. Boys would lose their lives if they went outside the camp to the nearby dry riverbeds. Being there by oneself would possibly lead to being killed by the Turkana.

There was a boy who had gone out of the camp to play soccer with his friends at the riverbed, and then decided he was tired and needed to catch some sleep under the nearby shade of a shrub while his friends remained engrossed in the soccer game. After the game, his friends decided to leave to go back to their dwellings, forgetting their sleeping friend. The Turkana got to him first and murdered him. It was shocking for us, but we could do nothing about it.

The Turkana community was unique. At times, the male members of the surrounding village would go on a cattle-rustling expedition all the way from Kenya to Southern Sudan. Had they been in the Kenyan Army, or had they any rapport with the Army, this border crossing could have been considered an invasion. The Turkana also have some very peculiar customs. One such custom is the ceremony of goat roasting. It starts by one Turkana old man donating a goat, and then a whole crowd of old and middle-aged men converge under the shade of trees.

The chosen location is also close to a water source, near a dry streambed, where water can be dug from underground.

After assembling, the goat is slaughtered, and then placed inside a burning pile of twigs and foliage, while the group converses. This goes on until the roast is ready to be served. It is then served, by being cut into pieces and distributed to the seated gentlemen. Everyone present sits on a nyacholong (a kind of chair), and has a nyakaparat (a specialized knife), for cutting.

At that time, despite the Turkana murders, some cousins and I decided we wanted to go buy some Turkana sugarcane from a sorghum field. Not that the cane was particularly sweet, but it was the next best thing after the real sugarcane, which was rare, expensive, and only brought from the Kenyan countryside. A few Kenya coins, 25 cents over a shilling, would buy someone a bunch. So, with a few coins, about five of us braved the Turkana villages to go to the one farther off to the distant hills. The Turkana along the way would look at us with questioning stares but said nothing, besides responding to our greeting, or we responding to theirs, "*Ajokaa*!" ("Hi!").

We would reply, "*Ejok*!" ("Hi!").

When we reached the field, the owner was only too glad to have paying customers. We went into the field, just like home, to get sugarcane (sorghumcane). After we had loaded up, near mid-afternoon, we decided to turn around and head back. The Turkana we found along our way began to shout in their language, which we couldn't understand, except to realize that they were asking questions and acting as if they didn't want us to be carrying the sugarcane. Sensing animosity, we made a beeline for our camp. Before we had reached the dry streambed, though, just on the ledge, a group of Turkana men were coming back from the camp where they might have gone to look for some economic benefit. They were with a dog, and they were carrying some sticks, and on their every wrist was what we all knew every Turkana male carried: a specialized knife called a Nyakaparat. The knife was like a bracelet or a bungle worn around the wrist, with the outer edge having been sharpened razor sharp, and having a piece of dry leather folded to cover the sharp edge, both to protect the wearer and to also preserve the sharpness of the edge. It was a prized possession and every Turkana who had one knew how to use one.

We also knew how bad a Nyakaparat cut was. The leader of the Turkana team must have been a comedian because he started shouting at us in Turkana and shooing his dog to go nip me on the side, trying to prevent us from getting into the riverbed and returning to the camp with our bundles of sugarcane. The comedian Turkana came right towards my cousins on my left. I was on the extreme right and he shooed his dog to get me, but I ran fast with my loot, with the dog missing me by a whisker. My cousin didn't fare well, though. He fell down and I heard his voice crying out, "*Mao!*" ("Mother!"). The rest of the group dropped their bundles. We could not laugh; we still had to outrun the Turkana. The Turkana got all the bundles they had dropped and then allowed the other boys to flee to the camp. I was the only one to hold onto my bundle. Later at the camp, I could not contain my laughter at the benefit of my cousin.

But, not all people were heartless strangers. An aid worker from Europe, a young woman who was assigned to the hospital, became friendly with the Sudanese, so that when it was her time to be rotated somewhere else, tears welled up in her eyes. How could it be that a lady all the way from Europe, and far apart from the Sudanese, could find it in her to be so bonded with strangers that they had become like family to her, and she would shed tears for leaving a part of her behind? This is what the human condition really is- kindness and love that embraces all humanity. I was more than impressed to know that it doesn't matter what ethnicity the person is, as long as they have love in them. They will give their best for the good of their neighbors, which led me to believe that the Arab northern Sudanese, especially the ones responsible for all the atrocities happening in the Sudan, were people who had lost that basic humanity, or had simply ignored it. They should listen to their hearts.

Group 52, the group whose members were the closest to the Catholic Church and among whom some served in the choir, as altar boys, catechists and other helpers, was a tough group to join, unlike the others in which you could be accepted by the head caretaker. So, when I decided to be a member of this group, the priest, Fr. Akot, made sure that the request went through the parish council chairman who knew me and who, together with the priest, welcomed me, after careful scrutiny, of course. But, before I knew the culture of the group, I came face-to-face with Fr. Akot in a very interesting situation.

The parish priest's house was secluded inside a compound of its own, while the rest of Group 52 was centered around a circle of huts for the boys. At the priestly compound, there were some nice Sudanese girls who were there to do some work for the priest. A friend asked me to accompany him to strike up a conversation with the girls, an idea that appealed to me, and before we knew it, we were enjoying a nice chat with lovely leggy girls, when the priest's car suddenly appeared in the driveway and we were caught. The priest would greatly frown upon such an act outside the church, but it was far worse given these circumstances. With this happening in his own compound, and by a boy who had just been admitted into the sacred Group 52, this act was beyond comprehension.

Sensing this, I was not far behind my intrepid friend who ran off before I could ask what to do, not even paying attention that the girls were then laughing. Off I went, past the priest who looked at me angrily. The following day at the Group 52 council with the good priest, I received a reprimand, issued by a fellow from our home county of Twic. He told me that the activities at Group 52 should never become a cat-and-mouse game. I took the reprimand, and learned the lesson. I didn't try to flirt with girls at the compound again, but outside this area I kept trying to woo the girls nonetheless.

The only things worth enjoying at Kakuma were school, dances and parties, church, sports, and the movies. Every Sunday, it was always good to dress in your very best, which usually would happen to be just a single shirt, a pair of shoes if you were lucky, a pair of pants and cologne. One thing, you had to be at your best, by the standards of the camp, to have any chance at the few girls around. Getting to be liked by the girls was always an uphill battle because there were so few of them, and they were kept on a very close leash of protection from their families. The competition was stiff. It helped if you did well in school. But this was also self-defeating, because if you did well in school, you would be given the reinforcing advice to "Please pay attention in school and stop thinking about girls. You will get them later on." It helped if the girl was also dedicated to schooling, and then she would be what is called in America, bitchin. So, if one did well in school, getting involved with girls would quickly nullify school performance, it was asserted.

The most interesting part about the churches in Kakuma was the way they differed. Every Sunday, you would hear the Episcopal Church, down near the river, under the large trees, belting out the *"Yin lo jik Nhialiny dit..."* song, which is the English equivalent of "Glory to God in the Highest...". When hearing that sung in Dinka by the largely Bor ethnic Episcopal Church on Sunday, you could swear that God was present among them. The Episcopal Church at Kakuma was truly a Dinka church. On Sundays there would be young men and women members of the choir dancing, and everyone singing those songs. Sometimes, people would fall on the ground, flailing, because the Spirit was with them. The service was mostly in songs and words, and you could hear great speakers talk about God in ways that made you believe that the speaker was a true believer in what he was saying.

In the Catholic Church, however, most prayers, and the mass, were more reserved, with only the priest leading. Services were mostly in English and occasionally in Arabic, while the songs were sung in Dinka, English, Arabic, Nuer, Toposa, Didinga and so forth. In a way, the Catholic Church was more inclusive in having the songs sung in the other tongues of South Sudan, but the mass was usually just in English, so it was a pretty good place to be if you wanted to speak in English the way it is spoken by the Western priests. However, compared to our fellow students who were mostly Episcopalian, the Catholic students were no better in English, especially when written.

The late, iconic Caesar Mazzolari, the Italian South Sudanese prelate of the diocese of Rumbek, is a leader I would never forget for what he contributed to the liberation of South Sudan, and to building its future.

He began to increase his support for the Southern Sudanese cause while we were refugees. The works of Mazzolari included building schools for, and sponsoring, students inside and outside of South Sudan. He also helped the families of the South Sudanese in the Kenyan towns, throughout the war, with their accommodations and schools for their children. Mazzolari the man was humble and kind, and his works will be long remembered, and will continue to bear fruits for South Sudan.

One of his last gifts to South Sudan was bestowed to the Embassy of South Sudan at Rome. He dedicated a private villa there, in southern Italy, for the use of the South Sudanese ambassador. Just five days after the July 9th declaration of South Sudan, the good bishop died of a heart attack while conducting and leading a celebratory mass for South Sudan. He was a blessing for our people from God the almighty.

The other priest of note was Fr. Vincent Donatti, or Vincenzo Donatti, an Italian Don Bosco priest who was funny and fatherly to boot. With his long beard, he would try to talk in Dinka and made funny faces and sounds just to make people laugh. Fr. Donatti was a great man of faith and he made us respect what it means to be a human being. He was more than a catholic priest; he was like a grandfather to everyone. One day, when the Sudanese bishop of Torit, Paride Taban, made a stop at Kakuma Camp before heading to the Sudan, Fr. Donatti was so happy to see him. He kissed the Bishop's ring and, laughing like old brothers, rushed the Bishop to bless his house and the dwellings of his staffers. It was as if a man from God had arrived to pay a visit to him. If I've become able to look past race, it was because of people like Donatti, Mazzolari and others like Sister Carolyn. They taught what it meant to be a Christian, and a human being, regardless of your ethnicity or how you looked.

There was a Catholic nun from Canada who prepared us for confirmation. She read to us a story in the Bible, from the book of Revelation, concerning how God gives us secret names, known only to us and to him, and that everyone was special in the eyes of God. She also read from a book of the gospels about when the apostles met Jesus. The story is that of Andrew and his brothers, and how Jesus narrated to them how he saw them before they appeared. The Sister asked for volunteers to enact the story, and I got the part of Jesus. This was pretty nice because I was the center of attention.

After that, I became an actor in the church drama series. I also changed my Christian name from John to Giovanni, the Italian version of the same name, during my confirmation because so many people were becoming John, thanks to the influence of John Garang. My choice of John, chosen at Panyido Camp, was inspired by an account from a friend of mine, Mabeny. He told me about John Kuleng, an SPLA alternate commander from his area, who crossed the line from Anya Anya II to be a member of the SPLA, reducing conflict and making the national cause more powerful. I admired the name John because of such a leader who would put aside his ambitions to bow down to national aspiration. I could have chosen the name John because of John Garang, but, surprisingly, that was not the case. To each his own, and I believe my choice honored John Kuleng. At Wau, in 1985, before I went away, an uncle of mine gave me the name George and would call me Giorgi Josef or George Joseph. I only remembered this name after I had already taken the name John.[71]

Another interesting priest was Fr. Tim. Irish Fr. Tim was a giant of a fellow, with a big heart, and he was as humble as only a great human being can be. Even though he was the parish priest, Fr. Tim, from Dublin, would wear mutwukali (lasting-beyond-your-death) shoes, made out of tires that would last a lifetime. Those were the shoes of convenience, and the cheapest affordable by anybody. They were so thorn-proof that you could run in them and step on a thorn bush, and nothing would prick you. Fr. Tim taught us to always remember to be humble, even if you were a giant. Indeed, Fr. Tim, upon hearing my lack of school fees while at Lopur, decided to pay my school fees. It is a debt I have not yet been able to repay.

Fr. Tim had a counterpart, and near polar opposite, in Fr. Neil. Fr. Neil (pronounced Nile) was also from Dublin. Whereas Fr. Tim was tall, Fr. Neil was short. He was funny, yet seemed to be mean, in that mean

---

[71] Had I remembered this fact in Ethiopia before baptism, I would have taken the name George during baptism

way Catholic priests can be forgiven for. He insisted on playing golf, even at Kakuma Refugee Camp, a place so arid that no grass typically grew, other than during the few months of the rainy season. But he would strike the golfballs, and then have some fellows go retrieve his golf balls beyond the further part of the stream. But, although he could be mean, he was also kind, if in a grudging sort of way. I found this out during the funeral of a member of the camp who had so sadly passed away after a sudden attack of malaria. Fr. Neil offered the use of his car to transport the body to the cemetery, and he was there to perform the funeral rites. Fr. Neil was greater than his diminutive self.

Another notable Catholic leader was the German, Armin Pressman, the director of the Don Bosco training institute at the camp. It was said that Mr. Pressman was the product of the German street, brushed off and made into a great, selfless man by the Don Bosco mavericks. We had a spat with him once, over our choice for secondary schools, but otherwise we got along all right with Mr. Pressman. Yet while he was nice, in a grudging way, he was also a no-nonsense man.

But, Mr. Pressman also provided a very important service for the boys stationed at Group 52, which was the original parish boys' camp where altar boys would reside, along with catechists, choirmasters, and other helpers of the church. The priests would admit to this group any boys at camp, whether they were exemplary or were having trouble and needed somewhere to stay near the church. Mr. Pressman decided to help the young ones by giving them employment. Don Bosco had started the planting of trees around its huge compound, and the boys would water the plants every morning and evening, and then be given some money by Mr. Pressman. So, Mr. Pressman was actually human. One day, he was on a motorbike coming from the main town of Kakuma to the refugee side, when he made a turn and veered into a Turkana lady, causing a grisly accident that almost cost him his life.

Before the time of Mr. Pressman, Don Bosco had many visitors, mostly from Italy. One day, a father and son team arrived to do some work on the carpentry machine just brought from Europe. The son was a catholic religious brother. Upon arrival, the pair went right to work, without even stopping to take a rest as most visitors would do. The brother was so engrossed in his work that I marveled at how dedicated he looked. That particular piece of machinery trained many lost boys to be professional carpenters, and its proper functioning was more important to the brother than his need for some rest. It was quite impressive for me to see such a total dedication to work.

Another interesting incident transpired, one which led me to marvel at how quite impossible it was to swindle or fool the priests. One fellow left the camp, on his own accord, to spend time in the countryside. A year later, he returned to the camp. He found that the Catholic Church was then looking for young men to be candidates for priesthood at their new facility being built in Kitale, Kenya, and that the major qualification, apart from the obvious requirement of good and exemplary character, was having completed and passed the Kenyan primary school certificate examination. This man decided to position himself for such a consideration.

The fellow told the parish priest that he had finished class eight and was already qualified to enter secondary school, even though he had never sat for the exam. The priest was convinced and took the fellow to be his helper at church until the time in December when the candidates for the spots would be appointed, with the understanding that he would be one of those selected. The fellow did his due diligence to be of help to the priest for all the time he was attached to the parish. But when it was time to reveal the candidates, the name of this fellow was not there, even after he had spent a whole year waiting for this chance. It was simply devastating, and a cautionary tale to never go around trying to fool priests. It was revealed to the priest that his candidate had never, ever gone beyond standard five.

Initially, the catholic priests at camp were Fr. Akot, a Dinka, and then some missionaries from the Republic of Ireland, and then later on the East African Apostles of Jesus, some of whom were from the South Sudan Equatoria region. The Salesians of Don Bosco, who were mostly Italian, were also present. Their technical school taught many people masonsry, carpentry, and other trades.

At times there would be groups of church youth coming from Italy to visit the camp. One such group, which included many young people, spent about a week with us. We got to know a few of them so well that when it was time for them to go, another friend was in tears. Among them was one who we called Sister, because she said that was her title, even though she didn't wear a habit. This Sister befriended us, and we guided her around camp while she asked us several questions. She was nice, and we spent a great deal of time walking under the tall trees along the dry riverbeds circling the camp. I guess we bonded and that is why my friend cried. I reckoned that she had to go back to Europe.

* * *

The rumor mill was always active at camp. The trouble was that refugees would pick up bits of information, then embellish the details, and soon hearsay would be presented as facts, which were inaccurate. A rumor could get out of hand in no time, and cause trouble to those who spread it without making sure that the information was accurate. One such rumor was that the Sudan Government had been allowed by the Kenya Government to secretly start bombing the Kakuma Refugee Camp. It was later found out that what actually started the rumor was that there was going to be a news bulletin for the camp, a regular publication. It so happened that the very first edition had a photograph of an aircraft that looked like an Antonov, and the word bulletin, emphasis mine. This set off the rumor and, before long, many were prepared to run for their lives. There were skeptics, though, who needed to hear the information on the radio, or actually see the paper. They were looking for hard data, which they only found when they saw the paper with their own eyes, and saw the word bulletin, which had been totally misunderstood.

Another rumor quickly spread when it was decided that the camp community should undergo a head count. Just to make sure that there was no one messing with the counting, there was going to be a mark made with purple dye on the hand. This started the rumor that it was the fulfillment of the warning in the Bible that the evil one would take over the world and would force everyone to have a mark on the hand. It was said that anyone who didn't have the mark would never be able to buy or sell products, or to participate in the life of the community. On the face of it, and without enough facts, one could be taken with this rumor, but there was enough information at hand, and it was not the first time that a headcount was conducted. The rumormongers failed to get what they wanted: a community that would be so scared that it would refuse the headcount.

Beyond Loki and Kakuma, another Turkana District town of note is Lodwar. The district headquarters, Lodwar sat at the confluence where the road leading to Loki, and that leading to Lake Turkana, converge. Perhaps the most notable thing about the town of Lodwar was the heat during the daytime. It was so oppressive that it kept people away, and made Lodwar look like a ghost town. All of the towns and villages of the Turkana District could become scorching hot, but Lodwar seemed the hottest. With the diurnal heat trapped in the rocky surroundings of the town, it never seemed a nice place to be.

But at night the view was something else, and the desert air would be cooler and suddenly, Lodwar was a place quite livable. The town held the seat of the Diocese of Lodwar, whose Bishop conducted confirmations of the Christians at Kakuma refugee camp. This Bishop Mahon, an Irish man, lived within the oppressive high temperatures of that town. One thing that I really hated about Lodwar, though, and also about Kitale, was the oppressive smell of the dead at the mortuaries of the two cities. But, it was always advantageous to avoid the smell; to get away from the heading direction of the smell.

While I was in Kakuma, my involvement with the church activities, like that of the rest of my fellow Christian faithful, was very important to me. Most of us found a sense of purpose and hope to carry on through our faith. Despite the onslaught of troubles, we had faith in God, believing that one day there would be a reason to smile and that the storm would pass. At that time, the three church activities that I enjoyed participating in most were the dramatization of the church's teachings, the reading of the word at the masses, and leading a small Christian community, the SCC.[72]

The so-called SCC (Small Christian Community) was a small group of churchgoers formed from people who attended church regularly on Sundays, and lived close by each other in the community. The aim was to make sure that the teachings at church were lived out properly by the members of the small Christian community, as we urged each other to stay true to the ideals learned at church, and to help each other be the consciences of our community. The major activities of the group were praying and reading the Bible together. I was the leader of one of our Christian communities.

Dramatizing the church teachings meant translating words into action, so that they could be better understood. Our dramatizations required a lot of diligent work, though it was ultimately worthwhile. And though we were amateur actors, we were organized and gave great effort. The plays, including those performed around Christmas and Easter, benefited the community by helping it see these stories embodied in real life. Because of that, the church pastors thought that I was one of the most brilliant boys at church, and sought to help me any way they could, including paying my school fees. They covered these costs while I was at school in Lopur, a small village in Turkana country, just north of Kakuma Refugee Camp.

Readings during church masses were a way for me to practice public speaking, if just to read words. At that time, reading at church was quite a fulfilling role for me, not only because it gave me satisfaction in the knowledge that I was contributing to the Church and learning at the same time, but I also gained a lot of friendship from sharing these good deeds.

At Kakuma, the Sudanese teachers were given what the UN called stipend to encourage them to render teaching service to the poor

---

[72] The Small Christian Community, SCC, was a church term for a group of five faithful, with their leader, invariably youth, who met regularly at a venue, at Church or in their homes to read the Bible and pray

unaccompanied minors. It wasn't a salary, per se, but an incentive, because offering them a salary would have immediately disqualified them from being able to receive the monthly distribution of camp rations given to the refugee community. Given this scenario, the teachers were well paid by the standards of the camp, and some enterprising women would take advantage of this situation to engage in the production and sale of a certain liquor. This liquor, known as aregi, was a local distillate made from flour or sugar, and distilled locally at the camp. It was so addictive that it almost couldn't be advertised. Aregi practically sold itself after the first few tastes, or once the consumer had time to adjust his palette and develop tolerance. Once this happened, the customer was hooked.

Being locally made, its alcoholic concentration varied with the distiller. The higher the concentration, the more successful the distiller would be, because through word of mouth, the quality of the brew would be communicated far and wide around the camp. Consumers would show up whenever the stipends had come in, or if they had developed a relationship with the distiller so that they could acquire the brew on credit, they would pay later, when the stipends came in.

It was in such a situation that a teacher came to have a drink of the hot distillate at the house of a relative of mine, at Group 15. The tall teacher came from an adjacent group for he had heard of the quality of the distillery from other consumers who had had a taste of my relative's liquor. That evening, as he continued to satisfy his palette, the teacher cracked jokes and told stories to the entertainment of those of us milling around. I stayed a little longer to listen to the wise old man cracking drunken jokes about many issues, in a way that made everyone laugh.

However, as every young person knows, if you hang around older people long enough you might be asked to run an errand. I was not surprised, therefore, when I was called upon to run an errand for the benefit of the old teacher in a drunken stupor. Only in my case, I was then asked to lead the visibly intoxicated teacher back to his group because he could not remember from which direction he had come. My goal was to lead him to his Group 17, and to point him towards his house.

I was reluctant, but felt obliged to help, being a young fellow and a Christian to boot. So I led him, by the hand, making sure that he didn't get lost, right into Group 17 until he was able to recognize the surroundings of his group. The teacher was so happy that he put his hand into his pocket and handed me a KSH 500 note. At Kakuma at that time, money was never easily acquired, especially for someone like me. And being offered such an amount of money was simply preposterous, unless the giver was flat out of his mind, which the teacher was. He was grateful and he wanted to thank me by giving me some gift, but giving me such an amount of money, which amounted to the equivalent of an American 50–dollar bill, at Kakuma around 1994, was simply out of bounds, and a clear indication of his drunkenness.

So, being the good fellow and Christian that I was, I refused to take advantage of the situation; I tried to give him back the money, to which he refused. He kept returning it to me. "Take it! I give it to you!" he insisted. Noticing that he was never going to take it back, I took the money, letting him go his way as I went my way. Sure enough, the following day, the now sober teacher came back to the relative's house, asking for the boy who helped him on his way the night before. "Might he have taken my money, because I have lost a KSH-500?" he inquired.

"Sure! Here is your money. You gave it to him last night and he handed it to me thinking you might want it back today," the woman told him.

The Kenya Certificate of Primary Education, KCPE, was the primary certificate gained upon graduating from the eight years of primary school learning. That certificate, and the national examination through which the students earned the certificate, were pretty much rites of passage for students, and important steps along life's journey. Passing well at that juncture would advance the student to a covetous spot at a prestigious national high school, leading to eventual success in further studies and a lucrative job and career upon graduation.

Failing the examination could mean the end of a budding academic career and the beginning of a life of great poverty, unless the individual was simply thrifty and could make it in the world of trade. Passing the

KCPE with flying colors was the way out of poverty, and the teachers would never hesitate to inform the students about this. The pressure to pass the exams was especially high on the Turkana students, given the backwardness of the Turkana District, with very few Turkana ethnic members in important roles within the Kenyan nation, given lack of a better education. For all of us, it was time to prepare.

At around this time, a group of prisoners, including Kerubino Kuanyin Bol, escaped from an SPLA prison. After successfully fleeing the prison, somewhere in Eastern Equatoria, Kerubino Kuanyin Bol left for the border with Uganda, where he, along with the rest of the political prisoners, now escapees, passed through Uganda undetected. They reached Nairobi, where they had a chance to meet with their families after a long absence. It was months later that this group of SPLA political prisoners hatched a plan whose details many people never knew. It was said that it had become clear that Kerubino, along with his comrades, were developing a plan to bring change to the SPLA. This was before the 1994 SPLM convention, where the movement ostensibly became more democratic.

We became aware of this plan when some people from our camp were called to Nairobi to meet with Kerubino and his allies. Some of those who went to Nairobi were Kerubino supporters who were promoted through the SPLA ranks by Kerubino himself while he was the SPLA Second-in-Command. Sometime later, the would-be rebels arranged a meeting at the home of Dr. Garang at Panyagor, in Bor. Among those who gathered at the rebel meeting at Panyagor were Joseph Oduwo, Riek Machar, Lam Akol and Kerubino. The meeting was unexpectedly brought to an end by the SPLA, which attacked the venue, killing the venerable Southern Sudanese politician, Joseph Oduwo, while the rest of the crowd, most of whom were soldiers, escaped unharmed.

Later, Kerubino was invited by some SPLA administrators in his home region to come pay a visit after so long. He was assured that nobody would attack him if he came in peace, but upon his arrival, he was met with fire. It was clearly a trap, and if he was to fight back, then his community would bear the brunt of the destruction. What transpired was a running battle between the SPLA and the Kerubino Bhar el Gazel Group, known as the Brigade. The rebellion only ended in 1998, when Kerubino returned to the SPLA fold, after successfully capturing the town of Wau, but then denied reinforcement. Asking for the SPLA to reinforce him ended in betrayal, yet again, and his forces left to be surrounded and defeated by a resurgent, but displaced, Sudan Armed Forces. Some of those people who left Kakuma were killed during the attempted capture of Wau. One thing that I liked about Kerubino's Wau battle was his capture of the Grinti Barracks.

But, before the incident in Wau, when Kerubino finally returned to the SPLA, the North Gogrial country had been left devastated. Young women were taken by force, to be married by soldiers, families were massacred, cattle looted and even grasses were cut during the growing season, before their seeds had ripened. It was so bad that when it was all over, goats and sheep had to be imported from the neighboring communities to help restock flocks that were decimated.

CHAPTER 27

LOPUR PRIMARY SCHOOL

We were confident that the Referendum voting we had just concluded was going to result in favor of secession. Though we didn't know by what majority, we were certain that it would be by a huge margin. South Sudan would be declared a new nation on July 9th, 2011. The official referendum results would be known in February 2011, as announced by the SSRC, but the preparation for a new state was already in high gear. Unless there was an invasion by the North, our independence was guaranteed.

A relative of mine befriended a Kenyan School teacher who was the headmaster of a school two hours walk north of Kakuma camp, deep in the arid Turkana countryside. The bush school was a standard Kenyan primary school, owned and funded by the African Inland Church. It must have been in the good graces of Kenyan President Daniel Arap Moi, who was a Church member and the nominal head of the AIC. The relative found a chance for me to study at that school. It was arranged for a few other Sudanese students and me to get ourselves to Lopur Primary School to enroll. Upon our arrival at the school, we all proceeded to go meet Mr. Oswana, the school headmaster. When we entered his office, Mr. Oswana informed us, "There is only one slot in class six. You are two too many. I need only one student to join class six." Apparently, Mr. Oswana and my relative never came to the particulars of the agreement, and so it fell to us contending students to decide who should remain and who should return to Kakuma Camp. This proposition was unpalatable.

The other student already had headway, and he was the one expected to fill the class spot. But Mr. Oswana, not wanting to get involved in what could have transpired, told the two of us contending students to, "Go outside my office and decide between yourselves who should fill the spot. Only one of you should come back here." While I thought I had the right to the chance, the other fellow was adamant that he was the one. We could not decide between ourselves because we were both ambitious and each wanted the spot for himself.

Sensing a misunderstanding, I informed the headmaster, "I will let this student take the spot. Between me and my relative, we should find another school if we are not going to get another chance here." I thought that the other student had no right to the spot and I was only leaving him the chance for two reasons: The fact that if my relative found out that I had left Lopur Primary School and not take the chance, that he would bring me back; and secondly, because I considered it unbecoming of a good Christian to argue over a matter like this.

Well, it turned out the happy camper had the chance and I went back to the camp dejected. However, a few days later, the headmaster, after having conversed with me, and after having seen me graciously yielded the spot felt that I might actually be a good student and someone good for the school. So, he sent for me. That is how I became enrolled at Lopur.

At Lopur, the headmaster became a good friend of mine, and he would ask me to come to his office to help him with his administrative work. I would read charts to him- just checking for accuracy. Slowly, I became a star student and very well regarded by most, yet also disregarded by some. Most Turkana students never paid attention in class and that led to lower grades and lower performance during national exams, including many failures and consequentially many dropouts. This all contributed to a social malaise in their community. So, to try to provoke some purpose into them, the teachers would employ the stroke of the whip to get their attention.

In some of the classes where the whip policy was severely employed, like the Mathematics classes, I became a recipient of the whip on a few occasions. The teacher, who was a kikuyu, would teach some topic for that day, and then the following day there would be a pop quiz on the topic of the day before. There were always ten Mathematics problems on the board, with the test timed for ten minutes, after which the notebooks would be collected, and then graded. The trouble came if a student had flunked any of the problems. Each failed problem would earn the student a single lash, so failing all ten would earn someone the whole ten lashes. Almost 99% of the class would fail at least one problem.

After a few of those lashes, I became one of the best performing students. I was second only to another student who passed all of his problems and received no lashings. I had improved steadily and markedly from my initial position, so that even the teacher took notice. One day, after two days of successfully avoiding the lashings, enjoying the benefit of excellent scores back-to-back, I was walking outside the schoolyard after leaving the hellish classroom. The uncompromising teacher saw me in the schoolyard and walked over to me. Surprisingly lighthearted, he asked, "Do you want to be number one?"

I didn't think that I could actually attain that rank. Surprised but grateful that such a tough teacher had even a sliver of confidence in my performance, I replied, still half-jokingly, "I don't know if I could pass enough problems to become number one, sir."

"I believe you can do it; if you study for it" he said. After that, we went our separate ways.

But, while I was having that exchange with the teacher, a few of our Sudanese students at the same school were seated under a shade tree, watching us talk. Afterwards, when I joined them in the shade, one of them asked me "What were you discussing with that teacher that made you grin? What could be good with that teacher?" he posed as sarcastically as he could muster. This surprised me somewhat, but I didn't think more about it at the moment. I told them about our conversation. This he replied to derisively with a laugh. "I think Mr. Kamau is out of his mind to even think that someone like you could beat Dhol. It has never been done before." He was defending the star student who was his friend and who was seated under the tree with them during our exchange. I joined in the derisive laughter, but the implication was not lost on me because I thought that the teacher was actually right- he had seen me rise from the bottom of the class to become the only other student who had successfully avoided the lashings. Until then, it was almost always only just one boy, Dhol, on whose account I was being badgered, who did well. But, I quietly promised myself, "Watch me," and I returned to our dormitory. Days later, the tough teacher left the school to look for other opportunities, but the dedication within me had just begun.

That term, I managed to do the unthinkable, at least to the fellow Sudanese who laughed derisively that afternoon. I became number one and not just once- I maintained that score, by margins, until I left Lopur near the end of 1995. Indeed, for the first time in my life, I ceased being a sloppy student anymore. I became popular with the teachers because I was passing their courses, which was an indicator that the teachers were doing their jobs right, and they would give assignments to me that showed their confidence and trust in me.

In the evenings, we would have chances to do homework and read by using the light of the pressure lamps. During those evening preps, some students would choose to make a lot of noise, to the detriment of other students. Complaints were being given to the headmaster, who would ask the teachers to stamp out the problem. The solution the teachers tried was to ask some students to quietly write the names of noisemakers, and to present the list to the teachers with the intention to punish the wrongdoers at the school assembly. But, those who would write the names would collude with the noisemakers, so nothing would come from the exercise. Noisemaking continued.

This happened repeatedly, leaving the teachers no choice but to look for someone who was trustworthy enough, and who wouldn't have fear about presenting such names. We were deep in the Turkana countryside, and some of those noisemakers had their relatives who were raiders, and who would go to the Sudan to raid their cousins, the Toposa, for cattle. They had guns at home and would not hesitate to use them against a Dinka, without redress.

But, it fell to me to write the names of such people and then to present the list to the teacher on duty. I decided to unabashedly do the right thing. The teacher, Mr. Eric, gave the paper to me. He told everyone reading, and doing homework, to read quietly. "Anybody making noise will have his or her name on the paper I have just handed to this student. Everybody, you better make no noise," he emphasized. The teacher, who was my friend, then left. My expectations were that the Turkana students would proceed to make noise no matter who was going to report their noisemaking. They thought that the teacher, a Borana, a member of a rival tribe to the Turkana, was never going to impose any punishment, or that perhaps a Dinka would never have the courage and the audacity to report on them.

The noisemakers went on making the loudest noise that had ever been heard in that study hall, prompting the teacher to come right back. Upon his appearance, the room went deathly quiet. We could hear the crickets outside, and the silent humming of the pressure lamp burning with the brightest light for miles around. However, the names were already faithfully recorded by me. The teacher approached me to inquire. "Do you have a list?" he asked.

To which, incredibly, I replied, "Yes!" I handed him the paper with the names of the most notorious noisemakers listed. That is what the teacher wanted.

The following day at the school assembly the majority of the noisemakers were found to be from the graduating class, class eight. The headmaster decided that the whole class was to be punished as a way to make them pay for all the trouble they had been causing at the school. The main culprit promised me, after their morning ordeal, that he would get even with me at a later time. Martin, the most notorious student noisemaker, whispered in my ear as he passed by me on the school grounds later that day, "*Utalia sana!*" ("You will cry a lot"). I knew that the threat was the easy part. If it is about me crying, I was ready to defend myself. There was no more noisemaking.

About a year after I had left the school, and was back at Kakuma Refugee Camp, one day I was walking along a road leading to the main town of Kakuma Town. Suddenly this fellow, Martin, came sauntering towards me along the same road. I thought to myself, "it is now or never." So there I was, finally approaching this fellow who wanted to take out revenge on me. We walked right up to each other, barely missing bumping into each other by a whisker, but without even a word uttered. He must have known that he was in the wrong, and that I did the right thing.

While at Lopur, church services on Sundays with the AIC were mandatory, given that the school was owned by that church. Two Turkana people typically led the church services. One was a youth leader, who led us in songs, and the other, an assistant pastor, who led us with some scripture readings and then prayers. The service never took more than an hour, because the assistant pastor didn't do any preaching beyond a few words of religious advice relevant to the students. The singing, the readings of the word from the Bible, and the short preaching, were all done in Kiswahili, the lingua franca of Kenya, and a mandatory school subject, just like the English language. There was also a pastor at school who was in charge of spiritual matters, even though he didn't always lead the services because he would be off preaching to the rest of the Turkana community in the surrounding villages.

It so happened that the pastor was given a brand-new bicycle, by the church, for his travels in the Turkana countryside. He never seemed interested in riding it around, though, being a man of God with little interest in material possessions. But, he would sometimes ask students to fetch him some water in jerry cans from the water well just ten minutes west of our school, near a seasonally dry stream. Seeing a chance to enjoy a bicycle ride, I decided to volunteer to fetch his water for him. I was so enthusiastic about it, asking him to lend me his bicycle every afternoon to fetch water for him after classes, and then staying away with the bicycle for quite awhile, that he began to be suspicious. Why was I the only Sudanese student so interested in helping him fetch water? Moreover, the other Turkana students were rarely too keen about helping out either.

Surely, there must have been something in it for me. He might've felt some guilt over somebody helping him, without receiving a dime. But, perhaps he realized that the altruistic fellow fetching water for him was actually enjoying riding the bicycle. Either that, or it was whispered to him. In any case, the pastor soon discontinued the use of his bicycle. Not surprisingly, I never returned to volunteer to fetch water for him using my shoulders.

Doing well at Lopur impressed the headmaster, so that he once told me, "I am glad I called you back to school after sending you back to the camp for lack of space at class six. If you have a good performance during the KCPE, a year down the road, it will bring the name of Lopur Primary School into great repute," he said. "I want you here!" he concluded. Thinking ahead, he considered that, no matter how well I did, going on to high school would be quite impossible because the Kenyan educational system would never allow a foreigner, even a well-performing one, to have a coveted place at one of the best schools at the national level. And so, he had hatched a brilliant plan: I would change my name to his, so that I would effectively be considered his son and therefore a Kenyan. "I want you to take my name, Joseph Oswana. Since your father's name is Joseph, the change should not be a problem," he said.

I thought it was really a great idea given all the benefits of studying at one of the most prestigious high schools in Kenya. It seemed a great way out of trouble, and a sure way to success for someone from the backwater of Southern Sudan, but my loyalty to my family and my family's name kept me in quandary. I told the well-meaning Mr. Joseph Oswana to give me time to think the issue over, and that I would get back to him in due course. There was still a lot of time, a year before I could sit for the exam. However, a year later, during my stay back at the Kakuma Refugee Camp for the August holidays, I decided to not return to Lopur. I elected instead to go to Iffo Dadaab Refugee Camp on the other side of Kenya, in the northeastern province, looking for a chance to get abroad from there. In effect, I was looking for an alternative way to a better education, different from Mr. Oswana's suggestion. Needless to say, Mr. Oswana was more than disappointed.

When I returned again to the Kakuma refugee camp in January of 1996, when there was still time to actually enroll in Standard Eight at Lopur for the national examination at the end of that year, I sent out a letter to Mr. Oswana to consider taking me back. I asked if I could be enrolled in class eight, but he replied that, if I returned to Lopur, I would need to enroll in standard seven, basically repeating the class, and then sit for the national exams in 1997. I refused to consider such a proposal because there was a chance to enroll in standard eight at my old school of Raja Primary, where I could sit for the national exam at the end of 1996. I didn't want to lose a year repeating a class.

So, I comfortably went back to Raja where I passed my exams relatively highly at the end of the year, and then got a chance to study at the Catholic Church's new school on the Kitale-Kapenguria highway in the Kenyan highlands. It was a wonderful chance that I took, and have never regretted.

And when the chance came to be considered for sponsorship at Kakuma, there were three agencies who offered wonderful chances for studies, though very little information to help considering which one to pick. There was the Jesuit Refugee Service, JRS, the Catholic Church at the camp, and the Don Bosco group.

The trouble with the JRS was that, even though they were willing to sponsor the best and the brightest, the options they offered for high school locations left a lot to be desired for a student who had gone to Nairobi and back to the Turkana District. While the JRS was really the top academic agency to associate with, the immediate offer was less than desirable, and this doomed it from the start. The JRS tried to offer uniforms of the destination schools to the Kakuma boys, in advance, and the immaculate uniforms did a lot to entice us, but those were just clothing and shoes.

The second group, the Saleseans of Don Bosco, had their strength in trade and technical education, such as masonry and the like. The other advantage was that they were willing to take students down country where the climate was good. They had taken students there, from Kakuma, the preceding years and the students were doing well, and so I assumed that they would do the same. Therefore, they seemed to really be the best choice.

The third group was the Catholic Church parish at Kakuma camp, staffed by the Apostles of Jesus order, who wanted seminarians, or future catholic priests. Even though I held no seriousness about becoming a priest at that time, this option was better than that of the JRS because there would be many chances to study abroad in whatever field one desired afterwards. Also, as a very prominent and wise relative once told me, being in the seminary was really a preparation for life afterwards, and not necessarily a waste of time, even if one was never going to be a priest. They taught character which, would be lacking in many other places.

So, for a while, a few friends and I dithered between these choices, while our answer to the sponsors was the simple "I am not sure yet". For me, the decision not to be with the JRS was really a foregone conclusion, because I didn't want to spend another four years close to Kakuma. I took my time telling them, though, because I was not sure if I really wanted to go to the Catholic Seminary, and it was said that the Don Bosco people were considering the JRS place of study, Kakuma Boys Secondary School, which is close to Kakuma. So, for me, waiting that confirmation, Don Bosco choice would fall on the way side. If Don Bosco offered scholarships to the Kakuma Boys Secondary School, I would decline their offer.

Finally, a JRS Sister had waited long enough for my decision. She asked me point-blank, one day, "Have you made a decision yet? I need an answer right now! It has taken too long."

I told her what I had already decided: I was not taking their offer. Though the English Sister was incensed, she took back the uniform, and left quietly smiling. I thought she might have been informed of my strategy, and likely choice. One choice was out, down to two.

Then, the Don Bosco people, in the person of the no-nonsense German Mr. Pressman, summoned my friends and me to their office. Once we were seated, Mr. Pressman asked us point-blank: "Who is going to Secondary School?" to which one of our friends replied in the affirmative. "And the rest?" he asked, to which the rest of us replied in the negative. Mr. Pressman uttered an expletive, and told us to leave his office. I think he must have been informed of our dithering in making a choice, given our other chances.

Therefore, by elimination, it fell to the Catholic Church parish to take us to the new Bakhita School in Kitale. The choice was arrived at by default. Even if I didn't want to go to that school, there was no turning back at that point. I made this choice because I really wanted to be away from the extreme heat of Kakuma, even thought it was clear to me that there would be no great learning there.

However, while there, we discovered that we actually got a wonderful education, to our surprise. In a way, we not only had the academics, but we also had the necessary character training. This was despite the fact that some priests thought that students such as us, with very high passing marks, shouldn't have gone to a school whose main aim was preparing priestly candidates for priesthood. It did happen that, of all the members of our seminary classes at Bakhita, only one eventually became a catholic priest. The rest are now all around the globe, and back home in South Sudan, where they are clearly leaders of their communities. Almost all of them are leaders in parliaments, governments, and in the private sector presently in South Sudan. One can never have enough hope for a bunch of brothers

In 1992, when we arrived at Lokichogio from the Sudan, the town was the launching pad for the OLS, Operation Lifeline Sudan, a UN aid relief program in Southern Sudan. And even though I didn't have the chance to fully explore Lokichoggio-being refuges, the Kenyan Authorities confined our movements to only the outskirts of the Loki and no chance to venture into town for any reason-to find out how developed it was, I never thought that Lokichogio was any different from Lodwar, the district headquarters. But when I had the chance to return to Loki in early 1997, five years later, it was interesting to take note of the development that had occurred in that time. In the company of the parish priest at Kakuma, who was happy that some of the brightest students had made his school their choice and was rewarding us in a way with a trip to Lokichogio, almost tripping over himself trying to please us, we came to a small compound belonging to the O.L.S. The level of development that I saw proved to me that even the arid regions could host towns. The little compound was surrounded with low fencing of barbed wire, lined by a flower bed, following the length and breadth of the fence. Also within the mesh, there were light bulbs for night-lighting, and within the center of the compound was a small Gazebo, perched like a small hut for congregating in the evenings.

It was inspiring to see that such a development could be possible in the arid region of the Turkana District. I thought that this could be an example for anyone interested in making Africa livable in the modern sense. Even the airport hub was a testament to the development-minded aid workers. Maybe it was the money that made Lokichogio. I guess money can actually buy development, as it did for the city of Juba, and of course Khartoum. As someone in the know once told me, by 2000, there was $18 billion spent on relief effort into the Sudan, over the course of many years, beginning around 1988, and therefore, Loki doubtlessly benefited from the aid money. But perhaps it was mostly the skill and engineering poured into development at Loki that made it a jewel overnight.

While at Panyido, our caretaker, Mabor, was issued a brand-new bicycle, which he would leave at the bookstore where I worked as the guard for the bundles and boxes of schoolbooks. Looking at the bicycle, it appeared to me that I could actually ride it, even though I had never ridden a bicycle before. While in South Sudan, before leaving for Ethiopia, I had been on bicycles, but they were ridden by someone else. One time, I got my feet caught in the rear tire spokes, while on a ride with my father to my birthplace at Chong. The ride was only memorable for the accident which was so excruciating. I was just a little boy and everything else was a blur, except for that pain. In Wau, I had chances to be on a bicycle ridden by someone, but to ride a bicycle myself was something I had yet to do. Only my confidence could convince me that I could do it. Still, I did not try to ride Mr. Mabor's bicycle. It was finally in Kakuma, though, that I had the opportunity to try riding a bicycle.

When I got to Kakuma camp, the Ethiopian refugees, who were more entrepreneurially inclined than the Sudanese refugees, opened a small bicycle training ground, located at the field at the center of the camp. A few Kenya shillings would earn a rider a few laps on the bicycle around a small track of bare ground. The track wound downhill a bit, into a gully that drained into the seasonal river meandering around the camp. This area was later named the Lazy Man Park. I was among the customers. The initial moment that I stepped on the bicycle, it was impossible to maintain my own balance, let alone the balance of the bicycle, but after several attempts over a few days, I was able to go for an enjoyable ride around the field. I ended up burning through several Kenya shillings to reach this victory, and I continued to celebrate every time I had some coins in my hands.

The rides became so popular that all the boys seemed to want to be there, drawing the attention of the camp managers. This especially drew the attention of Fr. Akot, who always made sure that any boy who was becoming a vagabond, and not paying attention at school, was called to task. He made sure that he preached about the vices, and encouraged good behavior. He counseled against some boys becoming sawalik, criminals, as much as he talked about the scourge of AIDS. I think that most of us pulled away from the bicycle rides because of his admonishing. Indeed, a word to the wise was enough for most of us. After Fr. Akot's departure from the camp, things changed somewhat. But while he was there, most boys were kept from crossing over to the dark side. Fr. Akot kept a lid on happenings like the bicycle rides, robberies at night, drinking, fighting, and the secretive videos of questionable imagery. In a way, Fr. Akot was the conscience of the camp.

But the ranks of the boys who spent their days riding bicycles still swelled, and as a consequence some suffered ghastly injuries to the limbs after falling from the bicycles which were so run down and old that they ought to have never been brought to the fields. It goes to point out that, even if free market is allowed, there must be regulation involved or the customer may not know how to tell the good items from the dangerous items. The customer is smart, but not wise all the time. Yet there were some benefits to learning how to ride a bicycle. Once one was confident on the bicycle, one could ride a few laps around the adult groups, where the few girls at the camp were based. It was always in order, if just to show the girls how smart on bicycles the suitor was. I had a tough fall once, where I grazed my hands and knees, but remained in high spirits because the fall happened after the desired impression was made.

It was an ongoing challenge to win the attention of the few girls available at the camp. One such girl was so beautiful that she became the most prized by the majority of the boys. She also caught my eye, and I decided to throw in my hat, even if it would be tough getting her attention, because she seemed to be a sophisticated Towner, while most of us were lacking in that manner. I decided to find a way to get to her heart, or to her proximity, which I did through a series of letters, including an English letter given to a teacher, to be translated to Kiswahili, as if it was a school paper, and then smuggled to the girl through the hands of a trusted cousin. I waited one week for a response. I received the necessary 'Yes' (The girl agreed to date). However, upon hearing this, and not to be outdone, the crowd of other boys descended on the same girl. My relationship with her was in tatters before it ever began.

There was a teacher at the camp who started using some of the money from his teaching arrears to open a business, retailing soda drinks and other goods. This brought him so much cash and profits that he became wealthy, by the camp standards, quite overnight. However, because he had no plan to manage success, the cash went away as fast as he got his hands on it. He ended up worse than when he began, and people snickered about it. But, his example did lead many people at camp in the entrepreneurial direction. The teachers didn't follow suit, however. No teacher thought that he could be a teacher as well as an entrepreneur. Indeed by the time the boys were leaving the camp to go to the US, a doctor at the camp, by the name Mr. Arokdit, had opened a shop, with his sons, for cold drinks. Their refreshment shop rivaled those of the Ethiopian traders, the businessmen of the camp. So, It took awhile for the Sudanese to develop the business savvy of the Ethiopians.

Indeed, in the Turkana District, trade was done mostly by the down country people, with the Kikuyu dominating the smaller shops and bazaars, while the Somali businessmen controlled the large stores, wholesale and retail. Though there would be a few Indians, the Kikuyu and the Somali mostly controlled the trade. When it came to the refugees, the Ethiopians controlled most of the luxury market items, followed closely by the Somali refugees, while the Sudanese really had nothing much to show, as far as business. A student from Germany, who I met at the University of Rochester in 2004, once asked me, "How can the Indians get so rich in Africa while you, the Africans have nothing?" He showed me a fellow student whose parents were so wealthy that their son drove a Mercedes at school, and said "they got that wealth from Africa!" This made me think that perhaps Mario, the atypically named German student, was right. Was it that we were never entrepreneurial? But I quickly found out that that was not the case. It was because of the economic set-up. Some Africans are cattle keepers or farmers, at mostly the subsistence level, with no reason to seek trade. The taste for trade goods isn't really present, as trade is simply localized. Learning is needed to push the Africans to be their own agents of development.

CHAPTER 28

DADAAB

In February 2011, the results of the referendum were announced by the Southern Sudan Referendum Commission, SSRC. Secession was favored by 98% of Southern Sudanese. The North swiftly recognized South Sudan, and promised to be the first to establish an embassy in the new Republic's capital, Juba. Yet we all knew never to trust anything coming out of North Sudan. Indeed, just two months removed from the formal declaration of independence for South Sudan, the North invaded Abyei. I was traveling to South Sudan when I heard of this news on the way. The SPLA decided to back down. Clearly war was the only option the North was left with to stop the South from seceding. They had thought the referendum would end in a unity vote. They were disappointed.

While I was at Dadaab's Iffo camp, there was a murder of a southern Sudanese man from the Kakua tribe by the notorious Somali bandits, the perennially rebellious Shifta. This incident made us painfully aware that the dangers of being in northeastern Kenya were simply much greater than we had first thought, and the risks were worse because we were unregistered and unrecognized refugees, without UN protection. It was said by some in the know that the murdered men, and his family, were actually from the Uganda Kakua community, posing as southern Sudanese to gain resettlement in the West, something that many Anywak and Nuer at the camp were also guilty of.

However, the real trouble at the spot was the continuous threat from the Somali Shifta bandits. They were known to have cut open the bellies of pregnant women,[73] who they found, without strong protection, outside the camp confines. It was simply unthinkable to be outside your compound at night, and also never advisable to be outside in the bush by yourself. It behooved the traveler to stay in a group. In that area, there was safety in numbers. The compound was surrounded by a thorn fence, and was properly secured by a gate which was closed and monitored at night. At these times, sometimes scouts would give quiet warnings to the dwellers, as a way to keep us safe, and alive. We also made a point to broadcast a rumor that we were tough on robbers at night. We made sure this was passed to the Somali community, because it paid to be seen as tough. There was speculation that some members of the Shifta were actually among the Somali refugees resident in the camp, but this was not admitted to by any in the Somali community.

So, when we were woken up at night by a gunshot, and the subgroup stirred into commotion to find that a man was shot, with the Shifta running out the open gate of the compound, I was not surprised. This was a recurrent episode from my time as a refugee. It happened with the Turkana night raiders at Kakuma. It also happened with the night commotions at Panyido, where we feared the legendary Nyanjuan, but faced the actual dire threat of the Tigrinya. Night shootings also occurred at Magos, where there was a fatal shooting at night of boys and an SPLA guard by the Toposa. And of course there were the Murahilin raids. All these prepared me for being woken up at night to the sounds of an attack. After learning of what had happened, I promptly went back to my sleep, which was cut short by the noise.

The following day, we found out that the wounded man had died at the hospital. His family had hopes for resettlement, but now they would have to go on without their father. Then ensued the culturally mandated

---

[73] This was more on the side of rumor than factual for I never saw a pregnant woman with belly cut open even though it was said the *shifta* would do it to any woman, even the Somali women. It was said that it happened to only fewer women. Moreover, apart from being stealthy, the *Shifta* could not be made accountable because there was no formal justice system in place

seven days of mourning, with drumming at night by the Kakua people. The forlorn drumming and singing became quite unbearable for the rest of us who wanted nothing more than a quiet night's rest. It was like the Muezzin blaring out *"Allah Akbar"* through the loudspeakers, waking up everybody in the neighborhood. However, we were sorry for the family and the community of Kakua, who were so stricken with grief. Even if they might never have been Southern Sudanese, they were relatives of Southern Sudanese.

Needless to say, the subgroup defenses were fortified further by having the thorny fence reinforced and the gate closed promptly at sunset and guarded, in turns, throughout the night. And if any straggler, who might have made a friendship with some Somalis, was outside the compound after closing time, this fellow would have to remain outside until the following morning. We would not suffer another intrusion. It was better to require that such a person face a night outside, then to endanger the rest of the people. I thought that was quite smart. It actually showed our resolve at staying out of danger, for we all wanted to survive this refugee experience. Nobody wanted to miss out on the promise and the beauty of eventually making it to a first world country.

Dadaab's Iffo camp was thoroughly Islamic. It often seemed like a little camp just outside Riyadh for the cacophony of the Somali children singing their hearts out at their Islamic madrasas, and writing the koranic verses to be recited on the small wooden tablets distributed to each student. For the Somali, as for all other Muslims, recitation of the Koran was the most important aspect of their education. The Islamic Somali community received aid from Saudi Arabia. This could partly be seen by the abundance of so much bala, or date fruits. This fruit was so plentiful that it seemed to have been grown somewhere north of the camp. It was said that the Saudi aid during Ramadan was a great contribution to the Somali needs at the camp. One other international non-governmental aid agency who provided help was the Danish International Development Agency, or DANIDA. This agency gave aid to the Muslim Somalis, even though the Somali children would sneer at us for carrying the holy rosary. One of them even insulted Jesus. We responded by, of course, happily insulting the Prophet Mohammed, for was he not responsible for the troubles in Southern Sudan? We were almost about to end up in blows, but other Sudanese standing nearby intervened. Not that the Somalis preferred blows. They preferred knives, and if a Somali had drawn a knife, he was going to use it, even on a woman. This puzzled us Dinka.

A truly comical incident happened once at Iffo. While the Sudanese community was housed in the three subgroups of Sudan I, II, and III, ethnic animosities were quietly simmering. This was fueled in part by the political fortunes of Southern Sudan back home, where the SPLM/ SPLA movement, the vanguard of the Southern Sudanese people in their struggle for freedom, was divided into two major camps. One was the SPLM Mainstream, or the Torit Faction, led by Dr. John Garang, a Dinka. The other was the Nasser Faction, led by Dr. Riak Machar, a Nuer, and supported by Dr. Lam Akol, a Shilluk.[74] The camp subgroups mirrored, more or less, those divisions. The ethnic and political whisperings reached a crescendo, so that one day a fight broke out in broad daylight, just outside the backyards of our two subgroups of Sudan II and Sudan III. Sudan II was a Nuer group, while Sudan III was group of Dinka and equatorians, mirroring directly the Nasser and the Torit factions as they were at home at that time. However, the major difference is that the men of Sudan III did flinch that day. Men who were never known to back down during a fight, and never to flinch if challenged by another man, did indeed show their worst selves that evening, for all to see. The Nuer men were left in stitches, and took advantage of the situation to herd the Dinka men back into their Sudan III area every time they developed the courage to get back at them. Even a single Nuer, throwing a spear, stone, stick or piece of wood at the Dinka men, would turn the whole cowering crowd on its heels, so that the back gate to the Sudan III compound was never wide enough for the fleeing throng.

The Nuer had a field day that day, and the Dinka women spectators were not amused. In fact, they were quite indignant, and one stalwart

---

[74] The Shilluk are a tribe of the Nilotic Community in the Upper Nile region of South Sudan

older woman stood up to drive men back, and lead in the charge against the Nuer, but then the Dinka men instead came rushing back at the sight of the Nuer coming at them, dancing and laughing away. It was simply a scandal of profound proportions, as we were reminded by the courageous women that night. Our group was so scared, or maybe they simply didn't want to get injured, given that the promise of freedom seemed close by. At Kakuma Refugee Camp, where the majority were Southern Sudanese refugees, going to a third country, invariably a first world country, was very limited. Only very few people got accepted. That was not the case at Dadaab. The majority Somali Refugees got a chance en masse to go to a third country in the western world. Southern Sudanese refugees who relocated to Dadaab Refugee Camp from Kakuma or elsewhere hoped to be part of the mass resettlement exercise at Dadaab. Being injured, or even dying in this manner, would simply be absurd. The sight of blood from an injured fellow would send the throngs fleeing again.

The greatest fear was injury or death, given that most hoped to get resettled within the space of a few months. We were prudent survivors, and it seemed like it made no sense to die in a fight whose objective was immaterial. Why would one leave Southern Sudan, cross the whole country of Kenya to come to Dadaab, only to die at the hands of the Ethiopian Nuer, not even our own Nuer. Such a thought was simply unacceptable. We were far away from home and we looked and acted the part. The UN had no part in it, given that most of those in the two subgroups were simply unregistered refugees and the UN didn't care to bring in the Kenya security to intervene. We were each persona non grata.

However, that evening, inside a hall, lit by lamps with the patter of rain outside, a war council was finally in session because our pride as the Dinka men who must never flinch nor flee from a fight was now wounded, seemingly beyond repair in the eyes of our women, and it was our duty to rectify the anomaly. We were to teach the Nuer a lesson to recognize who we were. The war council was convened to plan and to organize an overnight raid to the Nuer Sudan II area, and if need be, to engage in a fight with the aim of killing of some Nuer. There was going to be no holding back. The fight was now on, and nothing was going to stop it. Men were now men and the women in attendance started ululating, showing their approval. We were finally coming back to our senses. However, there arrived an emissary sent by the Nuer, and braving the Shifta in the dark of the night, with a message: Peace. The Nuer had been warned of a meeting, by the Dinka planning a vengeful attack that would devastate them. The Nuer had realized why the members of the Sudan III group initially did not want to fight: Because they were prudent. But the Nuer also realized that those members of Sudan III would return to fight after all, for their pride was now wounded. The Nuer wanted peace.

This message caught our leaders by surprise and gave them, and those who really never wanted to get injured or die in a senseless fight, the excuse they needed to stop the attack. The Nuer did not want to fight, and they felt sorry for their actions that day. With this, the fight was prevented. Had the Nuer not acted, I think there was going to be many causalities on our side and a massacre on the side of the Nuer.

In late 1999, the U.S. started processing minors to go to the United States. So, it turned out to be real. The planned move was known to camp managers back in 1995. That was when our group of refugees had left the confines of the Kakuma camp to go to Dadaab. After five intense months, our refugee community was forced to go back to Kakuma Refugee again.

The UNHCR loaded everybody who was willing to leave onto rented trucks for the journey back to Kakuma. The UN did not want the Sudanese Refugees to cross from northwest Kenya at Kakuma to northeast to Dadaab to seek resettlement in the West. It was too costly and dangerous. Dadaab was close to Somalia and therefore easy for Somalis but far from Kakuma and Southern Sudan. It was cheaper for Southern Sudanese to stay at Kakuma rather than in Dadaab. Moreover, Kakuma was relatively safer than Dadaab. The Turkana bandits were less atrocious than the brutal shifta and the security cost was lower for the UN at Kakuma than at Dadaab. Therefore, the Sudanese needs would better be addressed at Kakuma than at Dadaab. And if the UN had allowed the few Sudanese at Dadaab to go abroad en masse, the remaining Sudanese at Kakuma would all have traveled to Dadaab.

When everybody was in the trucks, and ready to leave, at the outskirts of Dadaab's Iffo Camp, we received a parting message. A Burundian Canadian, who was officiating, whistled to us and said. "Hey everyone, listen up. Goodbye, everyone. I apologize for you having to leave the Iffo Camp. You will be alright at Kakuma." However, at the end of his speech, he also said, "See you in USA." To me, it seemed to be a statement of mockery, and I am pretty sure I am the only who heard such a passing comment. For everybody in the trucks, the hope for a great life in the west was gone. I thought the camp manager was plain mean to mock us. I now know what he knew then- many Southern Sudanese were going to ultimately make it abroad, if they wanted. It proved to be true, four years later.

CHAPTER 29

BAKHITA

After the people of Southern Sudan were enslaved and persecuted for decades, they were now a free people. Southern Sudan had now become South Sudan; the rest was now history. The people of South Sudan had assumed their place among the peoples of the world. From here on out, none would pity them in the world. And as in the story of Bakhita, a tragic past was turned into a blessing for the people of South Sudan. Josephine Bakhita was a slave girl abducted from Khordufan, Sudan, in 1877, by Arab slave traders. After enduring mistreatment in the captivity of various owners, she finally made it to Italy, where she joined an order of Catholic nuns, and eventually became a nun herself.[75] The story of Bakhita has been retold countless times inside the Sudan for so many people, including Southern Sudanese. *Bakhita*, "Lucky" in Arabic, was among the lucky ones. Southern Sudan was also lucky. As Bakhita became a free human being once again, also South Sudan had become a nation, sovereign and free.

The Catholic Diocese of Rumbek built a school in Kitale, Kenya dedicated to the education of South Sudanese and named it Bakhita Formation Center. Most of those studying at the Bakhita Center High School were expected to become Catholic priests. Indeed, it was an expectation of the Diocese of Rumbek, Wau and El Obeid that those under training would go on to become members of what is known as

---

[75] Josephine Bakhita died in 1947 and was canonized by John Paul II in 2000.

the Major Seminary. That was where the real work of Catholic Priest formation actually began. The Minor Seminary at the High School level was for the fundamentals. Here was where the real candidates, who were fit and willing, were first identified, and where the virtues of a good priest were first inculcated. Indeed, one expectation was that the young men would never engage in any premarital relationship, and our little book of seminarian laws indicated as much: There was never going to be any relationship with the opposite sex that was of a physical nature. Engagement in direct relationship between a young man in training and a girl which could lead to intimate relationships and even fornication, was not permitted.

While fornication was expressly a sin for any catholic young person, it was especially frowned upon for anyone under formation to be a future priest. One might ask as to how someone under such an expectation, upon leaving the confines of the school and being away from the watchful eyes of the priests and the religious, would refrain from engaging in a relationship with the opposite sex. The answer is quite interesting, and it shows the maturity of the Catholic Church.

The young men were merely expected to observe the ruling, a law of the young seminarians. By agreeing to be a seminarian, under his own volition, where the door was always open to leave, the young man had submitted himself to be governed by such a rule of life. The rule was not only a pact made with the Seminary School teachers, but also it was fundamentally an agreement between the young man and God, the head of the church. By this agreement, the young person knew in his heart that he was always accountable. While the visible enforcer of the rule was sometimes not present, the invisible enforcer, God, was always present. This was especially true at times when the young man was alone, and when he might think that he could get away with breaking the rule because nobody from the Seminary School was with him.

This concept was emphasized one time during a visit by the co-founder, an elderly Italian Priest who, along with Bishop Mazzoldi, formed the order the Apostles of Jesus, made up exclusively of East Africans. When a question about celibacy, and the call to follow this way of life for the young men, came up, the priest gave a short hearty speech, delivered with humor and good grace, about the rule. He said it was a contract between God, through his Church, and those who so chose voluntarily to follow it.

"If someone decides to marry, there is no problem in such a choice because this is God's intention. And if someone has so generously decided to serve God that he becomes a Catholic priest, then God also blesses such a choice. Priesthood is contingent on a life of celibacy, though, as this is basically a sacrifice and a gift back to God, in the service of God and his people. Whether to marry or to remain celibate is all good in the eyes of God. The trouble is when one decides to serve God as a priest, and at the same time decides to marry. Such a behavior breaks the accepted and established Catholic Church's contract with God in the service provided by the priesthood. The Catholic Church has decreed that in order to serve God better in the service of priesthood, that those who so decide should remain celibate, as a tradition.

The Catholic Church also recognizes that one can serve God equally well in a married life, that both priestly and married life are good and pleasing to God, but separate with separate requirements and commitments. Therefore, if a young man who had decided to serve God as a Catholic Priest, then decides to date girls, he should simply change his mode of service to God by deciding to go ahead and marry, and to serve God as a family man. The call to marriage, and the call to priesthood, are both vocations but separate with different requirements and commitments," he lectured.

By this understanding, it was almost impossible to continue to maintain relationships of an intimate nature with the opposite sex, while professing to be a young man on the verge of becoming a Catholic Priest. Moreover, such a notion would not be possible knowing that the all-knowing God would hold you to account. Just because the Catholic enforcers were not there to witness the relationship, didn't mean that someone was in the clear with respect to the rule of Seminary life.

When the Bakhita Center was inaugurated, the administration made a point of making the school quickly self-reliant by making use of the lush and arable farmland it sat on, and by purchasing livestock in the form of pigs for pork and dairy cattle for milk. The rest of the fields would be used for farming corn and vegetables to supplement the diet of the students and staff. This policy was quite effective, and in the space of four years the number of dairy cows increased from two to eight. The school administration employed the use of artificial insemination, which the mostly Dinka student body considered a strange way to make the cows produce offspring. The Dinka, who were almost always cattle keepers and masters at anything to do with cows, believed it made sense to choose the best bull from infancy, and to make that bull the sole sire of all the offspring in the herd. The use of technology in merely extracting semen to be artificially inseminated was strange, however it worked!

One notable figure at Bakhita was Brother Ben, who taught Geography and Chemistry among other subjects, and who loved the outdoors, always walking the grounds of the school with his binoculars. Brother Ben was the man behind our popular country walks every afternoon just after the Sunday Mass, and lunch. We would leave in groups, usually by classes, to walk anywhere among the farms and the countryside of the Trans Nzoia District of Kenya. But we could never get further than a few miles, not only because we were on foot, but also because being absent for the evening adoration ceremony was tantamount to committing a sacrilege. We were known to all the priests, and even the staff, including John the gatekeeper. So if there was even a slight indication that someone was missing, it wouldn't take long to discover who had wandered too far on the country walk. It was simply unthinkable to even be late, let alone to be absent.

One might assume that we were deterred because of the kind of punishment we would receive, and indeed this was the case. While nobody was caned, as happened in the other Kenyan schools, verbal shaming and damning was the mode of punishment. Sometimes, the words at the school assembly would be so painful that even physical punishment would be desirable. Often times, the public shaming and damnation was too painful to endure, but there was no choice.

One morning Brother Ben arranged for us to visit the nearby Mt. Elgon Game Reserve. He took our whole group there using several

Kenyan matatus (minibuses), and by around ten we were at the top of the mountain. We took photographs and peered down upon the Kenyan farms in the valley below. We had a picnic and saw wildlife, including the nasty buffaloes who seemed never in the mood to be approached. At the top of the mountain, climbing became quite tough as the air grew thinner and cooler. Our lungs stung with the pain of exertion, leaving everyone gasping for more air and finding barely enough to continue climbing.

Lacking enough oxygen, the climb was tougher than we had thought, though we were all young and athletic. This showed how tough Brother Ben was, for he was right there with us. During the climb, we came to a dark cave frequented by elephants. The cave itself is at the lower levels of the mountain. Not right at the top of the Mount Elgon. The cave was so dark that you couldn't make anything out, unless you used torchlight. Even if you held your hand in front of your face, you couldn't see it. But the elephants would somehow still navigate in the dark and stay safe in the rocky cave, where they would eat the salts, which was mixed with the precipitates oozing from the ceiling of the cave.

How the elephants navigated through the dark was anyone's guess. For those who have lived in the Sudan, it is no secret how dark it gets at night, but even so, one can make out some shapes or at least sense that there is something in a certain direction. Not so in the Mt. Elgon cave, which one must visit to believe. Here in the pitch-dark cave, one couldn't see a thing, even during the daytime. It was quite a wonder to behold.

Of all the schoolteachers at Bakhita, Brother Ben was the most knowledgeable and sophisticated. Brother Ben's knowledge, mostly of Geography and Chemistry, was vast, and he taught with examples clear enough to be understood by the student. As for Geography, my favorite subject, Brother Ben taught it by showing examples from his country, New Zealand, and its two islands, the North and the South. He also discussed the inhabitants of these islands, the European settlers and the indigenous people, the Maori. Not only did we hear and read stories, but we also saw videos of these aspects of New Zealand's geography, peoples and history. This teaching aid was never employed by the other Kenyan teachers, owing partly to the lack of means, but also owing to teaching through rote learning, something that Brother Ben was already past.

And not only was his teaching based on textbooks and videos, he also made sure that we had plenty of outdoor learning. We took learning visits to museums, agricultural shows, game parks and reserves and commercial farms, and we took country walks to observe rocks and rock formations. It was empirical learning, where we were largely taught by example. He instructed so well that Chemistry, the other subject he taught us, became my other favorite subject, and the other one that I excelled in. In fact, when I got to the U.S., thinking that I would like and excel in Chemistry, I was surprised to find that I didn't do well in it there. The teacher was not as passionate about the subject as Brother Ben was, and it was my results that suffered. It takes a teacher who loves a subject and the art of teaching to bring students to success in learning the subject. My U.S. chemistry teacher struck me as someone who either never liked the subject, or simply taught in an uninspired way that led me to not do well in the subject.

Brother Ben also taught us about the geography of the great wide North America. Before I set foot in the United States and Canada, I knew about the lumberjacks, and how they would cut wood from the tall trees, and then send the logs along the river ways to the Pacific coast for export, and how the land of Canada freezes over during the winter. I also learned about the Russian Tundra, the frozen grassland that brings forth flowers during a short spring and summer, only to freeze over for the rest of the long winter months. I also learned about permafrost, where the ground, even the soil, stays frozen throughout the year, for years on end. Such facets of geography were simply amazing, and a reason one should travel the world.

Another distinct place visited by our class for field trips during my stay at Bakhita was the catholic girls' secondary school of St. Monica. One can easily imagine how the boys felt to be suddenly in a co-ed school surrounded by girls. As members of our all-boys school, we were expressly forbidden from having any intimate relationships with the opposite sex, but here we were allowed to visit another school made up of all girls, and permitted to intermingle freely for a whole day. It was the equivalent of an army graduating from a lengthy, strict training regimen, and suddenly allowed into a town to scavenge. But at St. Monica, even though we were allowed to spend time with the girls, we were basically just attending classes with them to shake up our mundane routine of four years of classes with only young men along with our teachers, among whom were a few females.

Upon arrival we were briefly allowed to intermingle with the girls, with each one of us quickly and happily identifying the girl we wished to spend time with and to sit next to in class. Then we were ushered into class sessions, one after the other, with strict attention demanded by the teachers at every class, and every whispering conversation severely frowned upon and potentially punishable, though mostly we avoided this trap. The girls were awfully smart and I couldn't believe how a girl could beat me in answering math problems on the board that took me a few seconds to decipher.

We soon learned that the girls excelled at these types of problems because they had been well-taught, using rote learning techniques. As was the practice by Kenyan High School teachers in preparation for the Form Fours before the national exams, the girls at the Catholic School were taught using a more mechanical method. As for us, our learning style was a little more modern and so, even though most of the problems the teachers were throwing at us were really relatively easy, the girls were far ahead in terms of having it all in their heads. But, the awe never escaped any of us. We were full of appreciation and joy later in the evening, as we boarded our school bus back to Bakhita, and addresses and contact numbers were exchanged, and even a few hugs shared.

A week later, the administration at Bakhita found it necessary to begin screening the letters coming through because it seemed we were all of a sudden getting carried away from our central purpose at Bakhita.

Another place we visited on a formal academic basis was the nearby Gosetta Farm which was a commercial diary and coffee farm. While the visit was in relation to our geography class, focused on how the Kenyan

Highlands, formerly the White Highlands, favored the growing of tea and coffee, and the keeping of the Western European milk cows, the teachers made more than that. They made sure that every student at our school was involved, treating the visit as both an outing, and also as an educational tour of the farm for geography, biology, agriculture, and even chemistry.

We took the usual tour of the machinery, observing the coffee machine that did the separation of the best coffee beans from the rest, and then watching cows being milked with milking machines. But, for Brother Ben from New Zealand, the practice was awfully wanting in hygiene, and he thought it was actually better to milk the cows by hand, as was done back home in Southern Sudan. Still, we never left the farm without being in awe at the sophistication of the Kenyan farmers, albeit within unhygienic conditions. The technology was simply awesome and we always appreciated the chance to be at Gosetta.

As much as Gosetta was fascinating, our country walks among the farms between Kitale and Kapenguria showed us even more about the Kenyan communities of that area, and how farming was the fabric of their lives. The volcanic red soil has sufficient fertility to produce enough yields from a small plot for a family to subsist on. However, the people were still poor and this was evident in the clothing worn, especially by the women and girls, and in the look of the countryside.

Indeed, while we made friendships with the folks we met, especially with those who might have previously traveled to the Sudan, including a former truck driver who was fond of the Sudanese, the walks themselves were rejuvenating. The exercise we gained from walking mile after mile through the valleys and hills, and breathing in the pure country air, cold and clean, was enough to clear our minds and rejuvenate our spirits to return to Bakhita and do well in whatever duty we faced. Indeed, without such country walks, Bakhita would have been a prison for all of us. Even though there was enough to be experienced every day inside the compound, from farming to sports to prayers to studies to the entertainment of movies, the change of scenery every week was essential, not to mention that it also provided another chance to meet some girls, especially towards the town of Kitale.

It was at this time that our beloved Monsignor Mazzolari was named the bishop of the diocese of Rumbek, which was based in exile at Bethany House in Nairobi, and ran Bakhita Center, our school. So it was with great pride and gratitude that I joined a group of students from our school to travel from Kitale to Nairobi for a surprise welcoming of the bishop at the Kenyatta international airport. He had arrived from Rome, consecrated, because such a ceremony could not be held in Southern Sudan due to the civil war. Khartoum would likely bomb the venue to pieces. The Bishop of El Obeid, an Arab, who had escaped to Kenya to administer to the displaced Christians of his diocese, was constantly hunted whenever he ventured inside SPLA-held territories with airplanes looking out for his small aircraft transports around the Nuba Mountains. It was a stealthy operation for the Bishops.

Bishops, when traveling or away from their flock, don't seem to be any different from anybody else. They will even hide their huge crucifixes in their breast pockets, so that only their white collars and black shirts could possibly identify them as clergyman or pastors, and I think this is done for their safety. Bishop Mazzolari would also travel in this manner. He seemed surprised, but joyous, when he was presented with flowers by the sisters, and greeted by a cross-section of the community who he represented, from students to clergymen to other religious leaders. The Kenyan airport staff, and the travelers, merely looked surprised, but maintained their professional composure.

Before long, we were back at the Bishop's residency for a party that evening, before retiring to our hostel later on. The following morning, we traveled back to Kitale, arriving at our school in the late afternoon. But, the bishop was grateful by such a show of gratitude, and he was ready to do more, not only for the Catholic Church he was leading, but also for all Southern Sudanese across the board. Bishop Mazzolari became more than just a churchman posted to the Sudan by Rome and by his missionary organization, the Comboni Missionaries. He also became a leader for all south Sudanese, for politicians and the peasants alike. If Daniel Comboni established the catholic faith in the Sudan, Mazzolari not only helped nurture it, but he also led the society politically and patriotically. He became a south Sudanese, through and through.

The Bishop of Wau, Rudolf Deng Majak, the tall, lanky Dinka churchman, paid us a visit once at Bakhita. Years later, when I returned to Wau as an adult in 2010, I had my picture taken with Majak and was surprised to find that I was a slightly taller than him. Yet, back then at Bakhita, he surely towered over most of us. The good bishop spent most of his time in the besieged town of Wau, rarely getting out to administer to the Christians in the vast Wau Diocese, let alone getting abroad to Kenya to lead the Christians of his diocese there. The diocese of Rumbek, therefore, under Mazzolari, had taken it upon itself to administer to the flock both inside Southern Sudan and outside it. But, here was a rare chance for the Bishop of Wau to finally make it over to Kenya to attend a meeting of the Bishops of the Sudan, and he finally made a sneak visit to our school (Our Bakhita School) at Kitale, Kenya, as well. He would have to go back to Khartoum and Wau and if a visit was made by him to Southern Sudan held areas by the SPLA, the Bishop would have been killed when he returned to the Sudan by the Sudan Islamic Government.

Bishop Majak is a man who all the students wanted to meet, especially those of us who hailed from the Bhar el Gazel area of his Wau diocese. We wanted to talk with him very badly, and so it was arranged for us to have an audience with him the afternoon of his visit, and we lined up many questions. Being trained to be priests and leaders of the people, our hearts were full of love for our people, whether they were at the camps, in the army, or still living inside southern Sudan. Our heads were also full with ideas about how to bring the war to an end right away, and bring a permanent peace. So, minute after minute, the bishop allowed us to present any complaints or questions we had, which mostly centered on why the civil population, both inside and outside Southern Sudan, was neglected by the Bishop, leaving them to the care of the beloved Mazzolari who has so much to do already. As students from the Wau Diocese, we felt we were becoming an added burden to the Bishop of Rumbek Diocese. I believe it hadn't escaped the good bishop that the complaints were really like those of a child who sees his peer from the neighbor's house receiving a nice cute toy. The child really wants to receive the same, but finds that his household may never have the means or the wherewithal to get the gift.

For once, the Bishop of Rumbek didn't discriminate upon his flock, whether we were from Rumbek proper, or from the extended diocese, or from elsewhere, we wanted to be heard, and we wanted our own largess, which was why the bishop was being grilled for possible negligence. Why didn't he leave the horrible town of Wau, come to the liberated areas and generally act like the generous Mazzolari, giving us a break? On and on we poured out our frustrations and hopes with the bishop writing in his notebook, seeming not to miss a word, while grunting quietly with approval and encouragement.

Once we were done with our questions, we eagerly awaited the response from the Bishop who we had so long wished to meet, and who we expected could bring instant changes for us. But, when it was his turn to provide answers to our questions, what he said in answer to each and every point provided words of calm, reason and wisdom, and brought us back to reality. "I can't leave the flock in town because the Sudan security would murder them all, or turn them into the human shields they want. It is a day-to-day life for everyone in the towns. In the absence of the bishops, massacres, disappearances, summary executions and extrajudicial killings would increase, and even as I speak, my heart is out there thinking about those who might need my protection at this hour," he said. "I have endured the brutality of the government of the Sudan towards the Sudanese in towns. They need a leader, a protector." Aspiring to be leaders ourselves, we quickly saw that the bishop was right to protect his towns, and thought that he should get back there soon.

Bishop Majak sympathized with us, though. "I do understand what is generating your frustrations," he said. "The arrangement with the bishop of Rumbek, is not just one-sided. The diocese of Rumbek under my good brother, Bishop Mazzolari, looks after the two dioceses in the liberated areas inside southern Sudan, and after the flock outside the country, mostly in Eastern Africa, while I, the bishop of Wau, look after both dioceses inside the government held-towns. This is a fundamental agreement that we two bishops have mapped out and mutually agreed on. If any person from Rumbek mistreats any person from Wau, then it is left to the person to state the fact. The two dioceses have merged thus," he declared. This was an eye-opener and the end of the meeting. We came away with more respect for the bishops, for they were smarter and wiser than the combined lot of us. After that meeting, none of us thought that the Bishop of Wau had evaded his duties, and we never felt out of place at Bakhita again.

When it was our final year at Bakhita, our class, the first high school class to graduate from Bakhita Center Secondary School, was ready to sit for the Kenya Certificate of Secondary Education. One requirement for every school was choosing an Agricultural Project, which meant choosing, cultivating, tending and harvesting a crop by every student, producing the very best produce possible under the conditions chosen and set by the school. Our school chose potatoes as the crop on which the students would be evaluated.

Starting during the farming season of the final year of our class, we first obtained the potato plant cuttings which were then placed inside mounds of soil. These cuttings soon developed the buds that became the stems of the new cuttings. Once these buds developed, the initial cuttings were removed and cut into several small pieces, and then these pieces were planted, spaced apart at distances along the ridges.

Making bigger ridges, and applying ample amounts of the relevant fertilizers and pesticides, would lead to better yields, or so the instruction manual indicated. So that is what I decided to do. When the harvest was in, the agriculturalist in me had produced the most yield. This came as a surprise to some of my fellow classmates who thought I seemed to never like tulba. Farming was something that I was introduced to at a very young age, though, at Wunlit village and at Zira in Wau. For me, seeing the seedlings germinating was more than magical. It is quite interesting that I never did go on to an Agricultural college in the U.S., nor have I ever considered farming as a profession. I suppose it can be a hobby.

Before we graduated, our class participated in a soccer game with the following class from Form Three. The game was 'Form Three' versus

'*Jadongo*'. Our graduating class, the pioneers of the Bakhita Secondary School, were known as the Jadongo Class in honor of the characters in our literature set book, *the River and the Source*.[76] We decided to go toe-to-toe to see who was to be the champions in soccer before leaving Bakhita. That afternoon, the whole school came out to watch the soccer game between the graduating Form Four, the masters, and the incoming Form Four, the boys as it were, to see who would beat who.

While most Form Four members were older and more experienced in soccer, the Form Three class had more mavericks and a lot of talent, but lacked the experience. The game lasted for the usual ninety minutes, yet at every turn and every chance, neither team scored. Each team tried to snatch victory, yet was unable. Whichever team had possession, and controlled the field, failed to score, however much they tried.

Form Three created more chances for scoring, and had some very close misses, but it was not to be. I helped make sure, as one of the defenders at our goal post, to never oblige our junior opponents, to deny them their very vaunted wish. We were determined not to lose at a time when we were stepping out, because it would have been a loss that we could never avenge. We simply held our ground. For ninety minutes, the tug-of-war went on unabated, with our juniors determined on scoring a winning goal and a victory, to forever gloat over.

It seemed that no team was going to score, and it slowly was leading to a draw, an outcome our team would be fine with, since we didn't have to prove anything, but something that the other team would see as a failure. Just about ten minutes before the final whistle, and after having maintained the ball near the other goal post, I decided to get closer to the action, while still maintaining my defensive chance to get back to our goal post for a quick defensive stop should the other team recover the ball.

I received the ball past midfield, passed to me by a teammate and I saw a chance, and without even thinking I kicked the ball towards

---

[76] The River and the Source was a Kenyan novel that was made a literature set textbook for Kenyan Secondary Schools Form Four graduating at the end of 2000. Jadongo is Luo Council of Elders invoked in the book-a narrative fiction.

the opponents' goal post. The ball floated up and above the heads of everyone, including my teammates, making a measured arch in the air. Everyone looked up to witness something not anticipated, and within a few seconds, there was a golden goal. Even the goalkeeper was left puzzled. We had scored! Our team then made sure that, no matter how hard our junior opponents tried, they were never going to score! Indeed, when the final whistle was blown, we erupted in celebration, while our opponents were despondent. It was a well-deserved victory, and up to this day our Jadongo class still looks back upon it with pride.

The defeated team, however, decided to look for other ways to effect revenge, or have a payback, but the rest of our proud class never gave them a chance before we graduated. I ended up being challenged to a basketball game, an area in which our class would have been utterly defeated by Form Three. While the rest of the wise men of our class refused to take the bait, I did go play with some members of the other class, if only to offer them a chance to assuage their wounded pride. It came down to me against a group of three of the opposing class, where I was defeated, with them claiming that our whole class was therefore defeated. But, the joke was never lost on our victorious Jadongo. We had prevailed.

The process for resettling the south Sudanese young men and young women, the now famous "Lost Boys and Girls", to America began sometime in 1998 at Kakuma Refugee Camp. At that time, I was not present at Kakuma, at least not on a regular basis, because I was in the Kenyan town of Kitale, in the highlands, studying through my high school education. By the end of 1998, I had one year of high school education under my belt, along with a great religious fervor as an added advantage. Our school, the Bakhita Center, was more of a religious educational center than a High School. It was basically a specialized High School, though my former schoolmates may not agree to this idea. They may see Bakhita Center as more strictly a religious school, since it was built and run by the Catholic Church.

The local Kenyan school administrators thought our school was even a college because the amenities were state of the art. We would spend the whole year studying at Bakhita, from late January to the end of November, and then leave before Christmas for our yearly recess anywhere in Kenya and Southern Sudan. It was at these times that I would go back to Kakuma Camp.

At Bakhita Center, which was built and run by the Catholic Diocese of Rumbek headquartered in exile in Nairobi, the diocesan officials were regular visitors to our school. Indeed, as the Bishop was our personal friend, his Vicar General was someone who we all took note of. And we all looked upon him with disbelief, therefore, when he would approach the altar at mass, due to his habit of genuflecting with his hands in his pockets. Everyone else at church would properly cross their hands over their chests while genuflecting in front of the altar, but the Vicar General was the odd one out. One assumed he must have been the member of some mafia, or that he was like the good Mr. Pressman of Don Bosco, a no-nonsense man, but also kind towards those who were battered by life. Such people are simply giants, even if they may seem a little grumpy and not too kind. Perhaps it is their way of fighting the social vanities that seem to keep people back and create pain among the weak.

Once we received visitors from Rome. They were young people in their 20's and 30's, men and women who were members of a youth ministry in Rome, but who worked in various capacities in Italy. Among them was a tax collector, of all professions. There were gasps of surprise when this burly gentleman introduced his profession to a group of us. We were essentially bible students who had spent countless hours reciting the last supper and the story about Jesus's struggle against the Pharisees, including his disfavor of some tax collectors. It was a happy surprise to meet a real modern tax collector, and from Rome itself, working for the Roman tax machine. Not that the students hadn't ever have met a tax collector before, though. There were tax collectors in the SPLA-controlled areas, and also in the Kenyan and Ethiopian towns, yet this tax collector was actually on a youth ministry of the church. This was a good tax collector.

Towards the end on 2000, when I was finishing up my high school education at Bakhita, the resettlement of the minors, now lost boys, had increased in intensity. Unbeknownst to me, just at that time, my file came up for interview. I later learned that the interviewers spent days calling out my name at the gates of the UN compound where those whose names were put on the camp's notice boards, would arrive in the morning to have their interviews. On the final call, a friend of mine who was present, later told me that the interviewer made the final call of my name at the close of the day and then muttered that perhaps Awak had decided he wasn't going to the United States. Little did he know that Mr. Awak wanted to go to the United States very badly because in Kenya, the chances for me to be educated outside of religious school and priesthood training, were slim. The interviewer stamped my file a "No-Show", where it would have become lost, except that someone came up a few days later to announce to the interviewers that he was indeed the Awak they were seeking. Therefore, my photograph was taken off and that of this other fellow was affixed. This was done without proper check. The file was put away, to await the next chance to be called up for interview.

Kenya is an agricultural country, even though it is the East African financial and technological powerhouse. Agriculture happens to be the second highest earner of foreign exchange currency, after tourism. Tea, coffee, and dairy are the most commonly produced agricultural goods, and the majority of Kenyans can be classified as farmers. It is with this backdrop that every year the Kenyan towns, especially those in the farming belt of the highlands, organize trade and agricultural shows where everything imaginable is showcased and sold.

At Kitale, the yearly Kitale Agricultural Show would bring in businesses, farms, agencies and corporations to showcase their services and products for the Kenyan public to see. Our school was always an annual visitor to these shows. From stall to stall, and from live show to live show, these days were fun and entertaining. And it wasn't all about agriculture. There were fashion dancers from Nairobi, and other major Kenyan commercial towns, showing fashion trends and state-of-the art technologies. Even the Kenyan Police chipped in for a recruitment drive. Those shows were a chance to learn about Kenya at its finest, for it was a time for the Kenyan workers to show what they produce best, and for all of us to see and shop.

Bakhita Center, our school, sat on a few acres of lush farmland, on a sloping terrain with its own creek. This farmland had been sold to the Bishop Mazzolari to build a school on. While most of the farm area was used to build dormitories, classrooms and the other school buildings, the rest of the area was left for farming corn and vegetables, and for raising pigs for pork, and breeding cattle for milk. Before long, we were happily subsisting on the work of our own hands, with enough milk to go around, plenty of corn and other vegetables, and abundant pork.

There happened to be one small tin-roofed hut that was part of the farm, left as it was, while the rest of the structures had been taken down to make way for the school buildings. Living in this forlorn, simple hut was one old man. This owner and sole dweller was ancient, and he was, until a short while before the acquisition of the farmland, the lone farmhand. It was also rumored that he was a veteran of World War II, who ended up on the farm as a farmhand, without relatives and nobody to care for him in his old age.

For sure, there were a few others like him: There was John Natondo, the large grounds man, whose job it was to tend to the grass, and the rest of the farm work which we didn't care to shoulder. But John was as poor as any uneducated Kenyan living in the lush farming regions of the Highlands. It seemed that the poverty of the uneducated and landless folks was a vicious cycle, so that from generation to generation, the poverty never ended. I never wanted to be like John, but as our Physics teacher, Mr. Mulyalya would tell us, we were better off because "Your country needs you." It seemed that Kenya had forgotten about people like John and the lone old man in the hut, who would walk silently out our gate in the early afternoon and return before sunset.

The School Administration made sure that this old man was allowed passage at these times, and he had his meals provided him at his hut regularly. Even our beloved Bishop Mazzolari made sure to pay the old man a visit the moment he landed at Bakhita, before he even had a chance to meet us. The old man was simply awaiting death, and the generosity of the Bishop was par excellence. Sometimes, some of us compelled by our love of God, and our readiness to perform good acts, would hasten to pay him a visit too, but usually we tried our best to stay out of his way, and to simply say hello whenever he was passing by.

For the Dinka, letting an old man be utterly alone like that would bring the wrath of God himself upon you and the rest of your living relatives. It was the duty of the offspring to care for the elderly, and such a sight would never be seen in Dinkaland, unless the immediate relatives simply had decided to care less about the wrath of God, or the ridicule of the rest of society. But here, the old man apparently had no relatives and nobody to help him out. Therefore, our generous Bishop, and our school administration, made sure that someone was always stepping in to be his helper. When I left the school in 2000, he was still there.

Just south of our Bakhita center, along the Kitale-Kapenguria road, was a creek, over which a bridge passed. And just west of Bakhita, and this road, were farmlands. One man claimed that he owned all of this land. He was a certain Kenyan businessman, a flamboyant fellow who seemed to be a man of influence around those parts. To our surprise, he went on to tell us that we were free to move about the area at our leisure, without any hindrance, because we were his kin.

Mr. Ayub went on to tell our group of students something after we bumped into him picnicking in the shade alongside the creek. He informed us that he was a Nilotic, and that since we were ourselves Nilotic, that we were like relatives. He went on to ask us a question; What is the most important aspect shared in common among all the Nilotic? This question puzzled all of us. Mr. Ayub then provided the answer: the 5–digit counting system, as opposed to the English 10-digit counting system. It took us awhile to consider this claim, given that our knowledge of the intricacies of our language was not our strength, given that English was becoming our major language of learning and formality. But we came to the realization that his claim was actually true. With every Nilotic language whose counting system we could muster counting to at least the 10th digit, there was the element of an addition in the counting after the fifth digit, invariably. We were sold.

Bakhita was only about five kilometers north of the town of Kitale. Not only was traveling between the two easy on foot, but it was also a great form of exercise. Groups of friends would often walk between the towns, and the walk was also favored by our premier schoolteacher, Brother Ben. Traveling on foot, even as far as the town of Kitale, was accepted so long as the prudent seminarian was cautious about avoiding trouble, either along the way or at the destination. Walking to Kitale was not absolutely approved, per se, given the situations that we could get into, but it was conditionally approved. As long as we remained prudent, sensible, and caused no trouble, always remembering who we were, wherever we were, we could be at Kitale, on our own without permission. The walks, in groups, through the farmlands of the countryside, were the most favored way to spend our Sunday afternoons.

Therefore, whenever we found ourselves at Kitale on a Sunday afternoon, on our own volition, it was always smart to plan to make it back to Bakhita on time. It was possible to return quickly thanks to the Kenyan Matatu minibuses, ready to whisk one to a destination without delay. The trouble was, however, the number of people who needed transport from Kitale at the same time, heading in the same direction.

On the one hand, poor Kenyan farmers would board the Matatus. They would have spent their mornings and afternoons at the public market in Kitale, selling their produce or buying a few goods, and would then be returning to their farms. They would be in great need of the services of the few creaky minibuses. And on the other hand, the poor Matatu minibus owners and drivers would be in need of enough cash to continue their operations, feed their families and themselves, and stay profitable. Therefore, caring less about safety, they would admit as many people as possible. The minibuses would be packed to the hilt, three times over, standing-room-only, so that the hind axle would be weighed down. To somebody watching from the side, the minibus might appear to be navigating a steep hill, even though it was on a flat road. And if one wonders what the police did, they were basically in cahoots. Most policemen, upon stopping minibuses which were clearly packed against regulation, could be bribed. They would ask and receive a small something for tea (Some bribe money), and then the packed minibus would continue to lumber on. This practice of over packing the Matatus was so bad that whenever there was an accident, the consequences involved fatalities: destruction was utter. While the Matatu drivers plied their trade, safety fell by the wayside, and the police turned a blind eye.

In our travels out of the Sudan, to Ethiopia and to Kenya, we were living by the skin of our teeth at times. When we were settled enough, like for the five years at Panyido, Ethiopia, and for the ten years at Kakuma, Kenya, we had some more security. The majority of the refugees at the camps received some very basic amenities which included clean water, perhaps nutritious food, some form of available medical care, access to education, and security. When we arrived at Bakhita, we once again lacked certain items. We didn't have enough clothing on our backs, and we lacked closed shoes to protect our feet from the cold and rain of Kitale. Yet, to the surprise of our beloved Brother Ben, who expected our group to arrive with enough belongings, we were grateful for the level of services and amenities we were offered. Soon everyone was given a pair of shoes, known as Safari Boots. This speedily brought to an end the cold feet. Then we were also given sandals, known as sleepers, which were convenient to use for the hot and cold showers. There were also wonderful toilets, not to mention abundant soap, and we had access to towels, one for each person, so that one could dry oneself after taking a shower, instead of waiting to be dried by the elements, the wind and the hot air.

In short order, we accustomed ourselves to the amazing amenities we never had while at Kakuma. Our Bakhita group enjoyed many of the same benefits as those Sudanese in the urban areas of Nairobi and Nakuru. The one thing we lacked, though, was sophistication or being urbane. I found this out upon traveling to Nairobi during holidays. When I would be introduced to the beautiful, sophisticated Nairobi girls, they would learn that I was studying to eventually become a catholic priest, and the fact that I was not allowed to have a girlfriend at that moment, nor to ever marry afterwards should I become a priest. This affected the countenance of the listeners, so that they seemed slowed in my presence. Some of them took pity on me. And if I asked any of them for a dance, I wasn't turned down.

Being teenage boys, and not allowed to be free with the girls, was much tougher than we thought. What really kept any of us from going crazy was the fact that each of us had made a commitment to submit to priestly preparation voluntarily. One of the requirements was to remain celibate, starting from the moment we entered seminary. It was even better if one never had any contact with girls before. Though we knew that we could walk out anytime, we stayed because we wanted to. There was honor and pride in submitting to God, and remaining celibate, as a gift in this service. However, we would still be drawn to girls, and it happened often, whether we were at the school or away on holidays. Even our female teachers, some of whom were still young, would tease us, knowing the strain we bore.

The student body at Bakhita came from various dioceses. The majority was from the diocese of Rumbek, followed by the diocese of Wau, and then the diocese of El Obeid. Thankfully, SPLA politics were largely absent, given that we never had access to telephones throughout the year, nor did we read newspapers, nor watch television. We only received bits and pieces of news about Southern Sudan through the monthly diocesan newsletter, through word from occasional travelers going to or coming from Nairobi, or just traveling the nearby Kitale-Kapenguria road, along which lived some Sudanese families, mostly of the SPLA high command. Our connection with SPLA politics was largely non-existent, though, and this gave us peace of mind.

At Bakhita, we were largely sheltered from the Kenyan Justice System because we hardly ventured away from school. When we did travel outside the school's confines, it was either on an official school trip, or on normal walks in the countryside, among the friendly farmers. On annual holidays, we would either go to a camp or have our little

Yearly Passes.[77] Being SPLM/SPLA sympathizers, the Sudanese Embassy in Kenya was never going to give us passports even if we could afford the transportation fare to Nairobi from wherever we resided in Kenya. Any encounters with the Kenyan Police in Kitale could be taken care of with a little bribe and the yearly pass. However, I once ended up in a Kenyan Courtroom, of all places, and willingly. Courtrooms are menacing for the first-timers, however I was not on trial. I had accepted the chance to go to the Kenyan Courtroom to interpret for a Sudanese prisoner, jailed on accusations of having carried out a murder of a Kenyan guard at the border town of Lokichogio. I only learned this fact, though, after my classmate and I were chosen to try to help this Sudanese man who was in a very unfortunate situation.

When the assistant priest at the school, Fr. Thomas, with halting English, invited my friend and I for a very important mission in town, I was not only glad for the chance to leave the confines of the school for awhile, but also happy for the confidence shown to me by the priest. When we arrived at the courthouse, I was asked by the lawyer representing the accused to, "Please acquaint yourself with my client, and get to learn a little bit about him," all under the watchful eyes of the judge and the group of lawyers present. Speaking in Dinka, I asked him quietly who he was and what he had done. The prisoner told me his name, then launched into narrating the whole story in a cursory manner, repeating the accusation. His lawyer acted as though he followed every bit of the conversation, nodding quietly as if he knew the Dinka language. I wanted to establish the truth outright, though, so that even though the rest of the Court was not going to hear it all, at least I would know whether we were defending a guilty human being, and whether he had acted out of self-preservation, or not. I was going to tell the court only what was in his best interest, but I needed to learn the truth for myself, whether the accusations he was then narrating were just baloney, or were true.

---

[77] The Yearly Passes were a sort of permits for foreigners staying in Kenya outside of the refugee camps and who lacked access to passports.

I asked him point-blank whether he actually did shoot at the soldiers to kill one of them. Hesitating briefly, he said, "They had threatened to kill me first. I was only defending myself." I nodded my approval. However, the lawyer immediately stepped in to change the subject. He must have noticed the line of conversation, and the meaning of the quick Dinka words being exchanged. The lawyer didn't want the judge to learn the truth. The prisoner was pleading not guilty and the judge, as he was watching our exchange, might have been receiving some flickering light of a confession. The lawyer brought to an end our little conversation. Not long after, the court was brought to session on the case. I was going to interpret for the court because the judge wanted to hear from the accused, and not his lawyer, the confession. I did my best to make the court know his pleading. I also explained to him the questions he was being asked by the court.

When it was over-I never returned to the courtroom and I don't know what the verdict was afterwards-my fellow schoolmate[78] and I ended up with a generous day's wage, a sum of 100 Kenyan Shillings each. I thought we deserved our wage. I encouraged my friend to use it to his liking. However, I had apparently violated one of the fundamental rules of seminarians: Everything was put in a common pool, to be shared by everyone. Such was the expectation of Fr. Thomas. When he learned what we had done, the priest was beside himself. He told me I had broken the sacred rule of our common brotherhood. He wanted us to hand over our money, apparently to be used for any group activity. Even though I felt the matter was too trivial to elicit such a judgment (the issue was not the sum, but the principle of sharing), the indictment was stinging. I made a promise to myself that as long as I remained a brother, whatever I earned would always be put towards this common pool of resources for the common good. Ignorance was no valid defense.

Rome decided that there was going to be another Catholic diocese, made from parts of the vast Eldoret Diocese encompassing the Uasin

---

[78] My fellow schoolmate said nothing throughout our time at the courtroom- he never translated for the accused, I did all the talking

Gichu and Trans Nzoia Districts. The new diocese was to be centered at Kitale. The Bishop of Eldoret, Cornelius Arap Korir, chose as his Vicar General a down-to-earth Monsignor, Matthew Crowley, from the Republic of Ireland. Mr. Crowley tied the rope of his cassock right around his waist, where modern men wear their belts, rather than tying it around his upper body just below the ribcage, as was the tradition of most of the clergy. This same fashion, of wearing belts just below the ribcage, can be observed with modern belts worn on uniforms of the SPLA brass at Bilpam, in Juba.

I met Mr. Crowley at a church rally at Eldoret where our school was invited, along with many other catholic institutions, including other schools, seminaries and nunneries. I don't quite remember what the celebration was about, but the presentations offered at the celebration grounds close to the Eldoret Cathedral, were a joy worth the travel. Aside from the prayer fervor of the high mass, a highlight was the dancing of the girls from Eldoret. Teenage girls dancing in front of a crowd of mostly teenage boys and young men, was simply a joy. This was in conveying the offertory, and I am sure that God must have been pleased.

As part of the celebration, Monsignor Crowley appeared, introduced as the Vicar General of the Diocese of Eldoret, and began speaking with his Irish-English twang. By reading the Gospel emphatically, he made the message ring out quite exceptionally, and made the words of the evangelist quite meaningful. Little did I realize then, that in just less than a year, there would be a Kitale Diocese and the Monsignor would be the Bishop. Within that time frame, the good Bishop stopped by our school to deliver a talk. On that occasion, he proceeded to admonish the African leaders for pandering at the UN, continually asking for aid when there is so much that can be done to bring development to the suffering Africans right from Africa. By giving the example of his own boyhood in Ireland, he underlined his message: the importance of self-reliance and knowing one's destiny. He told us of how he attended school with his siblings, miles from home, with no means of transportation except on foot. He said that he persevered only because he led a purposeful life, and had a goal of becoming a professional later on.

When it was time for him to be consecrated and installed at Kitale, the stadium at Kitale was swarming with people, including the Rome elite. One name at the consecration remained stamped in my mind: Cardinal Josef Tomko, who was the presiding cardinal consecrating the Bishop. The pomp and ceremony was breathtaking, and I believe it is something that the Catholic hierarchy lives for. The Bishop's family from Ireland was at the stadium to participate in the celebration, and at the end of the consecration there were many offerings made to the bishop and to the new diocese. All this was during the reign of president Moi, who some Kenyans, especially youths in the camp who opposed Moi, called M o one-MO1[79] for Moi.

President Moi was the shrewd politician who ruled Kenya from 1978–2002. During that time, his country maintained a tenuous peace. He took over from Kenya's founding president, Mzee Jomo Kenyatta. Under Moi, Kenya prospered, but quite unequally, and this caused consternation among many quarters. However, if there is anything President Moi should be credited for, it is really maintaining Kenya's edge in being the leading economic powerhouse it is, and in being a beacon of peace in the region. Whereas almost all the Eastern African countries were at war, Kenya was at peace and a place of safety for those fleeing mayhem in their home countries. The worst part, however, was the rampant corruption that had plagued Kenya and still does today.

The first time I saw President Moi was in 1998 when he made a pass by our school along Kitale-Kapenguria road. He was coming back from Kapenguria in a convoy of black government vehicles, with many of his government stalwarts in the cars. One prominent person we actually were able to see was the female minister, Martha Karua. Just before the convoy arrived at our gate, the road was cleared by the Kenyan security, with sirens blaring and whizzing past our school at intervals. Knowing how President Moi liked to commune with, and to give speeches to, the young and those in schools, we were well prepared. The teachers at our school, including the short Ugandan Catholic Rector, decided that we should dress in our full uniforms and stand outside our school singing

---

[79] For being the number one man in Kenya, the sovereign as it were

'*Nyayo, Nyayo!*' with the index fingers of our right hands raised in the air. Any school that didn't do this could be forced to shut down, and God knew we could not afford to be shut down. We complied to the good graces of the Kenyan establishment.

We stood there as sirens blared around us, with Moi a no-show so far. After a while, we began to feel that perhaps Moi wouldn't pass there at all. Suddenly, the road beside our school was crowded with black, heavy vehicles rumbling past, with sirens blaring and blue neon security lights flashing, and cars swerving with a frequency that would certainly confuse a would-be assassin, if there was one along the road. For a second, we thought they were never stopping. However, our high-pitched and frantic Nyayo chanting, with the proper finger jabbing, must have gotten the attention of the speeding vehicles, because the cars came to a sudden stop. Moi's car was at the far lane of the road. The door opened to reveal the large, wise man with a rungu, a big stick. The security apparatus was already spread within our little group of a few hundred Sudanese students, all black, tall, mostly young men, with a few women. Moi, who appeared like a Toposa for the two missing lower teeth, was not any different from the official government photographs of him.

One of our teachers, Mr. Wanjala, tried to make an approach to meet the President but the security men, whose black leather shoes had threadbare soles thanks to the apparent continuous running on asphalt, suddenly appeared from nowhere to bar his approach, throwing their strong arms across his chest and throat. This caused our teacher to backpedal to the lineup quite sheepishly. On the other hand, our short, burly schoolmaster, a Ugandan, wisely stood hidden at the back. Only our Luo teacher Mr. Otieno, and a Luo catholic nun in a habit, were allowed to approach the president so he could inquire as to which school it was, who owned it, and who the students were.

I was sure that every eye in the cars was turned towards us, taking in every motion and emotion of each person, for the cars were silent and the passengers had their windows rolled down, with faces turned towards us. These representatives of the Kenyan government were looking at part of the future of South Sudan! The President then seemed reassured. Still seated in his front passenger seat, he gave a short speech of encouragement. "Prepare properly to go back to your war-torn country as messengers of peace. Your country is very much torn by tribal wars. Prepare well to bring this to a stop," he said haltingly. Rather than say, 'torn by the civil war with the north', he said to prepare well to go back to a country torn by 'tribal wars'.

I thought that the speech was quite strange because the major conflict we believed we faced in Southern Sudan was not tribal war between our various ethnic communities, though that was actually a problem, but rather the primary conflict was with the north. All of our leaders, and nearly every southern Sudanese, knew that Khartoum was the problem. However, Moi was actually emphasizing our own needed unity in Southern Sudan, because unless we were united as a nation in Southern Sudan, we would not achieve any objective at all. In fact, the SPLA suffered most major losses throughout the war because of ethnic strife in Southern Sudan and disunity between the rank-and-file and the brass of the SPLA, and not because the Sudan Armed Forces, the SAF, were particularly strong.

Soon enough, it was time for the lumbering convoy to move on to Kitale. But first, Moi had some concluding words: "I am going to Kitale to address the people of the district there. It is my desire to tour your beautiful school and talk to you a little more, but I must be at that rally. I hope to have a formal invitation from your school administration to pay you a proper visit at a later date." He bade us goodbye as the convoy of cars left. I found that my ankles were killing me, something I had not realized while we were listening! That was how much we were paying attention, and that is actually how long Mr. Moi held audience with us. Our Nyayo chants were worth it, after all.

Later that same year, 1998, I saw President Moi for a second time. This was at a political rally at the Kitale stadium, while he was campaigning in the Rift Valley province to be re-elected as president for a final five-year term of office. Of course, nobody knew then that the next term would be Moi's last, after which he would willingly step down. President Moi arrived at the rally very early in the morning, in a large, black government vehicle that seemed quite the bulletproof. Yet he was standing in the middle of the car, through the sunroof, waving slowly to the crowd with his rungu, or staff, while the crowd at the stadium were led in clapping and chanting by the agricultural minister, Musalia Mudavadi; "*Baba wa Taifa, karibu! Baba, karibu!* (Father of the Nation, welcome; father, welcome)," welcoming the father of the nation.

When he had gone full circle around the running track inside of the stadium, President Moi went to the canopied dais. The crowd then sang the national anthem, as Moi raised his club in the air. And when the anthem was done, and the guard of honor had gone past, Moi went to take his seat in the shade. Some members of the armed forces, with quick movements, whizzed away the dais, something I had never seen before. After that, the President was officially welcomed by Mudavadi, with words that showed they were on good terms. When it was time for Moi to speak, the words he used clearly showed who was in charge in Kenya. Though I don't quite remember the speech, I think Moi made sure that the population at the stadium, and those listening by radio throughout the country, knew it was right to re-elect him, and to maintain Nyayoism, the continuation of President Kenyatta's systems under the KANU party, which Moi inherited. A friend of mine once told me that Moi actually did say at a separate political rally, to the Kenyans assembled, that "*Kenya ni yangu!*": "Kenya is mine".

Around this time, we became aware of the SPLA/SPLM relief wing organization known as 'The Sudan Relief and Rehabilitation Association's (SRRA) new controversial directive to the Non-Governmental Organizations (NGOs) working in Southern Sudan. The SRRA decreed that, in the liberated areas inside Southern Sudan, including in the Nuba Mountains and Blue Nile, any non-governmental organizations, NGOs, which were foreign would have to register with them. The SRRA was dubbed as the SPLA's relief wing, and buried within the registration clause was the requirement that those NGO agencies would have to pay some annual premium or tax to the SRRA. The commissioner of the SRRA indicated that all the agencies providing relief in Southern Sudan would need to register. The churches, including the Catholic Church which was financed from abroad, in the absence of a functioning government, were also required to comply with the registration fee. The churches provided most of our basic requirements, including healthcare and education, so they were required to register because they fit the relief description. The churches countered that they were indigenous, and therefore cannot be taxed, even if they were to register.

The SRRA gave an ultimatum to the churches that they could either register or pack up and leave. For the churches, it seemed like 1964 all over again. At that time, the Sudan government from Khartoum expelled all the church missionaries, leaving a very young church without shepherds. Yet this new demand was coming from the SPLA! Moreover, wasn't it around 1994 when the churches had met with the SPLA/SPLM to thrash out terms of engagement, culminating in a declaration by the chairman that the churches, grouped in their New Sudan Council of Churches, NSCC, as opposed to the overall Sudan Council of Churches, SCC, were now the spiritual wing of the movement? Those paradoxes befuddled the churches, and raised more questions than answers.

The result was animosity from the churchmen, especially those with generous hearts who would make trips to the West, returning with lifesaving relief for the poor of Southern Sudan. They provided their services, which included relief for groups studying in some of the most remote parts of Kenya, for free. They knew it was a thankless job, and they felt that the SPLA/M was just looking for a way to garner some economic gain, and the churches refused to budge. The beneficiaries of the Church's lifesaving relief became the victims in this tug-of-war between the SRRA and the churches. The Catholic Church, in particular, was providing more than its share of relief services all the way from Nairobi, for the urban Sudanese refugees, to camps, including our group in Kitale, with our school built and managed from funds from abroad, from the U.S., Europe and Oceania. The Catholic Church's relief services also spread across the vast country of Southern Sudan, all the way to the far north, to the Nuba Mountains and Abyei.

How the saga between the two ended, I have no idea, but I know that before long our chance to celebrate our national May 16th holiday at our school was banned, and any discussions favorable to the SPLM/ SPLA were frowned upon. We thought it was very bad to prevent us from celebrating what was truly our national holiday. It was left to a few of us to find ways to get out of our school to celebrate elsewhere. It was only in 1999 that we were allowed to celebrate our May 16th holiday once again with an invitation extended to an SPLM bigwig, from nearby Kapenguria, to be the guest of honor at the celebration. The invitee proceeded to leave the inviting priest, Fr. Otieno, in awe. The speaker was apparently eloquent about the war, Southern Sudan, Sudan and the political conflict overall. I was not too impressed, but Fr. Otieno was, and so he declared that the speaker was what he had ordered. Perhaps the priest was merely trying to make amends for our angry student body, who felt mistreated for being banned from celebrating past May 16th holidays.

At Bakhita, rebellion by the students was closer at every turn, and it was safer to rebel as a group rather than as an individual. It was also usually good to shout in unison with the group. Furthermore, one should never act as the ringleader, or be seen to be among the organizers, because the axe would fall on these few power centers, leaving the sheep behind. So, when rebellions occurred, it was advisable to be in the crowd, without seeming to be the mastermind, even if one was the mastermind. It was also foolhardy to remain behind, because the crowd might suspect you of being in collusion with the school administration. Moreover, the administration would not like you because those who rat on their brothers in the crowd, were simply not respectable. So, it helped to be a part of the group, without being ahead or behind or apart, because otherwise one became the victim of both the crowd and the administration.

In one such rebellion, the administration had chosen to expel about ten students for what the rector had determined to be a misconduct. These students were said to be guilty of a failure to attend the required morning mass on a number of occasions, which had become habitual, in violation of the code of conduct observed by everyone. Attendance at prayers and masses, as with every other item on the daily activity list, was paramount and a condition for continued stay at Bakhita. But these students, who were due to be expelled, decided to protest. They were joined by a few of their friends at first, and eventually they pulled in a whole crowd to protest with them. It took the whole day for the expulsion to be effected.

Indeed, when the administration realized that there would be violence involved in subsequent protests, the schoolmasters made sure that the students understood that they could be forceful too, a point not lost on the students. One religious leader, a favorite teacher of mine, came into a subsequent meeting where the students seemed to be heckling the rector for various reasons. This leader was the former global head of the Christian Brothers order, and a New Zealander, probably a rugby player. When the Rector allowed him to speak, he indicated to the students, in no uncertain terms, that he was ready for any attempt at physical violence. When he was done talking, he walked out saying, "Attack me!" and left the hall. Nobody was ready. The rector, for his part, took to wearing a cardigan with "Kick Boxer" emblazoned on it! But, it was just a test of wills, and our beloved Christian Brothers former leader had a strong will.

At this time, our long-lost, beloved church teacher and catechist, Samuel, showed up at Bakhita Samuel was a typical Dinka, whose values were those of the Dinka infused with the best of the church's teachings. If anyone wanted to have a model Christian Dinka, Samuel was the man. He was as kind as he was gentle and trustworthy. Another way of knowing the depths of his faith in God was through his Dinka songs of the church, which he taught. These hymns, mostly in Dinka, were about how the Christian faith was at home with the Dinka, and how that faith could save the population. One such song I learned by heart is about how the Dinka seemed to never pay attention to the word of God as taught at church, while there were signs of God everywhere within their lives. The song also referenced how the devil was always prowling around the corner, seeking to trap people, like a predator hunting other wild animals. When the song was being taught at church, I didn't pay attention, yet I later heard it being sung by a few of my friends. The song really sank in, though, and got into my head, when we were on a hunt at Pochalla. The feeling of us chasing down herds of wild antelopes, or thiang, brought the song to my mind. I understood the meaning. '*Ok a ye jongrac yop cimene e lai*' (The devil hunts us like the antelope)!

Samuel was universally liked by all the Christians in our community as we traveled from Ethiopia to Sudan and later to Kenya. I first came to know him at Panyido. When he appeared at the camp's Catholic Church, he was in rags! He must either have arrived from the Sudan, or he was perhaps coming from the frontline with the SPLA army. In any case, the church, under Fr. Akot and the catechists, including my friend Mayom, were quick to grant him everything he needed. It was not long before Samuel became an icon of the Christian faith, as understood by the Dinka.

It wasn't just his kindness, but also his simplicity that made people want to bow to him. Though he was not fluent in English, I believe he was mostly literate in Dinka, and he was quite the master Dinka speaker. To most of us, he was an elder brother as well as an uncle. Moreover, he was a hard worker in terms of what we knew as tulba, the manual work favored by the Catholics as a form of prayer. He had muscles to boot. One would say he was physically formidable and looked like a body builder, though that he never worked out, per se.

So, when Samuel showed up at Bakhita, he was ushered into our refectory. We all trooped into this dining hall to listen to him talk to us about many aspects of life, including strengthening our characters, to continue living in the way we had chosen. Finally we were able to hear from a popular Christian teacher, and our enthusiasm was not lost on the Bakhita clergy and religious staff. These jealous clergymen came running in to kick out the flabbergasted Samuel, to the chagrin and silent indignation, even anger, of the assembled student body. That was the last time I saw Samuel, and we were not happy with the way he was treated. It was indecent the way he was removed from our meeting with him, without being allowed to finish his short speech, which we had so much anticipated.

The Bakhita administration had determined that Samuel would be imparting information that might sow conflict in the minds of the students. People like Samuel were not the only ones prevented from giving unmonitored speeches to us; other visitors, including even priests, were not allowed to talk to us, as a group, or even in small groups, unless there was an expressed permission from the Rector, who would continue to be present during the speech. Samuel was really worse off, though, because he was speaking in Dinka. The Rector was a Ugandan, who didn't know a single Dinka word.

At another time, I was on a bus ride, on a trip from Kakuma to Nairobi. In the bus was a girl whom I decided to strike up a conversation with. After the niceties and introductions, I was surprised to find that she was a Tutsi, when my assumption was that she was a Kikuyu. The Tutsi had recently captured the imagination of the world for their close call with almost being completely wiped out. As someone who had faced a similar situation, I wanted to meet a Tutsi, and see for myself why they could be so hated. I had found my chance with this girl. I had wanted to know why one tribe tried to wipe out their people. The girl was dashing. I told her about our troubles in the Sudan, and she told me about how she lost her whole family. It was simply hatred. It must have been some kind of ethnic jealousy. We parted ways after that. After my stay in Nairobi, I returned to Bakhita.

CHAPTER 30

REBELLIONS AND BETRAYALS

While awaiting independence celebration, I spoke with Deng once again. "We are a go, my friend. This is it!" he said. I was at Wunlit participating in farming and awaiting independence. It was on June 23rd 2011 and Abyei had been captured by the SAF. The Northern Twic County, from just South of Abyei all the way to Wunrok was a beehive of activity, with the SPLA running combat vehicles and troops in rotation, containing the SAF in Abyei. The SAF sent the feared Antonov bombers even close to Wunrok, sometimes circling at the brand new Wunrok Bridge, where it was feared they might take it out but the SPLA Air Defense was just below the bridge, embedded and ready. It would cost the SAF dearly if the Bridge were targeted. At that time, rebels and loyalists, we were all united: We wanted a nation of our own, of our own making.

After leading a devastating rebellion against the SPLA, throughout the greater Bhar el Gazel, Kerubino Kuanyin Bol's SPLA Contingent finally hatched a plan to capture the garrison town of Wau. They planned to capture the town, which was the Bhar el Gazel headquarters, and to hand it over to the SPLM/SPLA, to mend frayed fences and to usher in a new era of friendship, cooperation and reconciliation with the SPLM/SPLA leadership, particularly Dr. John Garang de Mabior, the main archrival of Kerubino. It was Garang who had imprisoned Kerubino in the Movement's dungeons from 1987 until Kerubino's escape in 1992.[80] It was to be an era of new beginnings, a move welcomed by most people from Bhar el Gazel. However, it was not to be. Indeed, before Wau was delivered, the denial against Kerubino began to emerge.

Inside Wau, and in Khartoum, Kerubino had armed any Southern Sudanese man or woman who wanted to carry a gun, often telling the Khartoum Security that they were trained soldiers of his militia army, and Khartoum, hungry for fighting men and women, obliged.

Kerubino and his troops had amassed inside Wau, and in the Marial Bai suburb north of Wau. He had sent out secret information to the SPLA to help aid his troops in the capture of Wau from the government of the Sudan, of which he was a member. Indeed, the plot was so elaborate that it took the government of the Sudan by surprise. Even Dr. Garang later quipped by terming the incident the 'Mother of all deceptions.' Kerubino had tricked Khartoum by asking for the SPLA to send him contingents of their soldiers to aid him in capturing Wau. When the soldiers arrived, he announced to Khartoum, and the world, that a group of the SPLA army had surrendered to him at Marial Bai. Kerubino was not known to be given to trickery, so the Sudan government took the bait. But, sensing a likely trap, the government hierarchy in Khartoum asked for Kerubino to present himself to Khartoum. Perhaps Khartoum was warned about the impending, clandestine operation, but not knowing Kerubino to be given to trickery, perhaps they wanted to test the waters first, by taking him away from the scene of events. Khartoum was also aware that there could be some signs of an impending operation.

It came to pass that Kerubino refused to appear at Khartoum. Instead, he asked for the stalwarts of the National Congress Party, the NCP[81] to pay him a visit at his headquarters at Marial Bai. He was the military commander of the Southern Command, in charge

---

[80] See also Human Rights Watch, "CIVILIAN DEVASTATION: Abuses by All Parties in the War in Southern Sudan," (New York: Human Rights Watch, June 1994), p.300 for an account of the reasons for Kerubino's arrest

[81] Or as we all knew, NCP is the NIF, the fundamentalist National Islamic Front masquerading as a nationalist party

of his own army, and he refused to budge. Indeed, when a visit was made to his headquarters, by government officials from Khartoum, the visitors looked upon the event as Kerubino trying to have his way. They didn't recognize the situation as a security concern. Indeed, when one of the visitors, Shams Al Din, from among the highest echelon of government and security, returned to Khartoum, he reported that there was a lack of anything to be concerned about. It was then that the attack on Wau was to commence. The attack was to be coordinated between the larger SPLA army, along with Kerubino's forces inside Wau and in Marial bai, including those SPLA soldiers who had supposedly surrendered to Kerubino. The attack was going to be a surprise to everyone except Kerubino, his soldiers and the elite of the SPLM/SPLA. But, unknown to Kerubino and to his soldiers, the SPLA command had made a decision not to trust Kerubino, and not to aid him in capturing Wau. This was going to be a huge and deadly surprise to Kerubino, and indeed the beginning of new bad blood awaiting him in Nairobi.

On the D-Day, Kerubino's soldiers did capture Wau from the Sudan government, for the first time since the advent of the SPLA, dislodging the government army from its notorious Grinti barracks. Wau was in the hands of a new master. However, it was fleeting. When the expected SPLA army attack didn't materialize, due to being held back by the SPLA command who were uncooperative in the Kerubino scheme, the routed government army realized that it could take back Wau. This they did with devastating consequences, both to the Kerubino army and to Wau's southern civilians, including the police, game (Wildlife) and prison forces. I know about the devastation, for sure, because Kerubino's forces, commanded by captain Malek, were slaughtered, including Malek himself. Malek was the comedian at Kakuma who, without my knowledge, was among those who answered Kerubino's call to travel to Nairobi, to join Kerubino's army in 1993. This also led to the displacement of many people, to the countryside, where there was nothing for them.

After returning to Nairobi, and staying for a few months, Kerubino finally left there, to escape the new schism with Garang. Kerubino traveled to the Upper Nile, to stay with his warlord friend, Paulino

Matip. In the later part of 1999, Kerubino Kuanyin Bol, the man who fired the first bullet during the civil war in 1983 at Bor, and who later became pivotal in setting up the SPLA, prosecuting the war and becoming the second-in-command, was rumored to have been captured by the rebels inside Southern Sudan, and then killed in cold blood. The rebel executioner, Gadet, it was said, was acting on orders.

Kerubino Kuanyin had fallen out with Garang, the leader of the SPLA, and he was imprisoned towards the end of 1987. After spending years within the SPLA's dungeons, he was released by his friend, the one who had been promoted to Kerubino's former position of Deputy Chairman of the SPLM and Deputy Commander-in-Chief of the SPLA, William Nyuon Bany.[82]

After that unauthorized release in 1992, Kerubino went to Uganda, and then to Nairobi, and later joined forces with Riak Machar, and the other Garang opponents, to fight the SPLA until 1998. He then attempted to rejoin the SPLA by capturing Wau, only to fall out again with Garang, leading to his being inside Southern Sudan without an army when he was captured and killed. Having been branded an enemy by the leader of the SPLA, every southerner was against him, and when his death was announced, there was dancing. I don't believe there has ever been any death more celebrated among the Southern Sudanese than that of Kerubino- yet he is the hero of 16th May, 1983 and the man who became indispensible in setting up the mighty SPLA.[83] along with his colleagues.

---

[82] William Nyuon released Kerubino and fellow prisoners without permission from Chairman Garang-Nyuon actually rebelled against the SPLM/SPLA right after that incident.

[83] The 105th Battalion troops became the nucleus of the first SPLA soldiers

CHAPTER 31

UNENDING STRIFE

All Southern Sudanese knew that the SPLM/SPLA would have won the war in the Sudan in the 1990s if it weren't for the fall of the Mengistu regime and the subsequent disarray of the Southern Sudanese. However, because of their steadfastness, Southern Sudanese were able to decide the fate of the Sudan itself. We had earned the right to vote and we carried the vote with enthusiasm to decide our fate. Though we knew we had come to the end of one perilous road, a road to independence, we knew it was not done yet. The strife would continue in one form or the other but the goal is achieved. Our martyrs had fallen for a prize, which we now hold. We will continue to defend it.

I returned to Kakuma on February 2001 after I had finished with final exams for the KCSE[84] from Bakhita School. Results would find us later but I was confident I had done well. Kakuma Camp was beset by ethnic strife, with conflicts sometimes turning into violent fights among the sub-Dinka ethnicities, as well as between the Dinka and the rest of the South Sudanese ethnicities. Everyone was at the neck of the other. Those conflicts that turned into violent fights, often around Christmas time, were a nuisance for those of us who had accepted Christ's mantra of forgiving your enemies and staying in peace with your fellow human beings. Indeed from 1994 onwards, the Dinka Bor ethnic group would

---

[84] The Kenya Certificate of Secondary Education, KCSE

be pitted in fights, usually against the Dinka Bhar el Gazel ethnic group, specifically the ones in Group 31 and Group 15.

The fights occurred during Christmas time, right on the 25th of December, just after the prayer at church, usually in the afternoon after the Bor Episcopalians were at the very end of their Christmas March. The marches themselves seemed to be preparations for such fights. The Bhar el Gazel group was invariably Catholics and the Bor Group invariably Episcopalians (We called them Protestants). The fights happened on Christmas day because that was when more visitors from the urban centers of Nairobi, and even from Southern Sudan where at Camp and with them came the political wranglings of the SPLM/SPLA Movement. The visitors brought with them the usual political squabbles that would end in the fights. The worst fight yet occurred in April of 2001, when most lost boys were leaving for the U.S.A. I was in the camp then, and the three day fighting was something never seen before.

When it ended, several people were dead on both sides, with a few more murdered in cold blood later, and the relationships between the two communities seemed quite irreparable. It started simply. Interestingly, this worst of all camp fights didn't happen on Christmas day, rather, it happened on an Easter day in April. This was at the height of the 'lost boys' resettlement abroad. Consequently, the camp had more Sudanese from the Kenyan urban centers and even from the Sudan seeking resettlement in the West- these newcomers had more connections to the SPLM/SPLA folks and therefore tend to delve in political squabbles more. A fight just erupted between some members of the Bor Group 17 and the Bhar El Ghazel Group 15. This fight quickly drew in other members of the two ethnicities, and lasted for three days, usually peaking in the afternoon. A petty incident triggered the fight. It happened that there were two neighboring houses, separated by a road. One house was on the Bor Group 17 side of the road, and the other was on the Bhar el Gazel Group 15 side.

Some young men in Bhar el Gazel Group 15 had their *hamman* (shower room) directly opposite this Bor household, and every time that a young man would take a shower, the wastewater would travel to the other compound. One day, with the young men of the Bor household milling around outside their compound, a girl from the same Bor compound came out, shouting to her neighbors about the wastewater. She said, "It is disrespectful to have someone channel waste bathwater into the compound of another."

The young man of the Bhar el Gazel Group 15 replied, "That is not true. There is no way we can stop the flow, since this area is where the shower room is located." The girl went on with the name-calling. Not to be outdone by the girl, the fellows insulted back. The insults against the girl riled up the young men on the Bor side, who then stormed out of their compound with shields, spears, clubs, sticks and stones, to fight the other young men. Some members of Group 15, who were nearby, came over to try to stop the fight, but received injuries to which the larger Group 15 rushed in, as did the rest of the Bor ethnic community. There was a call to fight, if you will, and thus started three days of the worst fighting the camp had ever seen. On the third day, a gun was used. There had never been a gun in the camp before. How it got through is something that is left to speculation. The fight itself was quite unavoidable, even for a prudent person. It was so encompassing that fighters would come to your tukul to fish you out, and if you refused to strike back, they would threaten to take your life. Everyone participated, even those who wanted nothing to do with it.

Along with the lurching crowd, I went, and it so happened that when the tide turned, our community finally had the chance to chase off the attacking community. I found myself with my friend, Majak, the two of us chasing away a crowd of people who, a few minutes earlier, had been attacking us and were about to pin us between two large converging groups. Only our fighting acumen helped us in dislodging the groups, by having our fighters divided into two groups, and attacking both sides that were attacking us. We also received some help from another group, who came just in time. Shouting a lot of baloney, the retreating fighters left behind some of their weapons and even a single boot. We ran after them until they were beyond the Catholic Church, which they had surrounded, inside of which were children and women. The attackers didn't realize that women and children were in there. They would have had a field day.

Then, right behind us, a call came that the Kenyan security and police were approaching with the authority to use lethal force against any fighting groups, and to arrest any number of fighters. Knowing the Kenyan prisons and the justice system, it was prudent to find somewhere to hide and to not be taken into custody.

Sensing the danger, and knowing that we were right next to the Don Bosco compound, with plenty of hiding places within its cavernous dwellings, I urged my friend Majak to step over the wire fence with me into the safety of the Don Bosco compound. I quickly stepped over to the other side. Apparently, though, he hesitated. He missed the chance to jump over the fence, and instead began running around the compound trying to find somewhere else to hide. He got nabbed, and ended up in a Kenyan jail for months, being housed with the rest of the hardened criminals. He later told me, when he got out, that the treatment he received in jail was something he had never experienced in his life, and that even his skin had started to peel after he returned. I felt sorry for him, but I also felt that he should have listened to me. It made a lot of sense to hide from those Kenyan police because their aim was not justice, but rather to teach a lesson that would strike fear into the communities. They were not necessarily looking for the wrongdoer, otherwise they wouldn't have been arresting anybody who was close to his place of abode. Those attacking should have been the ones caught, and brought to justice. We reserved our right to defend ourselves by fighting back, even though we were peace loving and law-abiding.

After one of the fights at the camp, my friend, Kuot, was seriously injured on his right leg, just below the knee. The wound was so bad that the fat, under the skin and muscles, was visible. Yet he remained at home without seeking medical help. That night, finding that there was nobody else available or willing to help me take him to the hospital about twenty minutes' walk away, I borrowed a wheelbarrow, placed him in it, and carted him through a neighborhood that had just fought with our group. It was said that passing through that neighborhood at night would result in the passerby getting struck in the head with a stone. But we went through, with me vowing to fight to the death to have my friend delivered to the hospital and receive help, rather than suffering at home in obvious, silent agony. In a way, even if I was not fully aware of this at that time, I was repaying him a debt I owed him from back in Panyido. When I had had surgery that threatened to become a major issue overnight, it was my friend Kuot who I woke up in the middle of the night to look at the wound and advise me on what to do. In my heart, I was so thankful to him for being there for me that night.

We braved the neighborhood and the dark night to arrive at the hospital where many of the injured, mostly from the other side in the fight, were being treated. The emergency workers were also mostly members of the community we had exchanged blows with. I proceeded to track down one of these fellows, who was a brother in every sense of the word, and asked him to treat my friend as soon as was possible. Knowing me, and being the wiser for realizing that this fight between the communities was simply stupid, the gentleman quickly tended to my friend. Before long, the wound was cleaned, sewn up and bandaged, and the patient was inoculated with penicillin and other necessary medicine to keep away infection and to hasten healing. We left the hospital, and made it back to our group without incident. My friend, Kuot, had a quick and full recovery and everything soon seemed forgotten. I wonder if he really appreciated what I did for him that night, but one thing I know for sure, he later became a medical assistant, partly because of this incident, and he is now helping to save lives.

The question about why there has been so much war in the Sudan is something that scholars have given a crack at, but in my own mind, it is because of resources, religion, ethnicity, history, style of governance, and politics. There have been several scholarly researches into the reasons why the Sudan has been at war with itself for so long. The modern Sudan, granted independence by Great Britain in 1956, descended into war right from the get-go. In fact, the southern rebellion started even before the Union Jack flag was lowered, and the flag of the new country raised on the flagpole. The Anya Nya I war started in Torit, in August 1955, months before actual independence.

For someone who has lived the horrors of the Sudan conflict, it is not difficult to see what the reasons for the conflict were, and still are, even if these reasons may very well be one-sided. Initiated by the Equatoria Corps stationed at Torit, the 1955 mutiny became the precursor to the Anya Nya I movement, whose stated goal was the liberation of the southern part of the Sudan to become its own country. The 1947 Southern Sudan Chiefs and Prominent Persons' Council decided that it would be appropriate for Southern Sudan to remain part of the Sudan because the southern region basically had very few educated people to run a successful government. That was the basis of the resolution, not that Southern Sudan was cohesive with the Northern polity. Indeed, the main causes of the Sudan conflicts stem from the fact that the people, even though all Africans and descendants of Afro-Arab communities, had many differences. Issues of religion, culture, ethnicity and equitable distribution of resources had driven a wedge between the people of the North and the South.

Take for instance religion. On the surface, it appears that the Sudan has Islam as the religion of the majority, while Christianity is the religion of the minority, with other African religions also having a part. It has been known that Christianity can live side by side with other religions, especially when Christianity is the religion of the majority, or if it comprises half of the population, as is the case in Nigeria. In Nigeria, a single riot between Muslims and Christians in one day can cause more than 1,000 deaths, among both sides. But the violence is still contained, and there will usually be a Christian president with a Muslim vice president, or vice versa. The religious violence in Nigeria, though it might cost up to a thousand deaths in a riot in a single day, it is contained because the Nigerians continue to live side-by-side and still maintain a tenuous unity-it never descends into a full-scale civil war the likes of the former Sudan. Nigeria still holds itself together.

But if the majority religion is Islam, then it will generally not accept living side by side peacefully with other religions, though there is an exception in the Middle East, and in other Islamic countries, where Jews are mostly not disturbed. This could be because Islam shares much of its roots with the Jewish religion and writings, and the three

Abrahamic religions are considered the people of the book. So, the situation in the Sudan happens to be a majority Muslim population, with Christianity and other religions forming the minority. In this situation, the Islamic fundamentalists in Khartoum have decided that it is a Koranic precept that a Muslim must never be ruled by a Christian. That is fundamentalism, and a root cause for great conflict, for I would have to change my religion to that of the majority Islam to be able to participate in political life, in my own country. This was considered abominable by southern Sudanese.

Another issue was ethnicity. Given that the majority in the Sudan was definitely African, and descendants of Africans, the Sudan was definitely first and foremost an African country. But not to the clique in Khartoum. They had decided that the Sudan was an Arab country, even if the true Arab population was much less than the 40% that was said to be Arab. Indeed, it is virtually impossible to find anyone in the Sudan who looked like an Arab from the Middle East. The Sudan is African, through and through. There was an identity crisis and the Sudan paid for it.

The other issue was resources. The distribution of the national resources among the population had been wanting. The clique regimes in Khartoum had decided to harvest resources from the peripheries, and then concentrate development in Khartoum, for a small minority that considered itself the owners of the land. The rest of the country was left without development, and only pacified with an army when it sought justice. It was sort of like the case of taxation without representation. For instance, in 1970, the U.S. oil giant, Chevron, discovered oil in the Upper Nile of Southern Sudan. This gave great joy to the people of Southern Sudan, who assumed that finally there was something that could lift them out of poverty. The government in Khartoum, however, simply decided to change the borders between Southern Sudan and Northern Sudan, so that the oil was found in the Northern part of the country. When proceeds from it were used for development in the North, the other parts of the country, especially the South, were left empty-handed. This was done so that the Southerners would have no much incentive to complain or incase the South sought secession then the resource is easily annexed North. Khartoum's clique regime employed ruthless state machinery that played ethnicities against each other, and murdered emerging leaders from the periphery. The eventual war between the South and the North was a consequence of this.

There is no doubt that Isaiah Chapter 18 refers to the Sudanese people. All that has been written in Isaiah 18 has quietly happened in the Sudan over the years of its endless conflicts. The Arabs invaded the 'Bilad es Sudan', Arabic for the 'Land of the Black People,' quite literally stated in the 7th Century A.D. Ever since the Arabs came to the Sudan, it has been trouble and strife. Even my Grandfather told me about how, in his time, they fought the Arabs. The Arab raiders would be on horseback, launching attacks at them, fighting them with large spears called 'Thuro'. The Arabs would take anything they wanted, including cattle and slaves, and would burn everything down. However, the swamps in the south gave my grandfather and his comrades the concealment they needed, and kept the Islamic invaders at bay.

When the Anglo-Egyptian Condominium ended in 1955, leading to the independence of the Sudan in January of 1956, our people had already taken up arms to fight the northern Arab jalaba. The war that started just before independence in 1955 went on until 1972. After a respite of some time from 1972 to 1983, the war broke out anew and more ferocious than it had ever been due to the presence of new and better weapons. "The birds will feed on them all summer, the wild animals all winter": so says Isaiah 18, and that was how it seemed to be for the people of the Sudan for 22 more years, until the Sudan Peace Agreement of 2005. The peace has largely held until now. So, on January 09, 2011, a new nation was born that would fulfill Isaiah's prophesies.

So, why were the Murahilin raiders attacking our countryside? The raiders were part of the Defense Forces of the Sudan Army. They were irregular forces, helped and trained by the army to use their firepower to fight and make raids into Southern Sudan, as often as they wanted every dry season. The government of the Sudan had the advantage of denying the SPLA its recruiting ground and its base of support. Indeed, the man who launched the Murahilin into Southern Sudan was none other than Sadiq Al Mahdi, who was then the prime minister of the Sudan before he was overthrown in a coup by Omar Hassan Al Bashir in 1989. Al Mahdi is personally liable for inciting murders of southern Sudanese leaders, and ordering the massacres of southern Sudanese civilians. The Murahilin raiders were his way of destroying the Dinka as a people. Indeed, it has been said that Sadiq himself lashed out at a prominent Dinka, saying that he would destroy the Dinka people for their rebellious ways. Indeed, the raiders mission was to go to Southern Sudan to raid villages and towns, take whatever they found as their pay, and destroy the rest. They sought to prevent the southern Sudanese from being able to regroup or regain means for sustenance, to deny the survivors the chance to rebuild their lives. In fact, were it not for the SPLA and mother nature,[85] the Dinka of Bhar el Gazel would have been exterminated.

Finally, the primary root cause was nothing other than the widespread injustice in the Sudan. For example, even if someone became a Muslim, given that being a Muslim in the Sudan would mean embracing the Arab culture to the detriment of your own, you were still considered a third-class Muslim. Unless you were a member of one of the three Arab riverine tribes, you were never going to gain access into the inner circle of power. There was nothing one could do to earn access into the clique regime in Khartoum. You were either from one of the three Arab tribes, or you were a nobody. The Islamic requirement was just bait to make someone less threatening. If you shed your culture and religion in favor of Islam, Arabic became your language, and the Arabic culture became your culture, so that you became a less threatening third-class Arab Muslim, with no incentive for complaining. Only recently, in 2003, did the people of Darfur, who are purely African Muslims, decide to throw off the yoke of Khartoum. They finally refused to be Khartoum's soldiers in Southern Sudan, and they demanded their rights. This resulted in

---

[85] The annual floods that cover the land bringing forth vegetation and insects offered ample protection to the local inhabitants to wither the Islamic Arab Conquest-this was the barrier that kept the Islamic Invaders away from Southern Sudan and still kept away the Murahilin at bay.

genocide—Muslim genocide against Muslims. It finally became clear who was being taken for granted.

In North Sudan, the African Muslims of Darfur, Nuba Mountains, the Blue Nile, the Nubians in the far north and the Beja in the northeast, all the non-Arab peoples who were converted to Islam after the conquest of the Sudan by the Muslims from the Middle East, long struggled under the Khartoum regime. They were treated as if they were not citizens, or were third-class citizens in their own country. Even though they had become Muslims, it wasn't about Islam. What could have been the reasons to continue to be unjust to a fellow Muslim? This showed that the root causes were not only religious, but also resource and ethnicity based.

CHAPTER 32

INDEPENDENCE

Leading up to the independence declaration on July 9th, 2011, various militia forces, with cohorts from Khartoum, attempted to scuttle this independence. Again and again they tried, but the SPLA, South Sudan's Army, kept them in disarray. On July 9th, Southern Sudan became an independent nation, the Republic of South Sudan, as the whole world watched. "All you people of the world, you who live on the Earth. When a banner is raised, then you will see it, and when a trumpet sounds, you will hear it,"(Isaiah 18:3).[86]

In February 2001, I finally arrived at the Kakuma camp after completing my Kenya Certificate of Secondary Education, KCSE. I learned all about the issues surrounding my file with the U.S. resettlement authorities, so I made a call at the office a few days later, where I found that the processing staff was seriously considering closing out the no-show files for good. I had just arrived in time. Upon showing my credentials and documents, they were surprised to find that even though the name and the story were mine, the photograph on file was not mine, so they resolved to find out the truth. They asked me if I knew who had made the claim, and put his photograph on my file. I happened to know who it was: He was my cousin.

However, getting the staffers to look at our files was a formidable task. The process was coming to an end, and they were ready to close

---

[86] King James Version

our files for good. Every day we would come to the gate of the UN compound, asking for Mr. Fan, who was put in charge of our files, the no-show files. However, Mr. Fan was a wily staffer who would basically find a way to get away from the complaining crowd. He would tell them to wait for him at the gate, if it was morning, and then would proceed to stay away until the evening. Then, when he returned to the compound, where everyone would be clamoring for his attention, again he would proceed to tell them to come back the following morning. And then the process would continue like that. This went on for weeks, when he was around. And when he was not around, for a week or so, the other staffers would say he wasn't around, but that he would be back in a few days, "Check back tomorrow," was the staffers' common phrase.

It was a vicious cycle. One day, things came to a head. Mr. Fan had somehow spent the whole day inside the compound, without coming out, and everybody was waiting for him. The crowd had increased tenfold that day, up to 100 people. The folks were mostly urban refugees, from Nairobi or Kitale, from excellent schools, and they were then clamoring to get their chance to go to the U.S. Some members of the crowd had decided that either Mr. Fan was going to see them and solve their problem that day, or they would make sure that he was beaten up. I thought that shouldn't be the way to go about it, but I didn't tell anyone. I believed that if Mr. Fan was avoiding us, perhaps our case files were not going to be opened again. For me, Mr. Fan was actually our best friend, and we should have striven to find a way to have him help us, not force him to listen to our demands. I still had hope that he might do something, given that every time we asked staffers, nobody had ever told us that our cases were lost. However, we knew our window was closing very fast.

That evening, the gate opened as a car emerged with Mr. Fan and his driver. Everyone clamored to speak to him, and the car could not move. Someone asked him, "Mr. Fan, when are you going to open our files?"

Mr. Fan replied, "I am going to the old UN compound to help at the interviews of your fellow Sudanese young men. They are having their interviews done this afternoon. Don't worry. I will look at your cases tomorrow. Come tomorrow!" The crowd went wild. For a moment, it looked like there was going to be a riot, and that Mr. Fan and his driver would get hurt, or have their car stoned. Or maybe some members of the crowd would get run over by the car. There I was, just waiting for my chance to ask Mr. Fan when he might look at my file, but the tomorrow statement made things to get out of hand.

I seized the moment and shouted for the crowd to quiet down. "Listen up, everybody. Since Mr. Fan has clearly stated in his own words that he is going to help our fellow Sudanese get through with their interviews, we should let him go through. Those people are also our brothers. We should take Mr. Fan at his word. We must leave at this point, let his car go through, and then come back tomorrow morning to meet him as he has stated. Mr. Fan has spoken. Let us now take his word for it. Let us take him at his word. Should he fail tomorrow, then we can say 'He lied to us!' and then we can make noise. Please, let us give him a chance!" I implored the rowdy crowd. Mr. Fan looked at me and then echoed his approval; "Yes, come tomorrow!" I must say that I believed that Mr. Fan was lying, but I trusted that we needed to give him a chance to prove himself wrong in front of a crowd of 100 people! The following day was going to be critical. The crowd dispersed quietly, and his car was allowed to go through.

Early the next morning, we all trooped back from our camp dwellings to the gate of the UN compound. The doors opened, surprisingly, to allow us all to enter and be in line. Everyone who recognized my plea the evening before gave a nod of approval as we marched in. I was lucky enough to be near the front, third in line. I waited eagerly to be called in to state my complaint. I was prepared with a trove of my school documents to prove that the name on file was actually mine. Mr. Fan, seated at the table, recognized me but said nothing. He waited for me to be seated, before asking me to state my name.

I stated my name as it appeared on the file. I also stated my case number. This number was critical, and a lack of it would have doomed my case completely. I also gave to Mr. Fan the accompanying school documents, proving that I was the owner of the file. Going through my documents, and knowing me to be the fellow who calmed down the crowd the previous evening, Mr. Fan was only too glad to have me go through. Upon checking my documents, he informed me that I was ready for the next step, and that I would be called for an interview in a few days. Some days later, I was called to the U.N. compound to meet an American lawyer who would verify the truth about my claim to the file. She would be the one to give the final approval to go to the next step. The lawyer looked at my school documents and, after authenticating, showed me that I was then cleared for the next step.

Several days after that meeting, my name appeared on the camp notice board to go to an interview. Some friends told me that, even though at that stage some people still failed to be granted relocation, they didn't worry that I would fail. On the day of the interview, I met with a burly lawyer from the Joint Voluntary Agencies (JVA). He asked me a few questions to prove that I was the same person on file, even though my photograph already gave that away. He then asked me a few more questions about my life story, and then put down his pen, crossed his arms on his chest, and asked me, "What will you be when you get to the U.S.?" I understood the question to mean what sort of a career path would I take. The question was quite unexpected, having been primed by my friends only to stick to the script, stick to my story and act a certain way. But I knew that I wanted to do something in law, so I said, "I will be a lawyer or a police officer." The lawyer stood up and shook my hands vigorously, only stopping short of saying 'welcome to America'.

I wasn't sure if I had passed the interview, but I felt in my gut that I had. It had been said that when some minors, who had been suffering for years in refugee camps in Ethiopia and Kenya, failed the interviews and were handed rejection letters, it was crushing. Some of them were then young adult Dinka, who were expected never to cry in public, so they would go far away to one of the numerous Turkana dry streambeds to cry their hearts out. On the other hand, some never even wanted to go to the U.S. A friend of mine refused several times to go for the interview, and consequently never set foot in the United States or anywhere else in the western world. He is now a medical assistant (a diktor), who actually operates on patients, including pregnant women. In my case, though, I certainly wanted to go to the U.S. A few days after being interviewed, several of us were asked to appear at the International Organization for Migration's (I.O.M.) little clinic to have our medical checkups. These were thoroughly done to find out if we had any medical conditions, from simple ailments to major diseases rampant in Southern Sudan. I was glad to pass the checkup.

After about a week of waiting and forgetting, I was playing some dominoes with the remnant refugees at camp, most of whom had arrived directly from South Sudan. They had never really experienced the hardships of the unaccompanied minors, or lost boys, and therefore had no chance of getting the U.S. Some of them asked sarcastically as to why I was still in the camp, when almost all of my colleagues were gone and enjoying life in the West, to which I could not find a great answer, except to say that my time would come. Some of these newly arrived refugees filled their free time with fights. There was one fellow who kept scaring another young man with a knife, and he would not listen to us when we tried to stop him. The young man who was being threatened ran away from the attacker. The attacker followed him up to the nearby hut. A moment later, the same pair emerged, with the knife-wielder now running from a spear-wielder. The knife-wielder who had started it all came running back to us, where we were playing dominoes, and kept running around in circles, pursued by the spear-wielder, crying for us to help him. We were just plain laughing! How could he keep scaring someone with a sharp object, without listening to reason, only to come back to us asking for reprieve when he was the one who started it? We had to help the situation anyway.

It was during one of those domino games, wiling away my time, when someone appeared and announced that there are names on the camp noticeboards, and that my name is among them. And sure enough, I was slated to go to Rochester, N.Y., U.S.A.! Even though my high school education, and my own reading about the world's geography, including reading the National Geographic and Time Magazine, had shown me a lot about the rest of the world, I had never paid attention to a town called Rochester in New York. Nevertheless, I was ready to settle in any U.S. town, whether it was a small town with just a single gas station and a shop, or a major city. I would always have the chance to go to the university. This was in the first week of September 2001.

Our flight to Nairobi, and then to Rochester, was going to be within the month. I started preparing, and even threw a little party, with some cash I had received from a relative. I even rented a small video camera to record the festivities. The party went fine, and I resumed waiting for the day of our flight. But on September 11th, the U.S. was attacked by terrorists. We saw it on CNN news, at our local TV café. I thought that the world was going to have a World War III. I was convinced of this, and I all but forgot about going to the U.S. Days later, though, past our intended day of flight, a new list, with a new flight date, September 28th, was put on the noticeboard. So we were traveling anyway, but we now wondered how good would it ever be. Even if America was welcoming before, I was quite sure it would not be the same again. We were mad at the terrorists.

On September 28th, we boarded a chartered flight that served as a cargo plane sometimes, and flew from Kakuma to Nairobi. We arrived at Nairobi's Jomo Kenyatta International Airport in the afternoon, and were taken to the GOAL Accommodation Center in Nairobi's Kilimani neighborhood, to await the flight to the U.S.A. in only a few days. But first, we would have to undergo further processing, including further medical scrutiny, by taking medicine for worms, and having the C.D.C., through the I.O.M., verify that nothing of concern was entering the U.S. However, the flights from East Africa, and elsewhere, especially for people going to the U.S. for long-term stay, including for our program, were put on hold. So, even though the doctor had stamped my file "Expedited", I was going nowhere.

I spent Christmas in Nairobi, waiting for the New Year to see what else would happen. We were all wiling away our time. Refugees were waiting to go to Australia, Canada, the U.S. and to Scandinavian countries. Within the YMCA-like accommodation center in Nairobi, run by GOAL, some bored refugees started having illicit ideas. Here was another tragic example of how human beings commit actions that are truly bestial.

There was a Rwandese woman of the Tutsi tribe, who had been married to a member of the Rwandese Hutu tribe. The man died in the Rwandan genocide, but not before she had two children by him. This alone was trouble, and had almost cost her her life, and that of her children, right under the noses of the Kenyan accommodation staff. The lady was informed that she and her children were scheduled to go to Australia. She was elated after having waited for some two years for this chance. Being joyous, she invited the rest of the Rwandese residents of the accommodation lodge to come to her apartment to celebrate with her. It so happened that she had befriended a couple, also Rwandese, but Hutu, who had been at the accommodation center for more than three years waiting to go abroad. The night ended with her friends leaving for their quarters. However, towards the early morning hours, the woman was groaning in pain, as her two children lay in their beds dead, with their throats slit. Her struggle with the attacker woke up the neighbors, but when the neighbors finally arrived, the woman was dead, and the attacker, and the attack knife, were gone. The accommodation security was sure that there were no outside attackers, that nobody had breached the security to get inside the accommodation center, which was really their focus.

They thought that the people in the accommodation center were particularly in danger now, and would need protection. Everyone in the accommodation center was a suspect. Everyone took to sleuthing, to help find the knife used in the killing. The knife was eventually found behind the public bathrooms, near a window. It was a kitchen knife, one belonging to the accommodation center's kitchen utensils. From the look in the eyes of the Hutu couple, everyone thought they were involved with the killing, but there was no proof, except that they had the motive and the likely expertise. The killing method had puzzled the Kenyan crime police, for the attacker, or attackers, were professional. It was a sad incident for the aid workers, and for everyone else.

Another incident had similar connotations. Two Sudanese young men from Didinga, Equatoria were granted a chance for asylum, but they needed to wait to leave, and so they ended up in the accommodation center. But they decided that the wait was becoming too long. They informed the UN staff that they feared for their lives at the accommodation center, because there were many Dinka people there. They hoped that this would compel the staff to expedite their resettlement to the U.S. Instead, though, they were simply taken elsewhere in Nairobi, to continue awaiting their chance to be resettled abroad. Their strategy had failed. So, at their new place, they decided they should attack each other, and then report that they were attacked from the outside by somebody who wanted to end their lives, an approach which should force their caseworkers to have them sent abroad pretty fast.

But, because of the past incident, their trick was discovered. And worse than that, their stunt turned into a tragedy because one of them ended up dying from knife wounds after they jabbed at each other. Obviously, desperation was everywhere, so it was a good thing to be realistic and to keep one's sanity. We tried to keep in mind what the West was, or could be; it wasn't just a place for easy success, but it would provide us a chance to work hard to achieve something that nobody could take from us. We desired to be resettled abroad, but at the same time, if we didn't make it abroad, we would see that it wouldn't mark the end of the road.

After 10 years in Kenya, I was ready to go to another country where I knew I would go to school and earn a university degree. This dream was also espoused by my fellow southern Sudanese students, and had been drummed into us by the leaders of the Sudan rebellion. We were going to be the builders of a new Sudan that would come out of the war of liberation. I was on my way to becoming a part of the new intelligentsia that would help usher in the New Sudan. I finally was leaving Nairobi on August 13th, 2002. Our plane, the Kenya Airways' KQ plane, landed in Amsterdam, Holland, for us to change planes and board a KLM flight to NYC. We landed in New York City on August 13th to spend the night there. The following morning, before going to LaGuardia Airport for the afternoon flight to Rochester, NY, I came outside of our hotel room, and stood before a main thoroughfare. The cars were moving so fast that my friend yelled from behind me to get back in, because a car could crash into me, but I knew better than to step on the pavement. I had just come from Nairobi, where the cars were fast, but not this fast.

When I landed in Rochester that afternoon, waiting for me was Susanna, from the Catholic Family Center, her boss, Jim and Dale from the Presbyterian Church, ready to welcome me to the United States. There were also several 'walking boys' who had been in Rochester for about a year or so, and they were happy to welcome me. "You are brave!" said Susanna.

Assuming that her statement meant that she was amazed to see me come into an unknown country after having passed through so much trouble, I replied, "It was simply the right choice of action." But I felt that I had come to a place where I didn't know where to begin. The following day, Dale took a photograph of me with my new roommates, fellow walking boys, as they were being called in Rochester. In the picture, I noticed that I had my hands to my cheeks. I believe I must have been a little unsure where I was and whether it was worth the entire wait. The first thing I wanted to do was to find a way to go to the best university in the area. But before that, I needed to be self-sufficient. I needed to get another medical checkup, take driving lessons, get a job and then I could find a way to go to school.

Just days later, one of the sponsors of the lost boys asked a group of five of us to travel with him to the St. Lawrence River, for a weekend outing at his family's vacation house on the river, and to help him get their boat into storage for the winter. When we reached the house that evening, we collected firewood outside where we had supper and refreshments while we chatted about issues including about immigration and poverty in the U.S. We retired to bed early that night, only to wake up very early in the morning to spend time on the river, in the boat and doing some swimming. It was all good. The water of the St. Lawrence River is quite clear and, as our host told us, fresh, even though it is connected to the ocean. Steamers and other ships would pass through it to get to the ocean. On the final evening, a Sunday, we helped hoist the boat out of the water and put it on a trailer for the ride back to Rochester where our host would keep it until the next summer season. And as we were traveling towards Rochester that evening, there was a downpour on the way. It seemed that the sky was going to empty itself before the end of summer. That was my introduction to my first

American summer. At that point, I didn't know how cold it would get just three months later, when it became winter. I was looking forward to my first snow.

In September, I went, along with Dale, to visit the nearest university, the University of Rochester, arguably the best in the area. Dale took me to one of the admission counselors, an African American pastor. This man listened to my story and my need to get accepted at a university, but then proceeded to pour water on my dream. First, he asked me, "Do you have money in the bank amounting to $30,000?"

"No!" I replied.

"In the U.S., education costs money, and if you have no money, then you should not be thinking about getting into a university such as the University of Rochester. I don't think you can ever get a degree at all in the U.S. It costs so much!" he declared. I thought that was ridiculous. The sole reason, the only real reason for me to want to get to the U.S. was for a chance for an education, a superb education which I would never get if I were in Southern Sudan or in Kenya, and to have someone of authority tell me point-blank that I could never get such a thing, after waiting for months and agonizing as to whether I would ever get through, was just unbelievable to me.

Perhaps seeing my stunned disappointment, he told me that there was a cheaper community college that I could get into as long as I would be able to generate a little money to pay my way through it. That brought some relief to me. Five months later, I was enrolled at Monroe Community College where I would be studying during the daytime and then working at a local hospital overnight. How does one do that? It was just plain hope and grit that pulled me through to even pass my courses, but I did. I never failed a single course, though I was not at the top of the game. I now believe that this performance, and work ethic, actually affected my academic performance in later years. In any case, that community college beginning finally got me into the University of Rochester a year and a half later!

I decided to study the toughest subjects possible, and to make sure that I did them well. I studied physics and mathematics. Though I struggled with them both, given that I took on a huge load of five physics courses and mathematics to graduate in the shortest possible time, I did pass them all, and then graduated exactly two years later. I then decided during graduation that I was done with schooling. I wanted to work and create a life for myself, for the reason being that it would be tougher to continue on to graduate school in physics, while still taking care of my family back in South Sudan and in Kenya. I had decided that physics was not for me, and I would be better off doing law.

When I first arrived in the U.S., I was more than prepared for what I was going to find and how I was going to build my life. First, my goal was to get a job, no matter what the job was, and to do it well, honestly, and to go above the call of duty so that whenever I got paid, my employer would know he was getting more than he bargained for. I wanted to be a hard, and an honest, worker who made the employer happy, and wasn't a burden on the United States public.

Secondly, I wanted to use the benefits of my work to improve my own life as well as help my family back home. I would trace their whereabouts, and then be in contact with them to help them with their problems in the war zone of Southern Sudan or anywhere else they were.

Thirdly, I was going to apply to the best schools and, if given a chance, would study well and earn a degree to improve my own life, and that of my family and my future family.

Fourthly, I wanted to raise the awareness of the American public to aid the people of Southern Sudan, the SPLA and the churches, to bring to an end to the war and to save the people. This was my personal agenda for my own life, my family's and for the larger Southern Sudanese people.

However, when I was then free to pursue those endeavors, it became quite clear that it was not going to be easy. I was sure that I had no easy alternative but to go through the trials, and apply myself as best I could. This I did so well that some Americans, who had volunteered to help, knew that I was applying myself to the best of my abilities. I decided to get a job immediately after graduating. I landed a job on July 25, 2007 at a Rochester Optics Corporation, and held the job for the next three years. At the company, I worked as a test technician, a less than desirable position when I had hoped for an engineering position given my physics background. But I took the position and applied all of my energy and commitment to it, hoping that by it, I could create something for myself and then build a life for myself in the U.S. Although I received praise such as "Oh my, you are so smart, you studied physics!" I never got a better position than I had hoped. I wanted to be independent and so I stuck to my job of testing grating products on interferometers, and analyzing data on metropro software.

That data analysis would yield pictographs that would elaborate on the minute contours on the grating surface,[87] where grooves had been sunk with a patented machine which only this company owned. These products were highly sought after in the optics industry worldwide. I was made to believe that as long as I came to work every day, and did my job diligently, that I would never lose my job. It seemed to me that promotion and better pay, which I clearly deserved, were sacrificed for job security, and I was only too glad to keep quiet. They even asked me to work in the evenings rather than the mornings and to use any time in between the tests of the products to read a book or do anything beneficial to me. I chose instead to comment on the issues affecting our new budding, self-governing entity of Southern Sudan, and I was part of the group prowling the internet making sure that the CPA, the Comprehensive Peace Agreement, in southern Sudan was being implemented to the letter and spirit.

It was challenging to write something of substance that would be of help to my people miles away, something that would help them make better decisions, and help see them through to the nationhood and peace they had so craved for generations. I would spend considerable time thinking about ways in which peace could be achieved in Southern Sudan, and I would then write my comments, either stand-alone or in reply to any issue, be it a crisis or just a debate in progress. Doing so, I later found out that I had actually made many enemies everywhere for seeming to think too highly of myself. Little did those people know that I was so much consumed by the Sudan's problems, and my love

---

[87] A glass surface were microscopic grooves are mechanically sunk and used to view the stars in telescopes and sattelites by agencies like NASA

for the Sudan, that I sacrificed personal safety, and that of my family members, to say anything that would help our country gain peace. I felt that I owed a debt to the SPLA soldiers on whose words I was raised, and began to feel that I had a responsibility after they were gone, to make good on their sacrifices for the Sudan they had died for. Anything less than the achievement of the goal they died for would have been a waste of their lives and a betrayal to their ideals. They must rest in peace knowing that their lives were not sacrificed in vain. I tried to take some precautions, however, to try to stay ahead of those who would hate me for what I was doing for my country. I would try to never reveal where I came from in Southern Sudan, or who I am related to, so that I would keep my relatives and friends protected. I thank God for having brought our country safely ashore, even though we have lost so many people in the process leading to independence. Dr. Garang died in a helicopter crash on July 30th, 2005, one month after operationalizing the CPA. Then on May 2nd, 2008, a plane crash claimed the lives of more than twenty of the most prominent of our Twic community inside South Sudan. Both tragedies altered so much about South Sudan, because they took away several of the people who led, and participated in, the struggle.

While I was doing my work at my workplace, and commenting on issues affecting Southern Sudan, I found out later that my bosses were looking over my shoulder, unbeknownst to me. It seemed that they didn't entirely approve of what I was doing for the Sudan on the internet, but it appeared that I was doing my work well, because the bosses never complained, and I continued writing on the internet. It came to be that many people, Southern Sudanese especially, began to follow my writings and this continued to earn me online fame and enmity. I decided that I would make a return trip to Southern Sudan. But, while I was working at that company, I realized that if I went to Southern Sudan, there was a chance that I might never make it back, so I decided to become an American Citizen before I made the trip. The immunities of the United States Citizen could earn me benefits I might need while out there. So, in March 2008, I finally became a U.S. citizen, but had no money to make the trip just yet. Only in 2010 was I able to afford the ticket to travel to go see my family. I was happy that I was returning to Southern Sudan. When I asked my bosses if I could have some time off from work to go to Africa to see my family, after such a long absence, they seemed to like the idea and consented that I could go.

CHAPTER 33

SOUTH SUDAN

"We have done a good job. The country we fought for is now free," Deng told me when we met again at Syracuse, nine months after South Sudan became independent. Politics was now left to the politicians.

The Sudan war was fought for justice, equality and progress. The war went on for nearly fifty years. When the Anya Nya I war started, with the Torit mutiny by the Equatoria Corps in August 1955, the stated goal was the full liberation of the then Southern Closed Districts, or Southern Sudan. While the Anya Nya forces were honest in their objective, they were deficient in strategy, borne of a lack of knowledge about the continental politics of post-colonial Africa. When the war started in 1955, no country in Sub-Saharan Africa had yet achieved independence, so the Anya Nya I army shouldn't be faulted for not foreseeing the now defunct Organization for African Unity's[88] policy of never altering the borders of independent Africa. However, by 1972, the Anya Nya forces should have realized what the OAU was saying: There was never going to be any altering of the post-colonial border. Therefore, no chance for an independent South Sudan. Seen in this light, the Anya Nya I and II rebellions were doomed struggles.

When the SPLA was created in 1983, it came armed with this knowledge. The strategy from the start, as stated by the leadership, was for a socialist Sudan were everyone is accorded a fair chance. As declared

---

[88] OAU-The precursor to the current African Union, AU

by the SPLA/M Chairman, Dr. Garang, "Our bullets will fire first at the separatist." This not only appealed to the Khartoum establishment, but the OAU also liked the sound of it. The SPLA/M was fighting for a united Sudan. The colonial borders would remain unchanged. Not only that, but to also appeal to Mengistu, the Ethiopian socialist dictator, and host of the SPLA/M, the war was for a socialist Sudan. Though there was no proclamation of an African Socialism model like that of Julius Nyerere of Tanzania, the SPLA/M message appealed to leaders like him as well. Thus, while the rank-and-file of the SPLA soldiers, and the people of Southern Sudan, wanted their own independent country, the higher leadership espoused a united Sudan goal.

But, how true to this goal was the SPLA/M leadership? Indeed, there were questions asked often of Dr. Garang during the 22 years of the war. Questions came not only from Southern Sudanese, who felt confused, but also from Northern Sudanese and from elsewhere. In Northern Sudan, the likes of Al Mahdi wanted to know why, if the SPLA/M was fighting for a united Sudan, did they use the word 'liberation'. "Liberation from whom?" was a question asked by the wife of ASadiq al Mahdi, the prime minister. Indeed, with the roots of the SPLA/M (the Sudan Peoples' Liberation Army/Movement), the word "liberation" was problematic. For Southern Sudanese, who were familiar with the Arab slave trade, the Murahilin raids and the Khartoum government's brutal rule, liberation meant getting away from such a yoke. It seemed that ASadiq al Mahdi's wife was considering the same meaning. She must have suspected what the Southern Sudanese thought, and she must have been prepared, along with her fellow northern Arabs, to counter it. However, the movement's leadership gave an explanation that must have puzzled the Khartoum elite. It was liberation from what, not whom. The what being want. As illustrated by Dr. Garang, if a Sudanese woman who would spend hours walking five miles to fetch water, was able to get that water through a pipe right in her own house, then the SPLA/M had liberated her. This notion must have appeased the northerners, and cooled them to the idea of liberation. This took away the argument from Sudan being in a racial war, to being in a war on progress for all the peoples of the Sudan. A war against want and ignorance. The SPLA/M got it right. However, the Southern Sudanese, who bore the brunt of the war, did not stop complaining.

As the war dragged on, homes and villages were left devastated, and men, women and children were killed, starved to death, or died of disease, while thousands of soldiers were mowed down by the Khartoum Army and their associated Mujahedeen. The war became costly, and the goal of capturing the whole Sudan became a distant dream, even as the political winds began to change at the geopolitical level and within the Eastern Africa region. The SPLA/M lost its benefactor, Mengistu Haile Mariam, in 1991. With this, the SPLA/M was forced to change course and to begin the necessary strategic refocusing. While it's stated goal was still a united Sudan, socialism was replaced with democracy. The SPLA/M changed to the SPLM/SPLA, and the new goal became a democratic, secular, united Sudan.

Southern Sudanese could not see how they could single-handedly capture the whole of Sudan. Moreover, even though northern Sudanese were among the rank and file of the SPLA/M, that wasn't enough. Some southern politicians felt that the leadership of the SPLM/SPLA took Southern Sudanese for granted, and sought to rectify this by restating the Anya Nya I goal of a liberated Southern Sudan. Indeed, while South Sudanese still debate whether Dr. Garang was a unionist or a separatist, there was plenty of evidence to show that Dr. Garang treated the SPLM/ SPLA vision as a strategy for the benefit of all the stakeholders. The Machakos Protocol, signed in 2002, gave birth to South Sudan. Our independence, sought for more than 50 years, finally came on 'a golden plate', to rephrase Dr. Garang.

EPILOGUE

Much has changed in my life since that day in 1987. I have grown into a man and have learned a great deal along the way. In the process, I have met men and women of great repute and character who not only helped shape me, but also have imparted knowledge about how the world works. I might not have become too much wiser as a result, but at least I am not bitter for all the life experiences I went through on my own. Even though I was not orphaned, I know what kind of a life an orphan lives because I have lived like one. The experiences of my life have made me a better person, and I would not resist too much if I were forced to go through them again. I am a better person as a result. If it weren't for the situations I went through, I bet that I probably would never have gone to the prestigious University of Rochester, nor would I be trying to change lives for the better back in South Sudan.

When I made return visits to Southern Sudan, between 2010 and 2012, I was changed anew. I saw that the people were now settling down, and it seemed that the peace was taking hold, but the needed services were still lacking. I found that there was no way that I could remain in the United States without helping these people in my home area. I therefore made a pledge to myself that I would find a way to help them. One of the ways to help was to build a school for the local village children, a village where I spent the first few years of my childhood (Though the dream is not yet fulfilled, it still is alive).

The Sudan, that troubled country, has changed a lot since my childhood days, as well. It is now two countries, seemingly distinct and still at loggerheads. When I returned to Southern Sudan in March of 2010, and again when the region had become independent in 2011, the changes that one expected to have occurred in terms of development, especially for the rural population, hadn't seemed to have materialized. There were emphatic promises by the SPLM party, the new political masters of the new country, yet seemingly not much progress to show for it. While it is expected that a rebel movement might take time to prime itself for governance, it seems it is taking longer than expected, even though development in towns has accelerated faster than for the rural areas.

The political situation in South Sudan is now officially changed. In 2011, as the world came to know, the southern part of what was the Sudan split to form the new country that is now the Republic of South Sudan, with its own army, judiciary, parliament, executive branch and other branches of a modern democratic state. The SPLA, the former rebel army, has been transformed to be the independent nation's army, while the nation has become a member of, and signatory to, a number of international organizations, including the United Nations. The new nation is even mulling joining the East African region in the near future. Its ambassadors are posted to nations far and wide that have in one way or another supported the cause of the people of Southern Sudan, or just happen to hold major influence on the world stage. We now have ambassadors in China, Japan, the U.S., Canada, Britain, Australia and other nations.

But there are challenges still facing the country. One among them is the rampant corruption that has seeped into public life, tarnishing the nation's international image. South Sudan is beginning to look a lot more like the nearby Republic of Kenya in everything except name. The new President, though, has made a vow to fight the graft, and to make South Sudan unique in this regard, rather than copying Kenya, which is the region's economic powerhouse, but corrupt to the core.

There is good news on the local front, though. It is especially a relief that the Murahilin menace seems to have receded into the past. In the northernmost areas of the former Bhar el Gazel region, which is now divided into four states, the Murahilin can't try to attack with impunity. They can't race into the region to steal cattle, to maim or kill people, or to destroy property by torching homes and grain.

Then, there was an issue with the region of Abyei. This region had been transferred from the Southern region of Bhar el Gazel to the Northern region in 1905. Abyei's status was prescribed in part of the CPA, South Sudan's new peace agreement. The region was to hold a referendum simultaneously with the Southern region in January 2011. Yet, this agreement seemed to be losing strength. In January 2011, when the Southern region was holding its referendum, the Northern Government failed to provide a conducive atmosphere for a referendum in Abyei, and continued to obstruct any attempt to fulfill the agreement. Moreover, just when South Sudan was about to declare independence in July, 2011, the North forcefully annexed Abyei, and dissolved the regional administration, replacing it with a military one, basically carrying out a coup. It was with restraint that South Sudan stopped itself from striking back, a move which would have plunged the two regions back into a devastating war, and would have helped scuttle South Sudan's Independence.

But negotiations continue with North Sudan to find a way to solve the issues of the border demarcation for Abyei, as well as for the areas of Blue Nile and the Nuba Mountains. There is also the controversy surrounding the oil that flowed from South Sudan through a pipeline through North Sudan, to the Red Sea, for the international markets. South Sudan shut down this flow early in 2011, to protest Khartoum's intransigence and possible unauthorized oil migration to the government of Sudan's hands. This controversy led to a few days of standoff with North Sudan, and the capture of a very strategic town, leading to an international spat between South Sudan and the international community. The situation calmed down after South Sudan agreed to withdraw its troops from the seized area, which the South and the North each claim as their own. These disputes are yet to be hammered out, and peace still isn't fully secured between the two neighbors and bitter rivals.

Moreover, the popular consultation clause of the CPA for Blue Nile, Southern Khordufan, and the Nuba Mountains, was never implemented. The duly elected governor of Blue Nile, Malik Agar, a member of the SPLM/SPLA was overthrown and replaced with a military governor. The government then made sure that their candidate in the Nuba Mountain won the vote. That result rendered the solutions to the northern part of the Sudan problem null and void, leading the northern members of the SPLM/SPLA to don their military fatigues to fight back. The good news might be that the government of the National Congress Party, NCP, in Khartoum is now teetering on collapse, with an Arab Spring-styled uprising likely to happen. While the government downplays such an eventuality, it looks like there is a real chance it could happen.

Much has changed about the culture in South Sudan. Whereas in the villages dances still take place, they are not as they used to be. While there will still be the drums and drumming, the young men and women that attend those night dances generally dress in modern clothing now. It is interesting to take a note of the fact that in cities, traditional dancers wear dancing costumes designed to look like skins worn during the dances at the villages in the prior days. They try to emulate the 1980's, and sing songs that were sung then, songs now forgotten at the village level. In fact, it would be a curiosity now, to see someone dance in the old traditional costumes, or hear them sing the old songs. So, traditions now remain in the towns more than in the villages.

The English language is becoming the general language of South Sudan, likely displacing other languages, including Dinka, unless an effort is made to increase literacy in Dinka and to make it a mainstream language. The best way to do this is to encourage literacy for the adult population in the indigenous languages, like Dinka, since those languages are already known and this can bring basic literacy to most everyone in less than six months. Dinka should be learned alongside English. Encouraging adult literacy education in the English Language defeats the purpose.

Another aspect of Dinka culture that is quickly fading away is the traditional form of cattle keeping. At the villages, the number of cattle owned by the average person has increased due to the absence of the raids by the Murahilin and the Nuer, better disease control, reduced hunger, and more monetary wealth used to acquire cattle. Yet the traditional cattle camp management, where young men and women would travel far with cattle, seeking water and pastures, is now fading. Most of those who actually own cattle are not the ones who look after the cattle. There is a new form of cattle ownership, where the owner of the cattle, now becoming more and more attached to the government of South Sudan, or in the army or security services, or with children at school, is too busy. So he will give the cattle to someone else to take care of, for a meager pay in cash and some of the surplus dairy products. The owner, though, still maintains ownership.

Yet another traditional aspect of culture that is being phased out is scarification, the rite of passage into adulthood, especially for young men. While scarification on the forehead is still a mark of adulthood, more and more people seem not to care about it, or simply have no time for it. It is still being practiced, yet it is likely to be discarded sooner, rather than later.

More and more people now seek paid employment. This is due in part to young adults finding their place in modern South Sudan. After many have been to Kenya, Ethiopia and North Sudan, they have simply seen how other people live, and have come back with some of these aspects of economic life, which they use to enrich their lives. Indeed, even a farmer, while cultivating in the field, instead of singing the latest dance songs, he simply puts a boom box beside him in the field, and then turns on the latest music from the budding South Sudan music scene, which is modern as much as it is traditional. The farmer also will have a cup of tea, rather than a gourd of milk, to give him sustenance while farming. In as little as two decades, South Sudan has completely changed.

And while the weapons of choice were once spears, shields and clubs, these weapons aren't seen much anymore, and they are harder to come by. Typically, one will only occasionally see a man carrying a spear or club, or just a stick, to use against dogs. There are still rare instances, though, of finding someone carrying a bunch of spears, a club, and a shield, and wearing a traditional militia uniform, a robe in the colors of the subgroup of the area. This is mostly done for ceremonial purposes. In 1987, this was the official dress code for a young man in those parts. Indeed, the traditional militia is now integrated into the national army so that every young man can join the army rather than be at home. He can train himself in warfare and become a local militiaman. SPLA weapons and uniforms are the new form of the militia requirement.

Traditional hunting is now outlawed by the government so that if someone is found in possession of a game carcass or a bird, there is a stiff fine, and probably imprisonment.

Marriage, as done traditionally, would first involve exchanging enough cattle as determined by the two families of the betrothed. Most of the community would then gather, culminating in a ceremony where the marriage contract would be sealed. This form now seems to be modified, with the modern wedding held at churches, and there seems to be a move towards weddings being performed at churches at the village level, too, as well as traditionally.

The furnishings for sleeping on and reclining have changed. Now there are beds, mattresses, chairs and mosquito nets, thus leading to a changed housing style. The traditional mosquito management was to build specialized housing for livestock, including cattle, goats and sheep, and separate housing for humans. The human dwelling would either be a house on stilts, with a small opening for a door and space between the roof and the walls to keep out the mosquitoes, or a hut, with a still smaller round opening for a door, and no windows at all to keep away mosquitoes.

As for the livestock, they have traditionally been housed in a byre with windows, and large doors, that allow ample air to circulate. There would be a lot of smoke from cow dung or goat droppings, which are dried and burned as fuel to keep away the mosquitoes and provide warmth to the livestock. The cattle byre is now getting improvements in design and building materials, though, with the byres of the very rich now being made of bricks, with windows made of wire mesh. And as for the human dwellings, the houses on stilts, and the regular houses, are now being phased out because no one needs them anymore.

There is now more deforestation due to the return to the area of the people who were displaced. More trees are being cut for fuel, and land cleared for new settlement, including for farms. This is leaving the area open to encroaching desertification. More must be done to curb desertification. Perhaps because of global warming, the regular annual floods are becoming rare, with some years without floods materializing at all, leaving the land parched, without growing grass, leading to low pastures for too many cattle. The lack of floods also leads to a lack of enough fish, traditionally a supplement to the diet, and a protein source.

Largely because of lack of rain and floods, species of grass, endemic to the area and used for roofing, are going extinct. While this lack of ample rain is the primary reason for the loss of grasses, another reason stems from the war. During the war, the infighting between the southerners made it necessary for the war to continue during the rainy season, when the grassland would receive enough precipitation to grow. But because the grasses would contribute to camouflage, the reason the Dinka evaded the Arab invaders for so long, the same grasslands would be cleared of the grasses before the species could produce seeds for the next precipitation season, and this led to swathes of country losing the grass species. This is now being felt. Another reason for grasses going extinct is overgrazing due to too many cattle in an area, overgrazing the fields and leaving grass without time to grow back to maturity, or to have seeds for the next growing season. It probably will be advisable in the near future for the population to maintain a reasonable number of cattle. If it is a free market economy, as indicated by the new country's government, the market forces would help regulate the cattle economy.

Pollution is also becoming a problem. Though the major economic activity is localized, and not a major environmental issue at this time, the real problem for the environment is pollution from the byproducts of the urban consumables, which include plastic and discarded clothing. These plastic bottles from soda drinks, which are now the drinks of choice available at every market station anywhere in South Sudan, along with the discarded plastic and nylon wrappings, are environmental hazards. They are also hazardous to livestock. These days, it is sometimes said that a healthy cow will start to get sick and, after defying all the presently available treatment and livestock medicine, it will succumb and die. When it is opened up, there are large pieces of clothing, plastic wrappings and the like inside, which the cow had inadvertently ingested, only to bring its demise. If the Dinka are going to continue to keep cattle, and healthy cattle at that, environmental dumping of the byproducts of the urban consumables must be regulated.

Also, with increased population due to people returning to areas further away from the northern border, forests along the Lol River are now being resettled. This tree clearing for settlement and land use, and the wood cutting for charcoal and firewood, causing stress on the environment. It causes soil erosion, due to more open spaces, and less rain due to the absence of forests which bring in rain, causing damage to water catchment areas. The overpopulation in the area is also causing animal species to emigrate, especially big game animals. The areas which used to host all the major wild animals from lions, giraffes, buffalo, antelopes and gazelle to elephants, now have virtually none of these. While this is directly attributed to the widespread presence of arms, and the sounds of gunfire, a situation brought on by the war, overpopulation, with the continuous encroachment on the grasslands and forests, including settlement on along water, are also a direct cause. This is leading to uneven distribution of wildlife species, with bird species now bulging in numbers.

After the C.P.A. in 2005, leading to the formation of the autonomous government of Southern Sudan, the Sudan government, and the new autonomous government, had been working hard to make better roads to most towns and villages in Southern Sudan. These roads and bridges now extend to most parts, including the really remote outposts, and are easily accessible from anywhere in Southern Sudan. This has benefited the small towns, which used to be isolated from each other and from the major cities, particularly during the rainy season. Commerce is now flourishing, and transportation between towns is cheaper and relatively comfortable. This has also led to towns developing faster, with some villages becoming towns in their own right, with shops starting to sell the usual soda drinks and biscuits to passersby.

Because of new tools like tractors, and the use of oxen for plowing, larger fields and better tilling, farming has improved. Greater yields are being produced from better seeds, which are being provided by the government and the non-governmental organizations. The use of better fencing methods, with mesh wire, also improves yields because it provides more security and protection from livestock.

There is also better sanitation, with enough clean drinking water from wells, especially in towns. In the 1980's, UNICEF was quietly introducing a clean water revolution in the towns, and all the major and minor towns have numerous water points now, where clean water can be found. There is also a major industry in bottled water, taking care of those who can afford the filtered bottled water.

Houses are being built with burned bricks, which are more durable, and even with concrete bricks, and roofed with iron sheets rather than thatched.

Communication has improved, with cell phone communication everywhere even in the deepest of villages, and easily accessible and affordable to most people. The wireless communication is so effective that security personnel will sometimes briefly shut off this communication if they need to curtail information, for instance the presence of a government official at a certain location, which might be broadcast through cell phones, causing harm. Even shops are sophisticated. One can enter a shop somewhere to get a cool drink from new coolers that are easily affordable. Electricity is widespread, generated by the diesel-powered generators which are everywhere.

There is a better administration of the police force, which are deployed even to the deepest villages. The police are so effective that they are causing problems of their own: anybody can be accused and brought to the police, and the first thing that the police will do is have that person put in jail for a few days before being investigated. If the person is found innocent, he is only told to leave.

Towns are also growing and spaced closer together. These days, it is quite easy for a villager to go to a local market to sell livestock, for example, and be back at home in the village in the evening, rather than spend days walking to the nearest major town to market his livestock.

Christianity is the main faith everyone is trending towards, even for those in the countryside. While Christianity was the religion of those who went to school, where it was taught to students, it is quickly becoming the mainstream religion, replacing all the traditional beliefs.

When the Christian missionaries came to southern Sudan, they found that, apart from the language barrier, which they quickly bridged by learning to speak the local languages and then putting those languages to writing, getting Christianity into the minds of the older folks was easier said than done. The local belief in God the almighty was so enshrined, and such a great part of life and culture, that Christianity didn't have a chance, despite the general peacefulness of the missionaries, who gave medicine to the young, and gifts of clothing and other goods to the old. The Muslims tended to use the sword, and came with a knack for conquest. But still, the Nilotes simply refused to be wholly Christian, even though they respectfully tolerated Christianity.

The missionaries shifted gear and tried to teach the young by opening schools to teach literacy and then impart Christianity, making the new religion one for those educated so that the word for the "educated" in Dinka is *mith abun* ("children of the priest").

As I found out, there is a little less superstition, and more belief in the physical manifestation of things. For instance, rather than have sickness be a sign of bad eyes, it is now seen as probably just from contaminated water, or from some bacterial infection. Low yields from the field can now be because the field had no fertilizer applied, and so forth. It is possible for people to seek medical attention at a clinic, rather than stay home to seek the help of the traditional medicinal healers.

Another thing that has changed is the reliance on, and frequency of, traditional blessings. Whereas it used to be that any family member arriving or leaving the household was always blessed with water, and with the invocation of God, by the senior most members of the family, the grandparents or the parents, this is presently absent, or curtailed, with people just saying "goodbye" and "do be careful."

There is no doubt a marked rise in the modern manifestation of human greed, and less reliance on God. For instance, it is quite interesting to note many men's attitudes towards church. To them, going to church is wimpy, and it is mostly for women and children. The man, on the other hand, must pursue economic gains and not waste time praying at church. But they don't realize that touching base with God is actually the best beginning for earning whatever a person so desires.

Theirs is a short-sighted approach to religion. Another major aspect of the Christian thought and teaching that seems to be integrating into the culture is about monogamous marriage. This seems to be quietly implementable, perhaps aided in part by the facts of modern economic realities. Indeed, monogamy seems to be on the rise, and the way everyone is going, as explained to me by an SPLA colonel. While polygamy is the tradition, strict adherence to Christianity, especially by the modern young women demanding a monogamous relationship, and the dictates of the modern economy, might force a move towards more monogamous marriages. But, if going by the standards of the rest of the African countries, with two leading examples being Kenya and South Africa, perhaps this proposition will take awhile longer to be effected.

Indeed, one can say that South Sudan is on its way to being a Christian nation, if tempered by its many traditions and customs. And as a very frustrated Dinka old man told me, "It is better that there are churches everywhere, where shrines to God used to be, because there is more freedom in Christianity than in the traditional beliefs in God. Traditionally, there is more reliance on the good works and good behavior on the part of the person in order to find favor in God's eyes, and even then, issues never seem to get better. Perhaps the God taught in churches could be more forthright, generous and less cunning than the traditional God." Apparently, the old man, who has lost so much in life, seems to be angry at a God he so trusted to make things work for him.

Apparently, an unknown calamity had ravaged his family and he was searching for meaning and repose in a God he could better understand. For people like that, Christianity is a ready respite. If there was a Fr. Matong, perhaps the old man would have found a priest who would have made the two sides workable for him. Indeed, Christianity, including the evangelical belief, was right around town during the time I was in South Sudan in December, 2011, in the form of a revival prayer meeting and healing. Only, this form is the same as the traditional form where families go to be prayed over and healed. This is something that has led to the frustration that the old man was in- this praying and healing never seems to work, according to him. But if there was any hope for a better life, then it would be found through modern medicine, especially with respect to disease treatment and eradication, something I was advocating for, and looking forward to help provide to the villagers. Unbeknownst to the old man, I could actually be the saving grace to his predicament, and perhaps I was going to be the instrument God was going to utilize in answer to his agony and to open his eyes. We are the instruments of God in the service of creation.

The former lost boys who traveled all over the region of Eastern Africa have now grown to be men, and have gained educations, earning them a variety of occupations and positions of authority. If there was ever a group of formidable young men, with vast experience of human endurance and pain, and with a determined disposition to gain an education no matter the odds and to go on to become more than what they ever had imagined, then the former lost boys are the men. One by one, the stories are coming out in books and movies and other projects, all aimed at helping the new country of South Sudan, which they have sacrificed so much for.

But perhaps more important is the absence of the Murahilin raiders, unsettling the life of the peasants. The primary worry faced by the locals, now, is the worry about where to find pastures and inoculation for their cattle, rather than the fear of having to avoid the looting of their property, and their cows, by the Murahilin on a seasonal basis. Cattle rustling has been curtailed, and is quite manageable, as there is a quick response to any cattle-rustling attempts. The police and the paramilitary, the titweng (the cattle guards), have better guns, and better training, leading to fast response times against the cattle raids.

Since 2005, the feared Antonov bombers have been absent. Their sole purpose had been to terrorize the civilian population and force them to leave the countryside for the garrison towns in the South, and Khartoum in the North, in order to deny the SPLA its base of support. It is a great relief that they are gone, but recently the Sudan Air Force has been bombing South Sudan, with bombing campaigns near the border areas. While the SPLA still has insufficient air power, the ground-to-air missiles forces are quite formidable, and this brings caution to the

SAF Air Force aircrafts on bombing campaigns in South Sudan. Given that the war is over, joining the SPLA, the new national army, is on a voluntary basis. As a result of lack of conscription, more young men are getting into business and into the government than being forced to join the SPLA.

Trade is conducted freely among the communities. Trade goods flow from eastern Africa, and even from North Sudan to South Sudan, despite the destruction of the bridge at Abyei.

The government of the Sudan, centered at Khartoum in the north, used to treat the parts of the country further from the center, and especially southern Sudan, as regions for resource extraction, with nothing given back in form of development money. One aspect of the solution to this economic exploitation and marginalization, though, has been spelled out in the CPA protocol on wealth sharing. Now, 2% of the share of a local resource is returned to the local population, wherever there was a resource to extract. This formula was initiated in 2005, and is still in use for the new government of South Sudan. This has removed economic exploitation and marginalization to a large extent.

The new government of South Sudan had succeeded most in one particular issue: Uniting the people of South Sudan. But it came at the steep price of diluting the rank-and-file of both the SPLA and the SPLM, allowing in people of questionable loyalty to the ideals the people of South Sudan fought for. However, as it happened, on December 15th, 2013, that unity came crushingly apart. Fighting broke out in Juba, with an alleged coup carried out by Riek Machar and his comrades, disgruntled with the government of Kiir Mayardit. This quickly turned into ethnically backed violence, which claimed an estimated 10,000 lives, and almost brought down the South Sudan government. The post-independence SPLA and SPLM are all in tatters, and the very fabric of a united South Sudan seems but a myth. It will take years for such unity to be restored. Meanwhile, the fight continues. Now that it is South Sudanese against South Sudanese, my friend Ongwec must feel vindicated.

INDEX